D1728291

TO OUR READERS

Welcome to the new *AM/PM* Guide. Whether you're visiting, newly relocated or happily residing in Northern California, *AM/PM* can help you enjoy San Francisco and its nearby getaways to the fullest.

AM/PM's easy-to-carry format and comprehensive listings have inspired confidence for more than a decade. We do our homework, and we don't cut corners on quality. Our commitment to excellence means we stay on top of what's happening in Northern California.

You'll find some exciting new features in this *AM/PM*: introductions by well-known personalities, a California wine section with tasting notes by Master Sommeliers, calendars of interesting monthly events, children's activities, sports and much more.

With this edition, guests in Northern California's best hotels and resorts now have access to hardcover copies of *AM/PM* in their rooms. And businesses are using our corporate customized covers to say "welcome to San Francisco" in a uniquely personal way.

Trust *AM/PM* to show you what's best in San Francisco and Northern California. Use it, share it with your friends, and don't forget to tell our advertisers that you saw them in *AM/PM!*

THE PUBLISHERS

ACCOMMODATIONS

NIGHTLIFE

RESTAURANTS

WINES & WINE COUNTRY

CARMEL & MONTEREY

**PLEASE FLIP BOOK OVER
FOR AM CONTENTS**

ACCOMMODATIONS

NIGHTLIFE

RESTAURANTS

WINES & WINE COUNTRY

CARMEL • MONTEREY

GUIDE TO NORTHERN CALIFORNIA

Publisher
ANA GLORIA HUSON

Co-Publisher
THIERRY ABEL

Associate Publishers
ANTHONY KALK   DAVID CLARIDGE
●
Editors
DONNALI FIFIELD   MAIA MADDEN

Production Manager/Wine Coordinator
CAROLYN DURYEA

Wine Editor
EVAN GOLDSTEIN
●
Design Director
MATTHEW FOSTER

Design Associates
RAOUL OLLMAN   JENNIFER T. POOLE

Photographer
JOSHUA ETS-HOKIN
●
Circulation Director
ROLANDO RODRIGUEZ
●
Director of Sales & Marketing
CAROLINE LARROUILH

Advertising Sales Executives
MADELINE AUSTIN   JAMES CASSADY
●
Business Manager
JENNIFER BAILEY
●
Interns
**BRADFORD CLARK   STEPHANE DEMILLY   JEROME BOESCH
SANDRINE CHORRO   MARC RIVOLLANT**

Published By:
AM/PM Publishing, Inc.
3027 Fillmore Street • Suite D • San Francisco, CA 94123
TEL: 415-921-2676   FAX: 415-921-3999
COPYRIGHT © 1993

Thank you: The Mark Hopkins Inter-Continental; Joey Chase, Jennifer Wolf, EPIC Model

A LEADING TRAVEL MAGAZINE, THE *CONDÉ NAST TRAVELER*, RECENTLY NAMED San Francisco the most popular destination in the world, beating out such traditional favorites as Paris, London and Venice. One reason is San Francisco's legendary beauty. Another reason is the quality of our hotels and restaurants.

Accommodations

San Francisco boasts the highest number of four-and five-star properties of any major city, along with the most sophisticated restaurants and services. Hotel companies have built their finest flagship properties here, and San Francisco is one of the only cities where hotel restaurants rival the quality of independently owned restaurants. In fact, here at The Donatello, the restaurant was so highly regarded that we changed the hotel's name from The Pacific Plaza to The Donatello. The trend toward elegant, small "boutique" hotels also began here, adding a dimension of choice that makes every visit special.

Wherever you stay, whether for a few days or an extended visit, ask your concierge to assist you in planning excursions. Why not take a bus ride with food basket in tow and spend a day in Golden Gate Park? Or hop on a cable car to Fisherman's Wharf and take a ferry across the bay to visit the charming villages of Sausalito and Tiburon? The concierge can tell you where to find the best food, the top values, and that special little place with gourmet picnics ready to go. San Francisco's concierges, like its hotels, are the very best.

Enjoy your stay in San Francisco!

Introduced by A. Cal Rossi, Jr.

A. Cal Rossi, Jr., is the president of the company that owns The Donatello Hotel and Ristorante Donatello. He is the former developer and owner of the Stanford Court Hotel and the Monterey Plaza Hotel.

Exclusively Your Option.

Uniquely Inter·Continental.

When you stay at the Mark Hopkins Inter-Continental,
you can receive 500 American Airlines® A'Advantage® or
United Airlines® Mileage Plus® miles per night, not per stay.†
Plus, you'll receive your choice of one of the valuable
amenity Options below. All for one great low rate. From $129*

☐ *Double bonus miles – 1000 total*   ☐ *Adjoining guest room*
   miles each night of your stay.   *for half-price.*

☐ *Upgrade to a one-bedroom suite.*   ☐ *$25 food or beverage credit.*

**For reservations, contact your travel agent or call
(415) 392-3434, toll-free 800-327-0200.**

MARK HOPKINS
INTER·CONTINENTAL
SAN FRANCISCO

Number One Nob Hill • San Francisco, California

HOTELS

ABIGAIL HOTEL
246 McAllister St. at Hyde / 861-9728

Built in 1923, the Abigail retains charming touches of the past. Brightened by modern impressionistic fabrics, the rooms are furnished with antiques, down comforters, rare English lithographs and turn-of-the-century paintings. The Abigail is conveniently located in the Civic Center area, next door to the opera, ballet and symphony, as well as all major government offices, and just minutes from Union Square. **Portico Restaurant** serves breakfast, lunch and dinner, specializing in fondue and international cuisine. It's no wonder the *San Francisco Chronicle* lists the Abigail as one of "San Francisco's Best Values."
Singles & doubles $79; suites $125

ALBION HOUSE
135 Gough St. at Oak / 621-0896

The Albion House is in the Civic Center area, three blocks from the city's opera, symphony and arts complex. This cozy, welcoming bed and breakfast is also minutes from downtown, Fisherman's Wharf and Moscone Convention Center. Each room is distinctively furnished with antiques. All have direct-dial phones, and most have color televisions and private baths, with robes supplied for added luxury. A full gourmet breakfast is served in the living room. Spacious, with a high beamed ceiling and large marble fireplace, this room is the inn's focal point. Guests can unwind here with a glass of brandy, courtesy of the house, and are invited to play on the grand piano.
Singles & doubles $75-$150

ANA HOTEL SAN FRANCISCO
50 3rd St. at Market / 974-6400

The Ana Hotel welcomes you to the tradition of hospitality one expects to find in San Francisco. In 1992, the hotel underwent a $28 million renovation and now offers some of the most beautiful rooms, meeting spaces and public areas in the city. Rising 36 stories and overlooking Moscone Center, Union Square and the Financial District, the hotel features panoramic views from the floor-to-ceiling windows in every guest room. Personalized service includes a multilingual staff, escorted morning jog, fitness center, Executive Club levels, business center and room service. California cuisine with classic elements of French, Italian and Japanese cooking is offered in **Cafe Fifty-Three**.
Singles $170-$235; doubles $195-$260; suites $300-$1,500

CAMPTON PLACE HOTEL KEMPINSKI
340 Stockton St. at Sutter / 781-5555

Just off Union Square, Campton Place Hotel Kempinski, with 126 rooms and 10 suites, is only a few minutes from the Financial District. Details are what make Campton Place so delightful — Wedgwood china, a marble lobby, a hideaway roof garden, Roman travertine baths. Accommodations are particularly attractive to the traveling executive, including generous work desks and secretarial, courier and telecopier services. Tranquility and a homelike ambiance are accompanied by European-style hospitality. **The Campton Place Restaurant** offers American cuisine that is among the best in town.
Singles & doubles $185-$320; suites $395-$800

CARTWRIGHT HOTEL
524 Sutter St. at Powell / 421-2865

Fresh flowers and antiques add distinctive, old-fashioned charm to every room, and the hotel's Union Square location is considered by some the best in the city.

THE DONATELLO
501 Post St. at Mason / 441-7100

The Donatello is a polished gem in a grand setting. Impeccable attention was paid to the interior, with fine Italian marble, Venetian glass, Belgian tapestries, lovely antiques, contemporary art and fresh flowers. Special amenities include extra-length beds, fine linen and the *Wall Street Journal*. **Donatello**, the hotel's Northern Italian restaurant, is ranked one of the best in San Francisco — for good reason.
Singles & doubles $175-$195; suites $350-$525

FAIRMONT HOTEL
950 Mason St. at California / 772-5000

One of San Francisco's finest hotels, the legendary Fairmont towers over Nob Hill. Sophisticated and elegant, the hotel recalls the city in its golden era. Personalized attention is only one of the features offered by the Fairmont. A glass-walled outside elevator whisks guests to the top to discover the **Crown Room**, where they can dine surrounded by a dramatic panorama of the Bay Area. Jazz artists perform in the **New Orleans Room**, and the **Venetian Room** is now a banquet and meeting room that accommodates up to 900. Available for receptions, the **Cirque Lounge** has been restored to its original Art Deco style. Vintage wines and gourmet dishes are served at the award-winning **Squire Restaurant**, open for dinner. For exotic drinks and Pacific Rim din-

ing, the **Tonga Room** is a spectacular sight, complete with hourly tropical rainstorms. The **BellaVoce Ristorante and Bar** features singing waiters who serenade patrons with opera and Broadway favorites, and **Masons** is the perfect environment in which to enjoy California cuisine with a French flair.
Singles & doubles $165-$285; suites from $500

FOUR SEASONS CLIFT HOTEL
495 Geary St. at Taylor / 775-4700

Fortune Magazine has named it one of the world's great little-known hotels. *Harper's Bazaar* ranks it one of the 13 exceptional hotels in the world and *Condé Nast Traveler* readers chose it as one of the world's top hotels. It is San Francisco's only five-star, five-diamond hotel. The Clift is by any standard a very special place. The plush **Redwood Room** off the lobby is an authentic Art Deco masterpiece, with piano entertainment featured nightly in the elegant cocktail lounge. The beautifully appointed **French Room** serves California/French cuisine for breakfast, lunch and dinner.
Singles $200-$310; doubles $200-$340; suites $355-$1,000

GALLERIA PARK HOTEL
191 Sutter St. at Kearny / 781-3060

Only three blocks from Union Square, Galleria Park Hotel is in a freshly renovated 1911 building and boasts the highest occupancy rate west of the Mississippi. The hotel's mix of classic San Francisco design with ultra-modern amenities and indulgent concierge service explains this statistic. Guests enjoy the roof park and jogging track, various complimentary treats, including nightly wine tastings in the Art Nouveau lobby, and an on-site parking garage. State-of-the-art meeting facilities and two adjacent, world-class restaurants, **Brasserie Chambord** and **Bentley's Seafood Grill**, enhance business and pleasure alike.
Singles & doubles $145; suites $175-$385

GRAND HYATT SAN FRANCISCO
345 Stockton St. at Post / 398-1234

A perfect blend of old-world elegance and new-world luxury, the Grand Hyatt concentrates on modern comforts with elements of traditional design. On the 36th floor, **Club 36** is open daily for cocktails and offers piano music until 2AM. The Regency Club, occupying three floors of suites and guest rooms, has a club lounge, new executive business center and state-of-the-art health club; the Penthouse Floor, a hotel within the hotel, provides a personal butler service.
Singles & doubles $175-$265; suites $350-$1,500

HARBOR COURT HOTEL
165 Steuart St. at Howard / 882-1300

The Harbor Court Hotel, featured in *Condé Nast Traveler* for its spectacular bay views, is located minutes from the

city's convention, business and tourist centers. Converted from a YMCA, the hotel is intimate and elegant, with a decor influenced by its 1920s Romanesque architecture. The lobby features marble floors, stone columns and hand-forged ironwork. Many of its 131 guest rooms have canopied beds with oversized pillows and luxurious comforters. On the eighth floor, the penthouse suite has a telescope for added views of the Bay Bridge and Oakland Harbor. Amenities include daily limousine service to the Financial District, access to the pool and fitness center next door and half-price entry on weekends to the hotel's wildly successful bar and grill, **Harry Denton's**.
Singles & doubles $120-$160; penthouse suite $250

HOLIDAY LODGE & GARDEN HOTEL
1901 Van Ness Ave. at Jackson / 776-4469

Located in Pacific Heights, one of San Francisco's most beautiful residential neighborhoods, the Holiday Lodge is close to everything yet as serene as a secluded hideaway. Guests are three blocks from the cable cars, five minutes from Fisherman's Wharf, Union Square, Chinatown and Civic Center. They return to a peaceful oasis: one acre of beautifully landscaped grounds, a heated outdoor swimming pool, and an even rarer city amenity, free parking. Many rooms have private patios opening on the lush inner gardens. All this for a price that makes the Holiday Lodge one of San Francisco's best-kept secrets.
Singles & doubles $85

THE HOTEL ATHERTON
685 Ellis St. at Larkin / 474-5720

For reasonable rates and clean lodging in the heart of San Francisco, The Hotel Atherton is a good bet. Originally built in the 1930s and recently revived, the hotel has well-maintained rooms and a comfortable lobby. A friendly staff caters to all personal arrangements, from booking city and wine country tours to getting the best theatre tickets and restaurant reservations.
Singles & doubles $51-$81

HOTEL BEDFORD
761 Post St. at Jones / 673-6040

The Hotel Bedford is a moderately priced European-style establishment small enough to provide a high degree of personal service, yet affordable enough for today's leisure and business traveler. The Bedford's renovated lobby and modernized guest rooms offer comfortable accommodations. Complimentary wine is served every evening. The **Cafe Champagne** serves breakfast and the mahogany-paneled **Wedgwood Bar** provides a charming retreat just off the lobby.
Singles $94; doubles $99; suites $155

HOTEL DIVA
440 Geary St. at Mason / 885-0200

A high-tech Italian flavor makes the downtown Diva a

standout. Its 108 rooms feature VCRs, down comforters, classic Bertoia chairs and beautifully detailed showers. Guests enjoy the morning paper with their complimentary full California breakfast. Hotel Diva also provides complimentary limousine service to the Financial District each weekday morning and a full-time concierge to help make every visit effortless. Minisuites, conference rooms and a complimentary fitness center and business center with personal computers are available. Don't miss the on-site restaurant, **California Pizza Kitchen**, serving California pizzas and gourmet salads. *Singles & doubles $119; suites $135-$300*

HOTEL GRIFFON
155 Steuart St. off Mission / 495-2100

Overlooking the waterfront, the completely refurbished Hotel Griffon offers elegance in true San Francisco fashion. Pacific Union Hotels joined forces with the successful Real Restaurants team (Fog City Diner, Bix) to create an intimate hotel with tailored, European-style rooms and highly personalized service. The result is a stunning 62-room hotel with an award-winning restaurant, **Bistro Roti**. The restaurant specializes in Country French cuisine and spit-roasted entrees prepared over a huge wood-burning fireplace. Continental breakfast and access to a neighboring fitness center are complimentary for hotel

guests. The Boardroom is available for private meetings and dining for 12.
Singles & doubles $125-$145; suites $175-$195

HOTEL MAJESTIC
1500 Sutter St. at Gough / 441-1100

The Majestic Hotel is in a 1902 building that has been completely refurbished and decorated with turn-of-the-century antiques. There are 59 rooms, many with four-poster canopy beds and fireplaces. The outstanding **Cafe Majestic** serves old-time San Francisco favorites and California cuisine for breakfast, lunch and dinner every day but Monday. A board room and a meeting room are also available to guests.
Singles & doubles $135-$185; suites $250

HOTEL NIKKO SAN FRANCISCO
222 Mason St. at O'Farrell / 394-1111

Located just west of Union Square, the Hotel Nikko welcomes guests to a beautiful two-story marble lobby and its 522 contemporary guest rooms, which include 20 Western-style suites and two Japanese suites. Unwind in the full-service spa and exercise center, complete with glass-enclosed swimming pool, then choose between fresh California cuisine with a touch of Asian spices at **Cafe 222**, or authentic Japanese fare at **Benkay**. Execu-

tive meeting rooms, business suites, banquet and audio-visual facilities, 24-hour room service and a multilingual staff make the Nikko ideal for international business travelers as well as vacationers.

Singles $205-$225; doubles $225-$285; suites $375-$1,300

HOTEL RICHELIEU
1050 Van Ness Ave. at Geary / 673-4711

Originally built in 1908, the hotel retains its classic San Francisco Victorian ambiance. Beautifully preserved garments of the period are displayed throughout the hotel's lobby and hallways. The hotel has 150 charming rooms and suites. Guest services include a nightly hospitality hour, courtesy limousine service in the morning and an executive gym. Stanley is a favorite at Hotel Richelieu. The resident house cat, popular with new and repeat guests, lounges in the lobby and has been known to wander into guest rooms when doors have been purposely left ajar. The hotel's conference room, recently remodeled, is perfect for business meetings or casual receptions.

Singles & doubles $89-$175

HOTEL TRITON
342 Grant Ave. at Bush / 394-0500

San Francisco's newest boutique hotel, Hotel Triton, is across from Chinatown's dragon gate. Its great location and stylish decor — silk-taffeta dervish chairs with wavy backs, murals with mythological themes, sapphire carpets with gold stars, and waxy gilded columns — have already attracted celebrities, including Lily Tomlin, Suzanne Vega and the Psychedelic Furs. The hotel's 140 rooms are playful and custom-designed. Guest services include valet and laundry service, complimentary wine served in the lobby, a meeting room and a fully stocked honor bar. **Aioli** and **Cafe de la Presse** next door offer French bistro fare for breakfast, lunch and dinner.

Singles & doubles $129; suites $169-$209

HOTEL UNION SQUARE
114 Powell St. at O'Farrell / 397-3000

The original boutique hotel, Hotel Union Square has 131 rooms located directly on the Powell Street cable car line. Catering to families and leisure travelers, the hotel offers both old-world charm and modern conveniences. The hotel's corner suites and rooftop penthouses are a valued luxury in the heart of San Francisco. Complimentary services include a Continental breakfast of coffee and croissants, and tea and coffee served each afternoon in the lobby. On-site parking is available at a minimal charge. For enjoyable dining, there's **Carmen Taqueria** next door. The restaurant, open for lunch and dinner daily, has a full bar.

Singles & doubles $99; suites $180-$280

HOTEL VINTAGE COURT
650 Bush St. near Powell / 392-4666

Two blocks from Union Square, the Vintage Court

offers stylish, comfortable rooms in the heart of the city. This attractive, 106-room European-style hotel is small enough to provide a high degree of personal service. A large fireplace and a richly textured sitting area highlight the lobby, where complimentary premium California wine is served at night and coffee and tea in the morning. The location on the cable car line makes citywide transportation affordable and fun for guests who want to explore San Francisco. In keeping with its wine country theme, the hotel dedicates each room to a Northern California winery. **Masa's**, rated San Francisco's top French restaurant by many critics, is open for dinner Tuesday through Saturday.

Singles & doubles $119; suite $225

HUNTINGTON HOTEL
1075 California St. at Taylor / 474-5400

An atmosphere of comfort and unobtrusive elegance prevails throughout this hotel, called home by prominent members of the finance, government and theatrical worlds. The Nob Hill address on the cable car line provides convenience as well as sweeping views of the city. The hotel boasts exceptional concierge service, and guests may request complimentary limousine service to downtown. Exercise privileges at the Nob Hill Club and banquet facilities are just a sampling of the hotel's special services. Accessible through the lobby is one of the most respected names in San Francisco dining, **The Big Four**, and the nearby piano lounge is a delightfully intimate spot for cocktails before or after dinner.

Singles $165; doubles $185; suites $250-$685

HYATT REGENCY SAN FRANCISCO
Embarcadero Five at Market / 788-1234

The Hyatt Regency, famous for its innovative design, presents an awesome spectacle of architectural planes and open space highlighted by a soaring rise to the sunlit roof of the atrium lobby.

INN AT THE OPERA
333 Fulton St. at Franklin / 863-8400

Only steps from the Opera House and Davies Hall, the Inn is an intimate luxury hotel. The 48-room hostelry was originally built in 1927 to house visiting opera stars. Recently restored to classic beauty, the Inn is returning to its original role: to serve performing artists, music and art lovers. Beautifully decorated rooms at the European-style hotel feature queen-size beds, large private baths, wet-bars, small refrigerators and microwaves. Breakfast, lunch, dinner and cocktails are served in the **Act IV Restaurant & Lounge**; a pianist plays most evenings.

Singles $110-$205; doubles $120-$165; suites $165-$215

THE INN SAN FRANCISCO
943 South Van Ness Ave. at 21st / 641-0188

With the charm of a bed and breakfast and the amenities

RENAISSANCE
Estate Bottled Wines from the Sierra Nevada Mountains.
Exclusively.

CAFE 222

Benkay

Authentic Japanese Cuisine

hotel nikko san francisco

222 mason street, san francisco, california 94102 415.394.1111

of a luxury hotel, The Inn San Francisco is the best of both worlds. Built in the 1870s, the fully restored mansion offers 22 completely unique rooms, individually decorated with antiques, marble and polished brass. The "Deluxe" rooms have private spa tubs for two, and a suite has a private hot tub. Under the shade of a fig tree is another hot tub, open to all guests, as is the garden, the rooftop sundeck and the elegant Victorian parlor. Marty Neely and Jane Bertorelli are the friendly innkeepers, who make sure that every guest is both pampered and well directed to the Bay Area's incomparable attractions. A generous breakfast buffet and complimentary beverages accompany the warm welcome.
Cozy rooms $75-$95; spacious $115-$135; deluxe $155-$175; cottage suite $175

JULIANA HOTEL
590 Bush St. at Stockton / 392-2540

From the beautiful teal-and-peach lobby to the 106 rooms and suites done in Laura Ashley prints, the Juliana Hotel is refined and comfortable. Each room has its own air conditioning and heat, television with complimentary HBO and a small refrigerator stocked with beverages and snacks. Every evening between 5PM and 7PM, complimentary wine is served around the lobby fireplace. **Vinoteca**, open for breakfast and dinner, serves superb Northern Italian cuisine.
Singles & doubles $119; suites $135-$155

KENSINGTON PARK HOTEL
450 Post St. at Powell / 788-6400

Only a few steps from Union Square, the Kensington Park mixes the luxury and intimacy of a small European hotel with modern conveniences. Set in the completely renovated 1924 Elks Club Building, the hotel blends the old and the new with style and comfort. Each of the 86 richly detailed rooms is furnished with Queen Anne mahogany furniture, Chippendale armoires and marble-and-brass bathrooms. A complimentary Continental breakfast is served in the morning. In the afternoon, guests enjoy complimentary tea and sherry in the marble lobby to the tunes of a baby grand. The Kensington Park offers valet parking and limousine service to the Financial District on weekday mornings.
Singles & doubles $115; suites $165-$350

THE KING GEORGE HOTEL
334 Mason St. at Geary / 781-5050

Superbly located near Union Square, the King George is a delightful European-style hotel with 143 guest rooms and a warm, friendly staff. Offering guests every comfort, including laundry, valet, business and room service, the hotel has surprisingly moderate rates. Dine Japanese-style in the **Ichirin** restaurant, or

enjoy the charming **Bread and Honey Tearoom** for high tea with piano entertainment, or order a daily Continental breakfast.
Singles $97; doubles $107; suites $186

THE LOMBARD HOTEL
1015 Geary Blvd. at Polk / 673-5232

Built in the 1920s, the Lombard Hotel welcomes guests with a warm, comfortable lobby and an attentive, friendly staff. Value is the key here, but amenities abound: a redwood sunning deck, nightly complimentary tea and sherry, and the **Gray Derby Restaurant**, open for breakfast and dinner. Weekday morning destinations are a breeze for guests who use the hotel's complimentary limousine service.
Singles & doubles $83-$89

MANDARIN ORIENTAL, SAN FRANCISCO
222 Sansome St. at California / 885-0999

High above San Francisco, the Mandarin Oriental, San Francisco offers unrivaled views and the grand luxury associated with this award-winning hotel group. All 158 rooms are located on the top 11 floors of two towers connected on every level by spectacular skybridges. The highly praised Mandarin Rooms feature every comfort, including picture windows in the large marble bathrooms with views of the TransAmerica Pyramid, Alcatraz and the Golden Gate Bridge. Other hotel features include banquet and meeting facilities, complete business services, same-day laundry and valet service and an off-premise health club and sauna. For dining, **Silks** serves outstanding Asian-inspired California cuisine in a very romantic pastel environment.
Singles & doubles $255-$390; suites $540-$1,200

THE MANSIONS
2220 Sacramento St. at Laguna / 929-9444

A hideaway to the stars, the Mansions is set in a twin-towered Queen Anne structure built in 1887. The two historic buildings are both registered historical landmarks, connected by an interior walkway. The hotel is appointed with Victorian memorabilia. The opulent decor includes a multimillion-dollar collection of fine arts and a major Bufano collection. Each guest room honors a celebrated San Franciscan and many feature a marble fireplace, with a private terrace or a ceiling that slants to the floor. Flowers are in every room. Adjacent to Lafayette Park's tennis courts, the hotel prides itself on providing a restful atmosphere reminiscent of turn-of-the-century San Francisco. A sumptuous breakfast, nightly magic concerts, game rooms and an unusual sculpture garden are other special features. The Mansions also has an excellent French restaurant, serving dinner Tuesday through Saturday.
Singles & doubles $129-$250

THE MARK HOPKINS INTER-CONTINENTAL
One Nob Hill, California St. at Mason / 392-3434

As soon as you enter the historic lobby of the palatial Mark Hopkins, you know you have joined the ranks of the fortunate. Many of the hotel's staff have been on duty for more than 20 years, and their personal touch contributes greatly to the Mark's success. They consistently ensure that guests at the hotel will be provided with every comfort and service. The world-famous **Top of the Mark**, an elegant cocktail lounge opened in 1939, is one of the first examples of a skyroom where patrons can enjoy a 360-degree vista. **The Nob Hill Restaurant** offers superb California/French cuisine.
Singles $180-$275; doubles $200-$305; suites $375-$1,775

MIYAKO HOTEL
1625 Post St. at Laguna / 922-3200

After a four-year renovation program completed in 1989, the Miyako has become one of San Francisco's showplace hotels. The renovation included completely remodeling the lobby and installing a Japanese garden and waterfall, designed by a leading Japanese landscape gardener. Anchoring the east end of Japan Center, the Miyako is popular with both American and Japanese visitors. Guests can stay in Western-style rooms with Japanese accents or in traditional Japanese rooms with futon beds set on tatami mats. Deep-tub Japanese baths *(furos)* are available in most rooms. Several deluxe suites have private redwood saunas and the hotel's Club Floor rooms have whirlpool baths. Miyako's convention facilities, staffed by a multilingual team, include space for meetings, receptions and large banquets. The hotel's award-winning restaurant, **Elka**, serves seafood, with fresh California preparations inspired by Japanese cuisine.
Singles $100-$169; doubles $129-$189; suites $180-$300

MONTICELLO INN
127 Ellis St. at Cyril Magnin / 392-8800

Although the Monticello Inn is only half a block from the Powell Street cable car line, it is an intimate retreat removed from downtown's hustle and bustle. Elegantly renovated, this five-story building, dating from the early 1900s, is furnished in Federal period decor. Wake up to a generous Continental breakfast and end the day with a complimentary glass of wine in front of the delightful library fireplace. **The Corona Bar and Grill** next door serves innovative Cal-Mex cuisine for lunch and dinner.
Singles & doubles $120; suites $145-$165

ORCHARD HOTEL
562 Sutter St. at Mason / 433-4434

The Orchard combines European elegance and charm with a commitment to gracious hospitality. The small 94-room hotel, built in 1907, has been meticulously reconstructed with traditional furnishings custom-made in Italy. Each guest room features a private bath, a refrigerated minibar and direct dial telephone. The adjoining restaurant, **Sutter Garden**, serves contemporary Continental cuisine for breakfast and lunch.
Singles & doubles $99-$130; suites $195

THE PAN PACIFIC HOTEL SAN FRANCISCO
500 Post St. at Mason / 771-8600

Service and comfort are the attractions here, with personal valets, Rolls Royce cars, 24-hour room service and complete business center services. In a dramatic 17-story atrium setting surrounded by marble, brass and original works of art, **The Pacific Grill** serves imaginative grilled specialties and spa food for breakfast, lunch and dinner.
Singles & doubles $185-$335; suites $550-$1,500

PARC FIFTY FIVE HOTEL
55 Cyril Magnin St. at Market / 392-8000

Parc Fifty Five brings a new element of elegance to Hallidie Plaza. Two blocks from Union Square, a block from the San Francisco Centre and a half block from the city's trademark cable cars, Parc Fifty Five offers 32 stories of luxurious accommodations. The hotel features elegant rooms and suites, breathtaking views of the city and private-access Concierge Club floors. Guests also enjoy the beautiful crystal-topped atrium, popular cocktail lounge, elegant restaurants and an executive health club.
Singles & doubles $155-$210; suites $340-$1,200

PARK HYATT
333 Battery St. at Clay / 392-1234

The Park Hyatt concept of European-style luxury, privacy and personal service translates into an incomparable hotel experience. All of the 360 elegantly appointed rooms and suites, many with balconies, offer bay or city views. Catering to international travelers and business people, the multilingual staff responds promptly to all requests and will even arrange for complimentary Mercedes-Benz limousine service. For dining, try the **Park Grill**, an upscale clubroom eatery serving specialties from around the world.
Singles & doubles $169-$295; suites $295-$2,000

PHOENIX INN
601 Eddy St. at Larkin / 776-1380

Often called an "urban oasis," the Phoenix Inn caters to the special guest who seeks a relaxing escape in a resort-like tropical environment — right in the middle of the city. The inner courtyard features a sculpture garden and a mural by Francis Forlenza in the heated swimming pool. Great food is right on the premises at **Miss Pearl's Jam House Restaurant and Bar**, offering critically acclaimed Caribbean fare at breakfast, lunch and dinner and lively fun well into the night. Two more pluses: complimentary Continental breakfast and free parking.
Singles & doubles $89; suites $129-$139

THE PRESCOTT HOTEL
545 Post St. at Mason / 563-0303

A leader of the "small hotel revolution," the 166-room Prescott Hotel emphasizes elegance, attention to detail and many complimentary guest services. The fully renovated hotel maintains the early California ambiance of its former namesake, the Hotel Cecil, but with a definite modern appeal. Some of that appeal centers on famous chef/restaurateur Wolfgang Puck's first Northern California venture, **Postrio**, located in the same building. The 150-seat restaurant, serving Puck's much-lauded California cuisine, provides room service to the Prescott.
Singles & doubles $155-$175; suites $205-$225

THE RITZ-CARLTON
600 Stockton St. at California / 296-7465

Located in a landmark Nob Hill building, the U-shaped hotel with dramatic, block-long facade offers guests impeccable service and rooms with a view — of the bay, city or courtyard. Two restaurants, **The Dining Room** and **The Restaurant**, provide four-star fortification, and a fitness center will rejuvenate even the most weary traveler.

SAN FRANCISCO HILTON
333 O'Farrell St. at Mason / 771-1400

Conveniently located just steps from the Financial District, Union Square, cable cars, theatres and Moscone Convention Center, the Hilton, occupying a full city block, is the largest hotel on the West Coast.

SAN FRANCISCO MARRIOTT
55 4th St. at Market / 896-1600

The San Francisco Marriott opened to great fanfare in October of 1989 after its dramatic modern architecture — magnificent fan windows and glass-and-steel stories descending like steps to Market Street — was completed. With 53 meeting rooms, the largest ballroom in San Francisco and a location just a block from the Moscone Convention Center, the San Francisco Marriott was designed as the ultimate convention and conference hotel in the city. The hotel's equally lavish health club provides guests with a large indoor swimming pool, spa, workout room and other amenities. Guests may choose from six restaurants and lounges from the intimate **Kinoko** Japanese restaurant to **The View Lounge**, a bar with spectacular views.
Singles & doubles $215-$235; suites $500-$2,000

SAVOY HOTEL
580 Geary St. at Jones / 441-2700

Here's a small hotel that offers privacy amid big city pandemonium. In addition to 70 regular rooms, 13 suites are embellished with jacuzzi tubs, spacious sitting rooms and ultra-elegant bathrooms. Pampering includes complimentary Continental breakfast, late

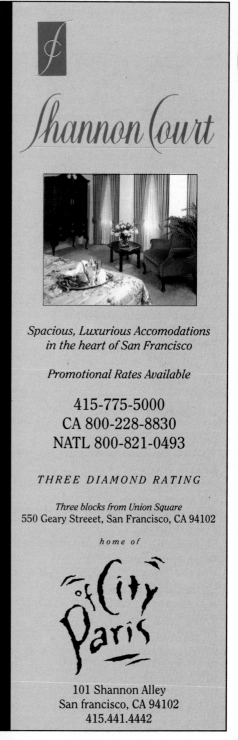

BED & BREAKFAST INNS

Often restored Victorians, San Francisco's bed & breakfast inns offer charm, intimacy and comfort at affordable prices. Many are furnished with antiques, and some even boast fireplaces, jacuzzis and views. If you need extra help with reservations, the bed & breakfast referral services are quick and reliable.

ALBION HOUSE
135 Gough Street 621-0896

ARCHBISHOP'S MANSION INN
1000 Fulton Street 563-7872

THE BED & BREAKFAST INN
4 Charlton Court 921-9784

THE CHATEAU TIVOLI
1057 Steiner Street 776-5462

EDWARD II INN
3155 Scott Street...................................922-3000

THE INN SAN FRANCISCO
943 South Van Ness Avenue 641-0188

JACKSON COURT
2198 Jackson Street 929-7670

THE MONTE CRISTO
600 Presidio Avenue 931-1875

PETITE AUBERGE
863 Bush Street 928-6000

UNION STREET INN
2229 Union Street 346-0424

VICTORIAN INN ON THE PARK
301 Lyon Street......................................931-1830

WHITE SWAN INN
845 Bush Street 775-1755

Referral & Reservation Services
BED & BREAKFAST INTERNATIONAL
....800-872-4500

BED & BREAKFAST SAN FRANCISCO
....800-452-8249

afternoon tea and an overnight shoe-shine, plus the essential business tools for traveling executives are available 24 hours a day. Downstairs the lively **Brasserie Savoy** further expresses the hotel's French elan.
Singles $89-$99; doubles $99-$109; suites $139-$149

SHANNON COURT HOTEL
550 Geary St. at Taylor / 775-5000

Built in 1929 with a unique Spanish design, the landmark Shannon Court near Union Square was completely renovated in 1989. Each of the 173 rooms and suites, decorated in contemporary and traditional American, has marble counter tops, full mirrors and Vidal Sassoon amenities in the bathrooms. The bright, spacious rooms accommodate king and queen size beds, as well as pull-out sofas. Complimentary Continental breakfast and afternoon tea. The hotel's **City of Paris** restaurant serves French bistro-style California cuisine and is open daily for breakfast, lunch and dinner.
Singles $90-$105; doubles $100-$120; suites $115-$275

SHEEHAN HOTEL
620 Sutter St. at Mason / 775-6500 or 800-848-1529

The Sheehan offers friendly service, affordable rates and an unbeatable location near Union Square. The 68-room hotel provides many personalized touches, including a complimentary Continental breakfast buffet featuring homebaked Irish Brown bread, muffins and assorted scones. Guests may also enjoy free use of the hotel's indoor lap pool and fitness center. The **Sheehan Tea Room**, open from 3PM to 9PM, serves freshly brewed teas, beer, wine and a light fare menu.
Singles & doubles $45-$95

SHERATON PALACE HOTEL
2 New Montgomery St. at Market / 392-8600

In 1887 Sarah Bernhardt stayed at the original Palace, Hawaii's King David Kalakaua died there in 1891, and the 1906 earthquake tossed famed tenor Enrico Caruso out of bed before the hotel succumbed to post-quake flames. The "new" Palace, completed in 1909, hosted Thomas Edison, Henry Ford, Woodrow Wilson and President Warren Harding, who died in room 8064 while still in office, to name only a few of the hotel's illustrious guests. Sixty-eight years and more than $100 million later, the Sheraton Palace is poised to attract today's luminaries. The restored **Garden Court** dining room resurrects a tradition of old-world elegance, while the **Pied Piper Bar** earns recognition as one of the world's seven greatest. **Maxfield's** serves American fare with an updated twist. Married to the Palace's magnificent history, state-of-the-art facilities, a new Japanese restaurant, **Kyo-ya**, and prime city location will take this landmark well into the future.
Singles $205-$265; doubles $225-$285; suites $400-$2,000

THE SHERMAN HOUSE
2160 Green St. at Webster / 563-3600

In a choice location one block from Union Street, The Sherman House is elegant throughout. Exquisite antiques and art combine with peaceful seclusion and luxurious dining to create the ultimate in overnight lodging. The century-old mansion has been beautifully restored to provide visual refinement, comfort and exclusive privacy. Each of the 14 rooms and suites is individually furnished with canopied beds, marble wood-burning fireplaces, stereo systems, refrigerators and whirlpool baths.

SIR FRANCIS DRAKE
450 Powell St. at Sutter / 392-7755

Welcoming guests to the Drake is a brightly costumed beefeater, who throws open the front doors with a jovial greeting. Although small in comparison to its neighbors, with 417 rooms and suites, the Drake is able to integrate the advantages of a larger hotel with a more personal approach to hospitality. Take the elevator to the **Starlite Roof** where you can munch complimentary hors d'oeuvres beginning at 4:30PM and then dance the night away. For breakfast, lunch and dinner, **Crusty**'s serves fresh California cuisine.
Singles $85-$125; doubles $95-$135; suites $325-$500

STANFORD PARK HOTEL
100 El Camino Real, Menlo Park / 322-1234

The Stanford Park Hotel offers elegant accommodations on the Peninsula. Conveniently located at the north end of Silicon Valley, the hotel is adjacent to Stanford University and the Stanford Shopping Center. Guest rooms are spacious and richly appointed, many featuring high-vaulted ceilings and fireplaces. Special amenities include deluxe minibars, in-room movies and three phones in each room. The hotel has a fully equipped fitness center with a whirlpool spa, sauna and a 40-foot lap pool. The **Palm Cafe** serves breakfast, lunch, dinner and Sunday brunch. Afternoon tea is served every weekday, and a pianist performs in the lounge Tuesday through Saturday evenings. The Stanford Park Hotel earned the 1992 Mobil Four Star and the AAA Four Diamond awards.
Singles $160-$250; doubles $175-$265; suites $195-$210

STOUFFER STANFORD COURT HOTEL
905 California St. at Powell / 989-3500

Erected on the site of railroad magnate Leland Stanford's mansion on Nob Hill at the cable car crossing, the Stouffer Stanford Court provides its guests with a gracious, residential atmosphere and the services of a European-style hotel. Highlighting the entry courtyard is a Tiffany-

style glass dome and sparkling fountain. The wood-paneled lobby, resembling a fine private club, is a perfect meeting place. In addition to telephones and televisions in the bathrooms plus many other amenities, the decor and furnishings at the renovated Stouffer Stanford Court are of a style and quality unusual in a large hotel. Its distinguished restaurant, **Fournou's Ovens**, features contemporary American cuisine.
Singles $195-$295; doubles $225-$325; suites $450-$2,000

THE TUSCAN INN AT FISHERMAN'S WHARF
425 Northpoint St. at Mason / 561-1100

Just blocks from Ghirardelli Square and the Cannery, The Tuscan Inn conjures the warmth and comfort of a European hotel retreat. Complimentary limousine to the Financial District, same-day valet service, an 80-person conference room and activities for children are just a few of this small inn's varied amenities. **Cafe Pescatore**, a classic Italian trattoria that offers outdoor dining on warm days, serves three meals daily and specializes in seafood, pasta and pizza.
Singles & doubles $158-$178; suites $198

VILLA FLORENCE HOTEL
225 Powell St. at Geary / 397-7700

The Villa Florence Hotel evokes romantic 16th century Tuscany. From the colonnaded entrance with its Giotto-style wishing fountain, enter the Italian Renaissance through a *trompe l'oeil* mural in the well-appointed lobby. The 177-room hotel has 36 suites and three meeting rooms that seat 10 to 60 people each. **Kuleto's**, the hotel's innovative Italian restaurant, has a tempting antipasto bar and serves one of San Francisco's most splendid breakfasts.
Singles & doubles $124; suites $189

THE WARWICK REGIS HOTEL
490 Geary St. at Taylor / 928-7900

A handsome 80-room hotel in the midst of San Francisco's theatre district, The Warwick Regis combines modern amenities with old-fashioned hospitality. Rooms are richly furnished in the style of Louis XVI, with French and English antiques, canopied beds, marble bathrooms, honor bars and remote-control color televisions. There are board and conference rooms, computer-equipped offices and a restaurant, **La Scene Cafe & Bar**, serving California cuisine.
Singles $95-$130; doubles $105-$205; suites $145-$205

THE WESTIN ST. FRANCIS HOTEL
335 Powell St. at Post / 397-7000

The historic Westin St. Francis has been a focal point for San Francisco social life since Charles T. Crocker built it in 1904. Dominating the very heart of downtown, the hotel has hosted many distinguished guests, including President Reagan and Queen Elizabeth. The spacious marble-columned lobby is one of the most popular rendezvous spots in the city, where friends meet "under the clock," or at the **Compass Rose** for tea or cocktails. Topping the tower is **Victor's**, the award-winning dining room, and **Oz**, an elegant nightclub. A brand new fitness and business center boasts state-of-the-art equipment.
Singles $150-$230; doubles $180-$260; suites $300-$1,450

THE YORK HOTEL
940 Sutter St. at Hyde / 885-6800

Just walking distance from Nob Hill and not far from Chinatown and Union Square, the York Hotel offers location and value. Stressing service and comfort, it has been a city favorite since it was built in the 1920s. The lobby has ceiling fans, elegant marble floors and, tucked in the back, the **Plush Room**, known for great cabaret.
Singles & doubles $95-$110; suites $175

HOTELS NEAR THE AIRPORT

BEST WESTERN EL RANCHO INN & EXECUTIVE SUITES
1100 El Camino Real, Millbrae / 588-2912
2⅓ miles west of SFO

For longer stays try these one- and two-bedroom apartments with kitchens and small patios. Twenty-four-hour shuttle, pool, jacuzzi, exercise room, coin laundry, restaurant and business services nearby.

CLARION HOTEL
401 East Millbrae Ave., Millbrae / 692-6363
½ mile south of SFO

Clarion offers one of the best business packages available. Services include a restaurant with heart-healthy items, 24-hour shuttle service, free parking, meeting rooms, executive and presidential suites and an outdoor pool with jacuzzi open year-round.

COURTYARD BY MARRIOTT
1050 Bayhill Dr., San Bruno / 952-3333
2 miles northwest of SFO

Amenities include an oversized desk, phone with 25-foot extension cord and coffee maker in each room. Restaurant, airport shuttle, indoor pool, whirlpool, coin laundry and business center nearby.

DOUBLETREE HOTEL SAN FRANCISCO AIRPORT
835 Airport Blvd., Burlingame / 344-5500
2 miles south of SFO

The Doubletree Hotel, located on San Francisco Bay, has spectacular views over the water. The hotel offers easy access to San Francisco and the Peninsula, with complimentary shuttle service to the airport. Guests are welcomed with cookies. Other inviting touches include a fully equipped exercise room and a jogging path along the bay. The hotel's 290 executive guest-rooms and suites are

spacious and well appointed with European furnishings. Conference and banquet facilities are available for business meetings, and for more informal gatherings, there is a relaxing guest lounge and library, warmed by a fireplace. The casually elegant **Chutney Grill** serves a wonderful selection of distinctive California cuisine, including a breakfast buffet.
Singles $109-$129; doubles $119-$139; suites $150-$300

HOLIDAY INN – CROWN PLAZA
600 Airport Blvd., Burlingame / 340-8500
3½ miles south of SFO

Participates in Holiday Inn's Priority Club, a frequent visitor program. Restaurant, 24-hour shuttle, meeting rooms, business services, exercise room, pool, sauna, jacuzzi, executive floor available for higher rate.

HOTEL SOFITEL SAN FRANCISCO BAY
223 Twin Dolphin Dr., Redwood City / 598-9000
7 miles south of SFO

Adding French flair to the mid-peninsula, Hotel Sofitel offers ample meeting facilities and 319 guest rooms with luxury touches. Each room has French toiletries by Nina Ricci, nightly turndown service, minibar and two telephones with dual lines and voice mail. Guests receive twice-daily maid service and professional concierge attention. Other guest services include a complimentary airport shuttle, conference and banquet facilities, a 24-hour health facility, an outdoor heated pool and full-service European spa. California French cuisine is served at **Baccarat**, the hotel's fine dining restaurant. **Gigi Brasserie**, a French-style bistro, serves breakfast, lunch and dinner daily. **La Terrasse** lounge offers entertainment and a waterfront view for cocktails.
Singles & doubles $135-$150; suites $198-$238

SAN FRANCISCO AIRPORT HILTON
At SFO / 589-0770

The only hotel in the airport, the Hilton operates a 24-hour shuttle to get you from the terminal to the hotel in minutes. Two restaurants, a business center, fitness facilities and executive suites are available.

THE WESTIN HOTEL
1 Bayshore Hwy., Millbrae / 692-3500
½ mile south of SFO

There's plenty of room to stretch your legs on the landscaped grounds, featuring palm trees and adjoining Bayshore Park. Amenities include two restaurants, 24-hour shuttle, business center, United Airlines check-in counter, health club and executive class service.

EXECUTIVE SUITES

BAYSIDE VILLAGE
3 Bayside Village Pl. at Beale & Bryant / 777-4850

Situated right on the bay just five blocks from the

ACCOMMODATIONS

Get to the Top ...

Location, Perfect. At the very top of Nob Hill, each elegant suite affords its own dazzling view. An exquisite retreat, while only a short walk or Cable Car ride to the Financial District and Union Square.

Service, Excels. An impressive array of business services, limousine and free use of the nearby Nob Hill Health Club, are all available.

For Reservations or Further
Information, Contact Us at

415 · 885 · 0636

"At the Top of Nob Hill"

1234 Jones St., San Francisco, CA 94109

Financial District, Bayside is also close to the city's cultural activities and nightlife. Amenities include deluxe furnished suites, a complete business center and a health club.

GEARY COURTYARD
639 Geary St. btwn. Jones & Leavenworth / 749-0101

Just minutes away from Union Square, Geary Courtyard optimizes city living with apartment homes that are contemporary and elegant. Distinctive amenities include modern appliances in every kitchen, 14th-floor Skyroom for private events, spectacular views and landscaped roof gardens, sun decks and terraces. A fitness center, attentive management and diverse neighborhood stores and services enrich everyday living, and nearby transportation eases daily routines. Minimum stay for furnished suites is 31 days; six months for unfurnished suites.
Singles $825-$1,700; suites $1,025-$2,200 (monthly)

HYDE PARK SUITES
2655 Hyde St. at North Point / 771-0200

In the center of Fisherman's Wharf, Hyde Park Suites offer both luxury and location. Each of the 24 luxury suites has a separate living room and bedroom and a fully equipped kitchen, with beautiful views of the Golden Gate Bridge and the bay. Ghirardelli Square and Fisherman's Wharf are within walking distance, and Chinatown and Union Square are just a cable car ride away.
Singles & doubles $165-$220

MARIN EXECUTIVE SUITES
82 Cypress Pl., Sausalito / 331-5534

In scenic Marin County across the Golden Gate Bridge from San Francisco, Marin Executive Suites has luxury furnished condominiums and townhomes available in Sausalito, Corte Madera and Larkspur for minimum stays of a month or more. Perfect for relocating corporate families and individuals, each one- or two- bedroom suite has a large, fully equipped kitchen, comfortable living room, television, video player, stereo, telephones, answering machine, washer and dryer and other amenities. In keeping with Marin's relaxed lifestyle, guests can unwind by playing tennis, swimming or using the spa facilities. Maid service, utilities and private parking included. Reservations may also be made in advance by fax (415-331-8039).
Suites $2,250-$3,000 (monthly)

NOB HILL APARTMENTS
1234 Jones St. at Clay / 923-1234

Located on top of Nob Hill and within walking distance from Union Square, the elegant Nob Hill Apartments are one of San Francisco's best-kept secrets. Individually decorated with distinctive artworks and furnishings, the 23 suites include designer kitchens and bathrooms. These luxury one-bedroom suites offer dramatic views of San Francisco Bay, North Beach and the Financial Dis-

trict. With its custom touches, the hotel has acquired a well-deserved reputation as a luxurious pied-à-terre for sophisticated travelers doing business in San Francisco. Limousine service available to the airport.
Suites $1,250-$2,500 (monthly)

NOB HILL LAMBOURNE
725 Pine St. near Powell / 433-2287

The Nob Hill Lambourne provides a full range of business services, available in the privacy of each suite. The services include fax machines, voice mail, personal computers and secretarial assistance. For the ultimate in comfort for the executive traveler, the hotel's concierge staff also makes travel and catering arrangements, schedules limousine pick-ups at the airport and offers health club memberships.
Doubles $175; suites $250

NORTHPOINT APARTMENTS & EXECUTIVE SUITES
2211 Stockton St. at Bay / 989-6563

With free parking in the busy Fisherman's Wharf, NorthPoint Apartments is an ideal location for executives who want to combine tourism with business. Guests can stay for a month or more in furnished studios and one-bedrooms with fully equipped kitchens.

SOUTH BEACH MARINA APARTMENTS
2 Townsend St. at Embarcadero / 495-4119

Towering above the San Francisco waterfront, the new South Beach Marina Apartments have spectacular views of the skyline and bay. Amenities for corporate residents include a shuttle to the Financial District, business services and concierge assistance. Minimum three month stay.

TRINITY EXECUTIVE SUITES
333 Bay St. at Powell / 433-3333

At choice sites throughout the city, including Russian Hill, Pacific Heights and the Union Square area, many of Trinity's luxury buildings have a lavish decor and breathtaking views of San Francisco.

2000 POST APARTMENTS
2000 Post St. near Steiner / 922-2006

Located in the up-and-coming Fillmore area, 2000 Post Apartments provides luxury living that is affordable. Open daily, 2000 Post offers studios, one- and two-bedroom apartments. Many have wood-burning fireplaces, bay windows and lots of sun. These apartments are available furnished, unfurnished and with short or long-term leases. Executives from across the world enjoy free aerobics and body-sculpting classes at its exclusive health club. Other health club benefits include a heated pool and spa relaxation. Corporate furnished suites are available, requiring a minimum 30 day stay.
Apartments starting at $795 (monthly)

SAN FRANCISCO IS A PARTY TOWN — AND I SHOULD KNOW. I'VE BEEN PARTYING here for 28 years, and it's been nothing but fun, fun, fun. We're lucky everything is close by because you can go to lots of places and never worry about drinking and driving. You just take cabs! Locals discovered that from the tourists. You ask the manager to call a cab and for five dollars you go clear across town.

Harry Denton owns Harry Denton's on Steuart Street, dedicated to "dames, drinks, dalliance and damn good chow."

Those who complain that San Francisco closes up at 2 A.M. miss the point: we like it that way. It's healthier. If you've had a good time, a really good time, who needs to prowl around for more at 4 A.M.?

For people-watching, San Francisco is the best. Try Bix, Postrio, Cypress Club or Stars on a Saturday night. I like to take my friends

Nightlife

from one to the other, always ending up at Harry Denton's for dancing.

In L.A. or New York, you find a great spot to hang out but when you return a few months later it's gone or empty. Here, places tend to last. If they like a place, people keep coming back. The bartender remembers them. They feel welcome, a part of the scene.

Only one thing is missing that would make San Francisco's nightlife the best in the country: more sidewalk tables. If only the city would loosen up, we could take the party to the streets.

Have fun!

Thank you: Nob Hill Restaurant; Andy Marshall, Jennifer Wolf, EPIC Models

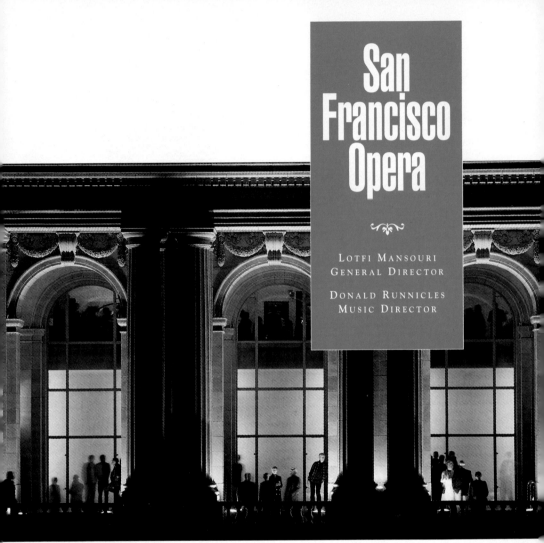

San Francisco Opera

LOTFI MANSOURI
GENERAL DIRECTOR

DONALD RUNNICLES
MUSIC DIRECTOR

Photo: Kit Morris

"THE SAN FRANCISCO OPERA
IS UNEQUIVOCALLY THE FINEST ALL-AROUND
AMERICAN OPERA COMPANY."

Spring 1992, Museo Teatrale alla Scala

For a complimentary brochure with complete performance details, call
415-864-3330

san francisco
OPERA

THEATRE

ALCAZAR THEATRE
650 Geary St. at Jones / 861-6655

The Alcazar Theatre is housed in the Islamic Temple, a San Francisco landmark. Two theatres in one, the Alcazar presents national touring productions and a variety of performing artists.

AMERICAN CONSERVATORY THEATRE
415 Geary St. at Mason / 749-2228

The American Conservatory Theatre is a leading repertory theatre and professional actor training school with an impeccable reputation. ACT won a Tony Award in 1979 and has conducted successful tours of the Soviet Union and Japan. Through its repertory approach, ACT affords the widest choice of plays during its October through May season. Because of earthquake damage to the company's resident theatre, call for venue information.

BERKELEY REPERTORY THEATRE
2025 Addison St. at Shattuck, Berkeley / 510-845-4700

The Berkeley Repertory Theatre enjoys both critical and popular acclaim, making it the theatre to watch in the Bay Area. An intimate 11-row, 401-seat facility, the Rep mixes strong commitment to fine new plays with a fresh look at the classics.

CABLE CAR THEATRE
430 Mason St. at Geary / 989-9132

An informal, 150-seat theatre, Cable Car is conveniently located near Theatre Row. This former speakeasy/restaurant is the perfect setting for comedies and revues.

CLIMATE
252 9th St. at Folsom / 626-9196

Climate presents national and local upcoming performers. The intimate theatre showcases experimental and avant-garde works. Some annual highlights include a performance festival in the fall and a contemporary puppet theatre festival in July.

COWELL THEATRE
Fort Mason Center, Pier 2 / 441-5706

The Cowell has excellent sight lines and state-of-the-art light and sound systems. You'll find a variety of programs, including theatre, music and dance.

CURRAN THEATRE
445 Geary St. at Mason / 474-3800

The Curran was the last major theatre constructed in downtown San Francisco during the 1920s. Performances have included opera, musicals, plays and ballets. Now it's primarily used for the "Best of Broadway" series, which showcases musicals and plays coming from or heading to Broadway.

GOLDEN GATE THEATRE
One Taylor St. at Golden Gate & Market / 474-3800

Quiet grandeur is the best way to describe the fully restored Golden Gate Theatre. Since 1922 it has played host to headliners such as Frank Sinatra, Carmen Miranda, Louis Armstrong, George Burns and Gracie Allen, and Lena Horne. In addition, most of the big bands of the '40s played this house. Live shows extended into the mid-'50s, followed by first-run movies. Since the theatre is too large for most plays, it is used almost exclusively for musical productions.

HERBST THEATRE
401 Van Ness Ave. at McAllister / 392-4400

Home to many of San Francisco's most beloved series and events, the Herbst Theatre opened in 1932 as the Veterans Auditorium and was the site of the signing of the United Nations Charter in 1945. Rechristened the Herbst after its renovation in 1978, the 928-seat theatre is hung with eight murals by premier muralist Frank Brangwyn, commissioned for the 1915 Panama Pacific International Expo. The diverse offerings here include the San Francisco Performance Series and the City Arts & Lectures series.

JULIAN THEATRE
777 Valencia St. at 19th / 626-8986

Established in 1965, the Julian is known for producing social and political works by new West Coast writers as well as undiscovered works from all around the world. The company is now in residence at New College.

LIFE ON THE WATER
Fort Mason, Building B / 776-8999

Comfortable seats and avant-garde programming make Life on the Water one of San Francisco's most innovative venues. International theatre groups, performance workshops, poetry, music and dance share the stage.

NIGHTLIFE

MAGIC THEATRE
Fort Mason, Building D / 441-8822

The Magic Theatre is one of the oldest and largest theatre companies in the country devoted primarily to the production of new works in American theatre. The theatre's season runs from November through July.

MARINES MEMORIAL THEATRE
609 Sutter St. at Mason, 2nd floor / 771-6900

Charles H. Duggan Presents took over the management of the Marines Memorial Theatre in 1982, and since then has brought one hit after another to its venerable stage.

MASON STREET THEATRE
340 Mason St. at Geary / 981-3535

Once a cabaret, this intimate theatre is located in the heart of downtown, two blocks from Union Square. The Mason Street Theatre presents musicals and revues.

NOEL COWARD PLAYERS
Fort Mason, Building C / 346-5550

Performing since 1990, the company presents two Noel Coward plays and two new productions a year.

ORPHEUM THEATRE
1192 Market St. at Hyde / 474-3800

The first Orpheum Theatre to titillate San Franciscans was built in 1876. Since that date, there has seldom been a time when the city didn't have an Orpheum. Today, the Orpheum mainly presents concerts.

SAN FRANCISCO MIME TROUPE
855 Treat Ave. at 21st St. / 285-1717

This 1987 Tony Award-winning political musical comedy troupe is the oldest and best known in the country. Don't expect a performance of silent mime; these are outspoken, provocative acts, on subjects as timely as today's headlines. In addition to touring the United States and the world, they perform free shows each summer in Bay Area parks.

THEATRE ARTAUD
450 Florida St. at 17th / 621-7797

Located in the former American Can Company, this 300-seat theatre serves as an arena for an innovative array of contemporary and experimental drama, music and dance performances.

THEATRE ON THE SQUARE
450 Post St. at Powell / 433-9500

Theatre on the Square, which brings in Broadway shows as well as local productions, seats 700 in an elegant and intimate setting. The Gothic-Mediterranean style of the building boasts gold-leaf friezes, wrought-iron metalwork, graceful archways and a hand-carved ceiling.

THEATRE RHINOCEROS
2926 16th St. at South Van Ness / 861-5079

Theatre Rhinoceros is considered San Francisco's most important gay theatre ensemble. Founded in 1977, the company has produced works by Lanford Wilson, Noel Coward, Judy Grahn and others.

THE WARFIELD THEATRE
982 Market St. btwn. 5th & 6th / 775-7722

Since 1922 Warfield audiences have enjoyed the live stage performers of their time, from Al Jolson in the early years to Carlos Santana today. Designed by G. Albert Lansburg, architect for the San Francisco House, the concert hall's cathedral ceiling and plush balcony and table seating create an old-world ambiance — a unique showcase for modern rising stars and legends.

BALLET

OAKLAND BALLET
Paramount Theatre
2025 Broadway, Oakland / 510-465-6400

The Oakland Ballet presents an annual fall season of performances at Oakland's Paramount Theatre and Berkeley's Zellerbach Hall. The company is internationally acclaimed for its preservation of master works from the Diaghilev and 20th century American dance eras, as well as for its presentation of innovative contemporary choreography.

SAN FRANCISCO BALLET
War Memorial Opera House
301 Van Ness Ave. at Grove / 703-9400

Among the country's foremost ballet companies, the San Francisco Ballet is also America's oldest professional company, founded in 1933. Currently under the artistic direction of Helgi Tomasson, former choreographer and principal dancer with the New York City Ballet, San Francisco Ballet offers a repertoire by some of the world's most distinguished choreographers, including George Balanchine, Val Caniparoli, Jerome Robbins, David Bintley and William Forsythe. The company launches its season every December with a lavish production of *Nutcracker*.

OPERA & SYMPHONY

SAN FRANCISCO OPERA
War Memorial Opera House
301 Van Ness Ave. at Grove / 864-3330

The 3,176-seat Opera House is a splendid example of Beaux Arts architecture and a handsome showcase for magnificent productions. Ranked as one of the finest opera companies in the world, the San Francisco Opera is directed by Lotfi Mansouri, whose career spans 30 years directing opera. He regularly directs at the Vienna

Opera, La Scala, the Metropolitan Opera, Chicago Lyric Opera, Santa Fe Opera, Paris Opera, Amsterdam, Geneva and Zurich Operas. San Francisco's fall season runs from September to December with an opera festival scheduled for June. All productions have supertitles. In June 1993, the opera presents a celebration of Richard Strauss, featuring *Salome, Der Rosenkavalier, Capriccio* and *Daphne*. The 71st fall season opens on September 10, 1993. Running through December 12, the performances include Verdi's *I Vespri Siciliani*, Donizetti's *La Fille du Regiment*, Puccini's *La Boheme* and *Turandot*, Janacek's *The Makropulos Case*, Wagner's *Die Meistersinger*, Mozart's *La Clemenza di Tito*, Bellini's *I Puritani* and Tchaikovsky's *Pique Dame*. To receive a complimentary brochure of the opera's season or for information, call 864-3330.

SAN FRANCISCO SYMPHONY
Davies Symphony Hall, Van Ness at Grove / 431-5400

Under the direction of Music Director Herbert Blomstedt, the San Francisco Symphony has achieved international recognition for its excellence. The symphony season also features presentation of the Great Performers Series, Pops, Joffrey Ballet, holiday concerts, and other festivals and special events.

BARS & CAFES

BALBOA CAFE
3199 Fillmore St. at Greenwich / 921-3944

Very popular with the Marina singles set, the glass-enclosed Balboa Cafe is decorated with dark wood wainscot, brass railings and tiled floors.

BOAT HOUSE
One Harding Park Road / 681-2727

Located on picturesque Lake Merced, the Boat House is home to an enthusiastic sports crowd.

BUENA VISTA CAFE
2765 Hyde St. at Beach / 474-5044

The "Bee-Vee" is famous for being the first to serve Irish coffee in the United States. Located at the end of the Hyde Street cable car line between Ghirardelli Square and Fisherman's Wharf, it's a convenient stop after a day at the Wharf.

CAFE ADRIANO
3347 Fillmore St. at Chestnut / 474-4180

This charming Italian bistro is a popular rendezvous for Marina residents. Cafe Adriano is casual and friendly. Moderately priced seasonal Italian dishes are served with selections from an ample list of Italian and California wines.
Tuesday through Saturday 5:30PM to 11PM; Sunday 5PM to 10:30PM

NIGHTLIFE

NIGHTLIFE

CAFE DE LA PRESSE
Hotel Triton, 352 Grant Ave. at Bush / 398-2680

Cafe de la Presse revives the sorely missed Sutter Cafe mix of international news and coffee. You can purchase newspapers and magazines from all over the world and read while you sip and eat. The cafe also has light French fare and wine by the glass or bottle for nighttime relaxation. *Monday through Saturday 7AM to 9PM; Sunday 7AM to 8PM*

CAVA 555
555 Second St. btwn. Brannan & Bryant / 543-2282

Everything about Cava 555 dazzles — from the neon glow at the entrance to the liquid ambiance of murals, metallic walls, shiny black surfaces and sparkling sprays of romantic lights. The club's theme is champagne and jazz; the mood is cool and elegant. Chef Patrick Rice has created an exceptional menu of eclectic California cuisine to complement the great selection of Champagnes and sparkling wines — there are more than 50 to choose from. There's also an impressive wine list and full bar. Cava 555 has live jazz Monday through Saturday. The club serves lunch Monday through Friday and dinner Monday through Saturday. You can also get a bite late into the night. Cava 555's late-night bar menu is available until 1:30AM Monday through Saturday. *Monday to Friday 4:30PM to 2AM; Saturday 6PM to 2AM*

COMPASS ROSE
Westin St. Francis Hotel
335 Powell St. at Geary / 774-0167

Decorated in the grand San Francisco style, the lounge is located just inside the Powell Street entrance to the hotel. A pianist, the St. Francis Strings and the Abe Battat Trio provide sophisticated live music in a lush environment of giant fluted columns, etched glass and marble, Oriental carpets and rich wood paneling. *Daily until 1AM. Luncheon 11:30AM to 2:30PM except Sunday; high tea served 3PM to 5PM (reservations advised); tasting menu 5PM to 1AM*

CORONA BAR & GRILL
88 Cyril Magnin St. at Ellis / 392-5500

Take a tropical vacation in the heart of San Francisco at the Corona Bar & Grill. Its Southwestern decor and tasty Mexican and Southwestern appetizers would be enough to delight anyone weary of city life, but this bar also has some of the best margaritas in town. *Sunday through Thursday 11:30AM to 11PM; Friday & Saturday until midnight*

EDDIE RICKENBACKER'S
133 2nd St. at Minna / 543-3498

Named after the famous World War I American flying ace, Eddie Rickenbacker's has motorcycles and war memorabilia hanging from the rafters.

GOLDEN GATE GRILL
3200 Fillmore St. at Greenwich / 931-4600

A Bermuda Triangle meeting place that attracts a large "bridge and tunnel" crowd, Golden Gate Grill is especially loud and lively on Thursday nights and weekends.

GORDON BIERSCH BREWERY RESTAURANT
2 Harrison St. at Steuart / 243-8246

Crowded since it opened last year, Gordon Biersch Brewery Restaurant serves three unique beers: Export, Marzen and Dunkles. Dan Gordon, a graduate of the elite Technical University of Munich, brews them with the finest hops and yeast according to strict German purity laws. You can watch them being made in huge tanks behind plate-glass windows. The bar is friendly and fun, and a popular rendezvous for the Financial District crowd. The cuisine features an eclectic California menu. Specialties range from Mediterranean to Thai dishes, and all complement the beers and the selection of first-rate California wines. *Sunday through Tuesday 11AM to 11PM; Wednesday & Thursday 11AM to midnight; Friday & Saturday 11AM to 1AM*

THE GREAT ENTERTAINER
975 Bryant St. at 8th St. / 861-8833

This is the city's largest billiard club-bar-restaurant: a 22,000 square-foot, high-tech setting for fun. The entertainment possibilities are limitless, with 43 pocket billiard tables, shuffleboard, table tennis, darts, foosball, basketball and a video arcade. There are private suites for small parties, or you can take over the whole place with 800 friends! No matter how many are in your group, The Great Entertainer will accommodate your taste and budget, with an array of menus, from hors d'oeuvres to complete four-course dinners. Come early on weekends, when everyone wants to party. *Sunday through Thursday 11AM to 2AM; Friday & Saturday 11AM to 3AM; 21 & over after 9PM Sat & Sun*

HARD ROCK CAFE
1699 Van Ness Ave. at Sacramento / 885-1699

Opened in September 1984, the Hard Rock remains popular and fun. Music is nonstop and the decor is unusual to say the least — visualize half a Cadillac coming through the wall. Great burgers, fresh fish, chili and thick shakes are among the menu listings.

HARRY'S
2020 Fillmore St. at California / 921-1000

In the middle of San Francisco's most upscale neighborhood, Harry's is an old-style, traditional San Francisco saloon and restaurant. Popular with young professionals, the bar's handsome room features striking deep blue walls, Italian lanterns and beveled glass. You can stop by for a drink at the mahogany bar where live music sets the mood every night, or you can stay for dinner. The California cuisine menu mirrors the extravagance of the room.

Daily 3:30PM to 2AM; restaurant service Tuesday through Saturday 5PM to 11PM, Sunday & Monday 5PM to 10PM

THE INTERNATIONAL BAR
Stouffer Stanford Court Hotel, 905 California St.
989-3500

Located in the award-winning Stouffer Stanford Court Hotel, the International Bar is perfect for cocktails and quiet conversation. The mix of international hotel guests and local patrons lends a cosmopolitan atmosphere to the elegant room.

Sunday through Thursday 5PM to 11PM; Friday & Saturday 5PM to 1AM

IRELAND'S 32
3920 Geary Blvd. at 3rd Ave. / 386-6173

This lively Irish pub attracts a mostly Irish crowd during the week and a mixed crowd on weekends.

JOHNNY LOVE'S
1500 Broadway at Polk / 931-6053

Named after co-owner Johnny Metheny, aka Johnny Love, one of the city's best-loved bartenders, this has quickly become one of the most popular hangouts. Johnny can be found behind the giant horseshoe bar, charming one and all and setting an upbeat mood in his inimitable way. Johnny Love's is perfect for a whole night of fun: enjoy cocktails at the bar, dine on critically acclaimed American cuisine, then linger for the live music, be it rock, blues or reggae. Featured performers have included Clarence Clemmons, Greg Allman and Curtis Salgado. Cover charge Wednesday through Saturday starting at 9:30PM.

Monday through Sunday 5PM to 2AM; dinner served until 10PM; bar/late night menu

JULIE'S SUPPER CLUB
1123 Folsom St. at 7th / 861-0707

A popular restaurant with singles, Julie's Supper Club has one of the liveliest bars South of Market. You'll like the Day-Glo decor and friendly ambiance.

THE LONDON WINE BAR
415 Sansome St. at Sacramento / 788-4811

"America's First Wine Bar," the London Wine Bar introduced the concept of offering premium wines by the glass and bottle. Today, nearly 50 wines by the glass are available daily.

NIGHTLIFE

LOU'S PIER 47
300 Jefferson St. at Jones / 771-0377

Located right on Fisherman's Wharf, Lou's has a big downstairs bar and restaurant serving great seafood, and an upstairs bar featuring live music nightly — everything from country rock to blues.

MARGARITAVILLE
1787 Union St. at Octavia / 441-1183

This Union Street watering hole features great margaritas and a bar crowded with young singles.

MASON STREET WINE BAR
342 Mason St. at Geary / 391-3454

Located right on Theatre Row, the Mason Street Wine Bar is an ideal place to taste and try wines, including champagnes, aperitifs, sherries and ports, whether it's before a performance or after dinner.

NOC NOC
557 Haight St. at Fillmore / 861-5811

Small and inconspicuous on the outside, dark and denlike on the inside, Noc Noc resembles a Mad Max movie. Lower Haight locals gather here to sip and talk.

PARAGON BAR & CAFE
3251 Scott St. at Chestnut / 922-2456

A favorite of Marina residents who appreciate good food and a warm welcome, the Paragon features live piano every night and jazz or blues Monday, Tuesday and Wednesday evenings. Past performers have included John Lee Hooker, Maria Muldaur and Jules Broussard. Plastered walls, beamed ceilings and a large fireplace give an old-tavern feeling, but the art and ambiance are definitely '90s. Quickly becoming one of San Francisco's most popular neighborhood bars, the Paragon is also well known for its superb American cuisine, served both in an intimate dining room and at the bar.
Daily 5PM to 2AM; dinner until 10PM

PAT O'SHEA'S MAD HATTER
3848 Geary Blvd. at 3rd Ave. / 752-3148

The awning on the outside of Pat O'Shea's reads, "We Cheat Tourists and Drunks," which gives you an idea of the atmosphere at this Irish pub-cum-sports bar.

PERRY'S
1944 Union St. at Laguna / 922-9022

Perry's is a long-time favorite Union Street watering hole. The clientele is sophisticated, outgoing and decidedly urban. The attractive interior is decorated with dark mahogany paneling, posters, tiled floors, brass rails and a pressed tin ceiling. Perry's sets the standard for old-fashioned American food. Whether you're enjoying dinner or a weekend brunch, you are assured of large portions, fresh ingredients and speedy service.
Daily 9AM to 2AM. Food served until 11PM Sunday through Thursday; until midnight Friday & Saturday

THE PLOUGH & STARS
116 Clement St. at 2nd Ave. / 751-1122

Long wooden tables with an Irish Republic banner create a warm, friendly atmosphere that attracts a large Irish clientele. Fine imported ales are served on tap, and traditional Irish folk music can be heard nightly.

POSTRIO
545 Post St. at Mason / 776-7825

Wolfgang Puck's hugely successful restaurant also has a comfortable bar where you can enjoy his pizzas, sandwiches and creative appetizers until 1AM — without needing to make a reservation.

RASSELAS
2801 California St. at Divisadero / 567-5010

Elegant yet casual, Rasselas has comfortable tables and chairs and a Victorian back bar, with live blues and jazz nightly. A small dining room serves spicy Ethiopian cuisine for lunch and dinner.

REDWOOD ROOM
Four Seasons Clift Hotel
495 Geary St. at Taylor / 775-4700

Located next door to the Curran Theatre and two blocks from Union Square, the Redwood Room typifies the opulence and grandeur of the Art Deco period, when it was built. Live entertainment is offered nightly by renowned pianist Ricardo Scales. The Redwood Room serves appetizers, light meals and desserts. For elegant dining, the Four Seasons Clift also offers classical French cuisine with a California touch at the adjoining French Room.
Daily 4:30PM to 2AM

SAN FRANCISCO BREWING COMPANY
155 Columbus Ave. at Pacific / 434-3344

Built on the site of the historic 1907 Albatross Saloon, the San Francisco Brewing Company is the city's first brew pub. The bar serves up to four different full-flavored beers daily, including Albatross and Emperor Norton lagers, all brewed on site in handmade copper brew kettles. Fresh, seasonal California bistro cooking is offered for lunch and dinner.
Monday through Thursday 11:30AM to 12:30AM; Friday 11:30AM to 1:30AM; Saturday noon to 1:30AM; Sunday noon to 12:30AM

THE SAVOY TIVOLI
1434 Grant Ave. near Union / 362-7023

The Savoy's large, open-air patio bar has been a favorite of North Beach locals for years. It's a wonderful perch for people-watching over cappuccino or a glass of wine.

SILHOUETTES
524 Union St. near Grant / 398-1952

Packed on weekends, Silhouettes is a lively '50s and '60s club catering to a young and young-at-heart, energetic crowd that likes to dance.

STARS
150 Redwood Alley off Van Ness / 861-7827

This warm San Francisco restaurant, made famous by Jeremiah Tower's inventive cuisine, has a bright, lively cocktail lounge located in the center of the restaurant. The large wooden bar with its adjacent tables is one of San Francisco's most popular places for a drink, especially before or after the theatre. An inexpensive bar menu is available, but the real treat is listening to the jazz pianist.

TOSCA CAFE
242 Columbus Ave. at Broadway / 986-9651

In business since 1919, Tosca is situated at the crossroads of San Francisco's famous nightlife district in North Beach. Opera buffs enjoy Caruso and other favorites from an old-fashioned jukebox while sipping Tosca's memorable cappuccino laced with brandy.

TWENTY TANK BREWERY
316 11th St. at Folsom / 255-9455

Twenty Tank Brewery is a popular place for hamburgers, nachos, chili and beer on tap. Several kinds of beer are brewed on site.

THE UP AND DOWN CLUB
1151 Folsom St. at 7th / 626-8862

Reminiscent of a 1940s New York saloon, the bar presents live blues and jazz. Downstairs, the restaurant serves French bistro fare.

VESUVIO
255 Columbus St. off Broadway / 362-3370

Nestled next to the historic City Lights Bookstore, Vesuvio maintains the bohemian spirit of a Beat generation bar.

WASHINGTON SQUARE BAR & GRILL
1707 Powell St. at Union / 982-8123

The "Washbag," as columnist Herb Caen has christened this popular restaurant and bar, is a favorite with the city's media and literary crowd.

SKY-HIGH BARS

CARNELIAN ROOM
52nd floor, Bank of America Building
555 California St. at Kearny / 433-7500

This elegant glass-enclosed room high atop Bank of America's world headquarters is a private dining room until 3PM. After that, the public is welcome to dine, sip cocktails and enjoy the heavenly ambiance.

CITYSCAPE
46th floor, San Francisco Hilton
333 O'Farrell St. at Mason / 771-1400

Dancing enlivens the sky-high view of downtown San Francisco from this sophisticated lounge.

CROWN ROOM
24th floor, Fairmont Hotel
950 Mason St. at California / 772-5131

At the top of Nob Hill, the Fairmont reaches high in the sky, crowned by a glass-enclosed cocktail lounge and buffet dining room.

EQUINOX
18th floor, Hyatt Regency
Embarcadero Five at Market / 788-1234

Take a 360-degree tour of San Francisco without ever leaving your seat in the city's only revolving rooftop restaurant and lounge.

OZ
32nd floor, Westin St. Francis Hotel
335 Powell St. at Geary / 774-0116

An outside elevator takes you all the way up; once inside, mirrors reflect the chic, international dance crowd and intimate decor.

SHERLOCK HOLMES ESQ. LOUNGE
30th floor, Holiday Inn Union Square
480 Sutter St. at Powell / 398-8900

Sherlock Holmes Esq. Lounge offers one of the finest vistas of San Francisco in town. Live piano music and comfortable stuffed chairs create just the right atmosphere.

STARLITE ROOF
21st floor, Sir Francis Drake Hotel
450 Powell St. at Sutter / 392-7755

Known to generations of San Franciscans as a romantic destination, the Starlite Roof is still very popular, whether for a quiet drink or a night of dancing under the stars. The views are spectacular.

TOP OF THE MARK
19th floor, Mark Hopkins InterContinental
One Nob Hill, California at Mason / 392-3434

What may be the world's most famous cocktail lounge, the Top of the Mark is a spectacular glass-walled room with an unsurpassed view of San Francisco.

VICTOR'S
32nd floor, Westin St. Francis Hotel
335 Powell St. at Geary / 774-0253

Victor's lounge atop this prominent Union Square hotel offers a quiet and romantic interlude with a beautiful view of the city.

THE VIEW LOUNGE
39th floor, San Francisco Marriott
55 4th St. at Market / 896-1600

The lounge's signature 35-foot fan window opens out onto dramatic vistas of the Financial District, Alcatraz and the Oakland docks beyond the Bay Bridge. With its backlit window designed to jut out like a cockpit over the city's skyline, the lounge offers an intimate evening, with piano and jazz entertainment, above the brilliant lights of downtown San Francisco.
Daily 11:30AM to 1:30AM

CABARETS & MUSIC CLUBS

BEACH BLANKET BABYLON
Club Fugazi, 678 Green St. at Powell / 421-4222

Beach Blanket Babylon is the nation's longest-running musical revue. Now in its 19th year of sold-out shows in North Beach, Steve Silver's zany, fast-paced musical revue has had more than 6,500 performances. The show revolves around Snow White, whose worldwide search for a prince leads her to encounter an ever-changing cast of celebrity caricatures such as Cher, Madonna and Elvis. With stops in Paris, Rome and Japan, she eventually returns to everyone's favorite city. The excellent cast sports stunning costumes full of visual puns and a dizzying array of enormous hats that tower upwards toward the ceiling. The choreography is fantastic; the gags come fast and furious; and the music is first-rate and fun.
Performances Wednesday through Sunday; over 21, photo I.D. required; minors welcome at Sunday matinees

BLUES
2125 Lombard St. at Fillmore / 771-2583

Blues is small and intimate, with live blues. The newly opened club is very popular on Saturdays.

CYRIL'S CABARET
Club Fugazi, 678 Green St. at Powell / 421-4222

Cyril's Cabaret is tucked away below Club Fugazi in the heart of North Beach, site of the wildly successful musical revue, *Beach Blanket Babylon*. Named after the late Cyril Magnin, Cyril's is an intimate showroom, vividly decorated with *trompe l'oeil* draperies, Renaissance-style murals depicting famous San Franciscans and Italianate balconies. The cabaret tables with shaded candles and the glittering chandelier recall the nightclubs of the 1930s and '40s such as the Stork Club and El Morocco. Steve Silver presents offbeat as well as traditional cabaret-style shows that reflect the club's elegant yet comfortable spirit.
Call for dates, information & ticket sales; box office open daily; over 21, photo I.D. required

ELI'S MILE HIGH CLUB & RESTAURANT
3629 Martin Luther King Jr. Way at 36th
Oakland / 510-655-6661

Eli's offers live blues and dancing Wednesday through Sunday evenings. *The Jazz & Blues Lovers Guide* voted the club the "best blues joint in the East Bay."

ENTREE TO MURDER DINNER THEATRE
A. Sabella's Restaurant, 2766 Taylor St. / 991-2583

Now you can take part in an interactive murder mystery while enjoying a three-course meal at A. Sabella's Fridays and Saturdays at 8:00PM. *Cafe Noir* by David Landou is a Bogart-style comedy mystery that takes audiences on a trip to the Caribbean, where they become patrons at the legendary Cafe Noir, host to smugglers, blackmailers and other lowlifes. It's an evening of fun in four acts. *Call for reservations; price includes dinner & two-hour validated parking*

FINOCCHIO'S
506 Broadway at Kearny / 982-9388

Finocchio's world-famous revue of female impersonators has stunned generations of visitors since the 1930s. It's great entertainment and all in good fun.

THE GREAT AMERICAN MUSIC HALL
859 O'Farrell St. at Polk / 885-0750

Celebrating its 20th year in business, the Great American Music Hall is San Francisco's most beautiful venue for live entertainment. Their lineups range from the best in blues (Etta James and John Lee Hooker), rock (Van Morrison and Leon Russell), jazz (Bobby McFerrin and Acoustic Alchemy), country (Johnny Cash and Suzie Bogguss), to folk (Indigo Girls and Joan Baez) and comedy. On the weekends, The Great American Music Hall often features dance bands to create a party atmosphere. Light meals, snacks and a full bar are available. *Call for dates, information & ticket sales; box office open Monday through Saturday*

JACKS BAR
1601 Fillmore St. at Geary / 567-3227

Jacks Bar is a fun club for live jazz and blues. The club has an easygoing atmosphere and an unpretentious decor.

KIMBALL'S
300 Grove St. at Franklin / 861-5585

Right across the street from Davies Symphony Hall and the Opera House, Kimball's is a great stop for a nightcap. Known as the "home of world-class jazz and cuisine," the club hosts a number of top performers in a comfortable setting with good sight lines. Kimball's won the 1983-84 Golden Cabaret "Best Jazz Club" award. *Tuesday through Saturday 5PM to 1AM; Sunday 5PM to midnight. Call for show times*

KIMBALL'S EAST
5800 Shellmound St., Emery Bay Market Place
Emeryville / 510-658-2555

The premier jazz venue on the West Coast is right in the Bay Area: Kimball's East. A large club that seats 350, with absolutely no sight obstructions, Kimball's East has an incredible Meyers sound system and top-billed national and local jazz greats. The club includes a full restaurant serving American cuisine and opens at 5PM. *Tuesday 5PM to 9PM; Wednesday through Saturday 5PM to 1AM; Sunday 5PM to midnight. Call for show times*

ODESSA BEACH
915 Columbus Ave. at Lombard / 346-6655

Odessa Beach features dancing to the big band sounds of the 1940s. On the second floor, you'll find the latest comedy and musical revues.

ON BROADWAY
435 Broadway at Montgomery / 398-1541

The historic supper club, built in 1886 and witness to the wild nights of San Francisco's Barbary Coast, is the perfect home for rock operas, musicals, cabarets, comedy groups, stage plays and screen readings.

PASAND LOUNGE
1875 Union St. at Laguna / 922-4498

Pasand is the place for a little jazz and lots of delicious Indian cuisine. Local jazz and blues combos play nightly, with no cover charge.

PIER 23 CAFE
Pier 23, The Embarcadero / 362-5125

Pier 23 is a lively waterfront club with some of the best jazz in town. Featured music is old-style jazz, R&B, Latin, reggae and Motown. Pier 23 Cafe also presents Zydeco and Latin music. There is no cover charge. The club offers a reasonably priced dinner menu, with dishes ranging from a bowl of clam chowder to grilled Monterey sole and a hot fudge brownie sundae. The entrees, emphasizing American cuisine, include a signature cioppino and various seafood specials. *Performances Tuesday through Saturday 9:30PM to 1:30AM; Sunday 4PM to 8PM*

THE PLUSH ROOM
York Hotel, 940 Sutter St. at Leavenworth
885-2800

The Plush Room is a cozy, luxurious nightspot tucked behind the lobby of the York Hotel, just a few blocks from downtown's theatre row.

YOSHI'S NIGHT SPOT
6030 Claremont Ave. at College
Oakland / 510-652-9200

Local jazz groups are featured during the week, name

NIGHTLIFE

acts appear most weekends. The SF Cabaret Awards has named Yoshi's the best jazz club in the Bay Area.

COMEDY CLUBS

COBB'S COMEDY CLUB
The Cannery, 2801 Leavenworth St. / 928-4320

The plush Cobb's is Northern California's premier full-time comedy club, featuring top national and local comedians seven nights a week.

HOLY CITY ZOO
408 Clement St. at 5th Ave. / 386-4242

A small, informal club in the Richmond District, the Holy City Zoo is San Francisco's longest running full-time comedy club, featuring live comedy and comedy workshops.

THE IMPROV
401 Mason St. at Geary / 441-7787

The Improv features both local comics and national headliners. There is a two-drink minimum for those 21 and over.

THE PUNCH LINE
444 Battery St. at Clay, 2nd floor / 397-7573

A sophisticated club where some of the best comedians are featured. Because of the long lines, it's advisable to buy tickets in advance.

DANCE CLUBS

CAL'S
2001 Union St. at Buchanan / 567-3121

Cal's has a cafe, two dance floors and three bars. The music mix is classic rock, hop, techno and popular dance music. No smoking.

CLVB DV8
540 Howard St. btwn. 1st & 2nd / 777-1419

Clvb DV8 is San Francisco's most stylish, ornate and "in" club. It's also huge, with three large dance floors open to the public on separate levels, modern dance music with four DJs, and several rooms for talking over a drink. Entertainment includes go-go dancers and performance artists. The fantastic decor is a startling mix of *trompe l'oeil*, pop art by Keith Haring, polished concrete and cracked Italian marble, candelabras and theatrical lights, mirrors and bizarre props.
Wednesday 9PM to 2AM; Thursday 9PM to 3AM; Friday & Saturday 9PM to 4AM. Cover charge

CLUB OASIS
11th St. & Folsom / 621-8119

It has to be seen to be believed, and it's well worth the trip South of Market. The indoor-outdoor dance floor is on a swimming pool, with live music and DJ dancing.

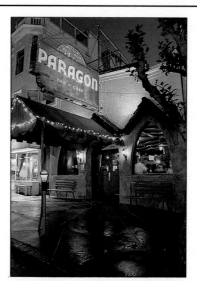

COVERED WAGON
917 Folsom St. at 5th / 974-1585

The Covered Wagon has dancing on weekends, with soul, rock, '70s funk and alternative rock programs.

DNA LOUNGE
375 11th St. at Harrison / 626-1409

DNA Lounge is an avant-garde club where you're just as likely to see a crazy fashion show or hear the latest poetry as you are to dance to a live band or the DJ's choice of mostly progressive rock.

EL RIO
3158 Mission St. at Army / 282-3325

On Friday, it's world sound, Saturday it's rock and Sunday you can dance to house music. El Rio also has margarita nights on Tuesdays.

ELBO ROOM
647 Valencia St. at 17th / 552-7788

Elbo Room has an eclectic program of live and DJ music, with dancing on Friday and Saturday.

END UP
401 Sixth St. at Harrison / 543-7700

The music at End Up is techno, house and dance music. The club has gay and lesbian nights and a Sunday tea dance with no cover charge.

FIREHOUSE 7
3160 16th St. at Guerrero / 621-1617

Firehouse 7 is a friendly club in a 1907 firehouse frequented by a local crowd ready to party, dance and have a good time.

KENNEL CLUB/THE BOX
628 Divisadero at Hayes / 931-1914

The Kennel Club features live music with national headliners, gay and lesbian nights and a world beat-reggae dance party every Sunday.

LE CLUB TOUCHE
300 De Haro St. at 16th / 861-8990

Le Club Touche is an elegant mainstream alternative to underground clubs. An elaborate sound and light system enhances the contemporary house beat.

MARTINI
1015 Folsom St. at 6th / 431-1200

Martini has three rooms with three different DJs. The music is top 40 and house. The popular club has a high cover charge.

NIGHTBREAK
1821 Haight St. at Stanyan / 221-9008

For danceable live music away from the mainstream, Nightbreak fits the bill. The emphasis here is on up-and-coming rock bands, and funk and rock DJs.

THE PALLADIUM
1031 Kearny St. at Broadway / 434-1308

The Palladium attracts a very young, lively crowd since it admits anyone 18 and up with valid ID. There are three dance floors, a food bar, a liquor bar for those over 21, a 12-foot video screen and a 13,000-watt sound system.

PARADISE LOUNGE
1501 Folsom St. at 11th St. / 861-6906

The Paradise Lounge has three stages with a mix of live music every night, from progressive rock to karaoke and the Fabulous Buddy Love Show.

PAULA'S CLUBHOUSE
3160 16th St. at Valencia / 621-1617

At Paula's Clubhouse, the music mix includes punk, rock, '70s funk and dance music.

THE QUAKE
1748 Haight St. at Cole / 668-6006

The Quake, formerly the I-Beam, gives as much as it gets. The sound system shakes the floor, and there is a different theme (and crowd) every night.

THE RAMP
855 China Basin St. at Mariposa / 621-2378

Perched on the bay, The Ramp's outdoor stage fills spring and summer weekend nights with exciting and diverse sounds, from rock 'n' roll to Brazilian salsa and jazz.

SLIM'S
333 11th St. at Folsom / 621-3330

Boz Scaggs converted this once decaying warehouse into a premier showcase for R&B and American roots music. Blues, country, rock, alternative and world beat musicians from throughout the country perform here.

SOUND FACTORY
525 Harrison St. at First / 543-9200

The Sound Factory is the largest (15,000 square feet) and wildest disco to ever open in San Francisco. The main dance floor has 84 speakers, and you can hear everything from techno to hip hop, R&B, alternative and salsa. Friday night is Life, a disco that draws a mixed crowd. Saturday night is Cyclops, a gay dress-up evening.

TOWNSEND
177 Townsend St. at 3rd / 974-6020

Especially lively after midnight, Townsend has R&B, rock and gay nights. Its newest addition, King Street Garage at the back of the club, has a separate program featuring raves and trash disco.

ZANZIBAR
842 Valencia St. at 19th / 695-7887

Zanzibar has reggae on Thursday, house on Friday and '60s soul on Saturday. The club is a restaurant before it turns into a dance club at 10:30PM.

NIGHTCLUBS

BAHIA TROPICAL BRAZILIAN CLUB
1600 Market St. at Franklin / 861-8657

San Francisco's premier Brazilian nightclub features top Brazilian jazz artists and stage shows with dancers dressed in extravagant Carnival regalia.

CESAR'S LATIN PALACE
3140 Mission St. at Army / 648-6611

A vast, brightly lit ballroom in the heart of the Mission District, Cesar's is popular with all who prefer traditional salsa to new wave rock.

HARRY DENTON'S
161 Steuart St. at Harbor Court Hotel / 882-1333

Harry Denton's popular restaurant turns into a night-club after 9PM. An R&B band plays every night but Sunday until midnight. In the back, you can also dance to DJ music on Thursday, Friday and Saturday from 10:30PM to 2AM. The atmosphere is fun and romantic. Antiques, ruby walls and rich drapery conjure a turn-of-the-century saloon, and the bay views are outstanding. *Monday through Wednesday 9PM to midnight; Thursday through Saturday 9PM to 2AM. Cover charge on weekends*

JAZZ AT BRASSERIE
3 Embarcadero, podium level / 981-5530

On Friday and Saturday evenings, this lively brasserie showcases some of San Francisco's finest jazz musicians and vocalists. Offering a full bar, extensive wine list and plenty of comfortable seating, La Brasserie is quickly becoming a San Francisco favorite. An extensive menu is served until 10PM, and parking is free with validation. *Open Monday through Saturday*

NEW ORLEANS ROOM
Fairmont Hotel, Mason at California / 772-5259

Located in the Fairmont's lobby level, the New Orleans Room offers jazz nightly. Solo jazz pianists perform Sundays and Mondays, and local jazz vocalists appear Wednesdays through Saturdays. Internationally famous jazz stars — from bebop to fusion artists — play for specially scheduled performances. The New Orleans Room serves cocktails and a la carte appetizers. *Daily 3PM to 2AM*

OZ
Westin St. Francis Hotel, 32nd floor
335 Powell St. at Geary / 774-0116

The wonderful world of Oz begins in the mirrored hall-way, continuing inside to a fanciful forest of leafy tree-tops, mushroom tables and thousands of twinkling lights casting their glow on the chic nightclub scene. On the 32nd floor of the St. Francis Hotel, Oz is reached by a glass-enclosed outside elevator, which adds to the illusion of traveling to a magical spot. Video screens feature the latest releases, while DJs play Top 40 and international modern music.
Sunday through Thursday 9PM to 1:30AM; Friday & Saturday 9PM to 2:30AM. Cover charge. Appropriate dress required

SOL Y LUNA
475 Sacramento St. at Battery / 296-8191

This lively Latin restaurant becomes a club after 10PM Wednesday through Saturday nights. The music at Sol y Luna varies, with an exciting mix of rhumba, salsa, mambo and flamenco. You can enjoy a wonderful selection of authentic Spanish-style tapas in between the dances. *Call for schedule and special events*

STARLITE ROOF
Sir Francis Drake Hotel
450 Powell St. at Sutter / 392-7755

Known to generations of San Franciscans and hotel guests, the Starlite Roof continues to offer easy listening, big band music, '50s rock and dancing under the "stars" on the 21st floor atop the downtown Drake Hotel. The spacious cocktail lounge provides one of the best views of the city in a low-key, refined atmosphere.
Monday through Saturday 4:30PM to 2AM; live music & dancing Monday through Thursday 9PM to 12:30AM; Friday & Saturday 9:15PM to 1:30AM

NIGHTCLUB TOURS

JAZZ CLUB TOURS
By reservation / 916-393-5266

Jazz Club Tours offers tours of the city's most elite jazz clubs. A 24-hour notice is required for reservations.

3 BABES & A BUS
Fridays & Saturdays by reservation / 552-2582

A great way to discover San Francisco's clubs and make friends while you party is a night on the town with 3 Babes & A Bus. Join Paula Sabatelli, Donna Lo Cicero and Susan Francke on their traveling party bus and be taken to four of the city's hottest dance clubs (the list varies nightly) ranging from the funky to the chic. A mere $30 includes pick-up and delivery from one of four locations. You'll pay no cover charges, and you'll also receive priority admittance, one complimentary cocktail and lots of on-board fun. And, if you want to return to a particular club that same night, you'll be admitted free. 3 Babes & A Bus is available for private parties. Reservations are required; participants must be 21 or older. VISA/MasterCard accepted.

NIGHTLIFE

when the newly rich sought the most exotic dishes to celebrate their wealth. Today, it is a mecca for those who seek the finest in food and service, and its mixed ethnic heritage provides a spectrum of cuisines unmatched in the world.

Introduced by Gianni Fassio

The Bay Area has always been blessed with an abundance of fresh produce and with the enormous selection of seafood from the Pacific Ocean. The quality and variety of these products

Restaurants

have increased thanks to the area's pioneering chefs, who demand the best to create dishes that are revolutionizing traditional cuisines.

Gianni Fassio owns two highly regarded Italian restaurants, The Blue Fox and Palio d'Asti.

One San Francisco tradition that remains unchanged is gracious service. Today, at both The Blue Fox and Palio d'Asti, we believe that service and ambiance are the keys to an unforgettable evening. It is the serving staff, whether in a formal restaurant or a casual bistro, that sets the tone for fun, romance, business and friendship.

San Francisco has so many great restaurants, both new and established, that residents as well as visitors need an easy way to keep informed. With *AM/PM*, you can turn to any cuisine you desire and find a restaurant to suit your mood, whether you want a romantic meal for two or pizza at midnight.

Thank you: Nob Hill Restaurant; Andy Marshall, Jennifer Wolf, EPIC Models

B.Y.O.B&B

à la chambre 914

B and B Liqueur. 40% Alc./Vol. Hiram Walker & Sons, Inc., Farmington Hills, MI © 1992

The French call it "joie de vivre". A joyous celebration of life's unexpected moments. Moments meant for B&B. With a taste derived from a mysterious combination of exotic spices, B&B excites the palate and delights the imagination. Discover it straight up or over ice. B AND B

RESTAURANT DIRECTORY

SAN FRANCISCO

QUICK PICKS

MARIN

For Marin restaurants, see the AM section,
page 103

LEGEND

$15 or Less Per Person	**$**	View	
$15 - $30 Per Person	**$$**	Full Bar	
$30 & Up Per Person	**$$$**	Romantic	
Reservations Accepted	☎	Dressy	
Off-street or Valet Parking	🚗	Fun	😊
Live Entertainment	🎵		

AFGHAN

HELMAND
430 Broadway btwn. Kearny & Montgomery / 362-0641
Lunch Mon-Fri, dinner daily

$ ☎ ▼

Helmand offers a unique cuisine redolent of garlic, yogurt, mint and delicate spices. Don't miss the pumpkin appetizer or the lamb.

KABUL WEST
2800 Van Ness Ave. at Lombard / 931-9144
Lunch Mon-Fri, dinner daily

$ ☎ ▼ 🚗 ▥

In a converted townhouse, Kabul West serves elegant Afghan cuisine in a romantic atmosphere.

AMERICAN

THE ACADEMY GRILL
625 Polk St. at Turk / 771-1655
Lunch & dinner Mon-Fri

$$ ☎ ▼

Catered by the California Culinary Academy's students, lunch features a weekly menu of grilled meat and fish. At night, the specialties are Italian.

THE ACORN
1256 Folsom St. btwn. 8th & 9th / 863-2469
Lunch Tues-Fri, dinner Tues-Sat, brunch Sat & Sun

$$ ☎ 😊

Homemade pastries and bread, hearty sandwiches, huge salads and excellent desserts bring back the pleasure of daytime dining and afternoon tea in a cheerful, light-filled space.

RESTAURANTS

BALBOA CAFE
3199 Fillmore St. at Greenwich / 921-3944
Lunch Mon-Fri, dinner daily, brunch Sat & Sun

Long a favorite Marina watering hole, the Balboa is also a great spot for hamburgers, brunch and creative American specialties.

BIX
56 Gold St. at Montgomery / 433-6300
Lunch Mon-Fri, dinner daily

Right out of a Hollywood film fantasy, Bix is one of San Francisco's premier supper clubs, with Art Deco light fixtures and a curving staircase that leads to the upper dining room. The bartenders serve potent martinis, manhattans and sidecars.
Specialties: Potato & Leek Pancake with Smoked Salmon & Caviar; Steak Tartare; Chicken Hash a la Bix; Pork Chop with Mashed Potatoes

BULL'S TEXAS CAFE
25 Van Ness Ave. at Oak / 864-4288
Lunch Mon-Sat, dinner daily

All sorts of Texas memorabilia, from cowboy hats to longhorn heads, stud the walls of Bull's. The Tex-Mex food is hearty and generous, as befits the Lone Star State.

CAFE SFA
Saks Fifth Avenue, Post & Powell / 986-4300
Lunch Mon-Sat

A relaxing oasis in Saks Fifth Avenue, Cafe SFA overlooks Union Square. The fifth-floor glass cafe offers a respite from the shopping rush. Here, you can enjoy a quick bite or time out for a restful lunch. The menu includes appetizers, salads and soups such as Saks signature sweet corn and crab chowder. The entrees, which change frequently, feature ahi tuna, filet mignon, salmon, swordfish and other specialties, elegantly prepared.
Specialties: Mini Crab Cakes; Herb-crusted Shrimp Salad; Black Pepper Salmon & Pasta; Pan-seared Duck Breast with Honey & Mint

CAMPTON PLACE RESTAURANT
340 Stockton St. at Post / 955-5555
Breakfast & lunch Mon-Sat, dinner daily, brunch Sun

Creative American cooking is showcased in a comfortable yet formal dining room. *Food & Wine Magazine* voted Campton Place Restaurant one of the "Top 25 Restaurants in America." The menu, which changes seasonally,
features fresh ingredients combined in exciting ways. Don't miss breakfast at Campton Place — it's hearty, original and thoroughly satisfying.
Specialties: Seasonal Menu; Game Ravioli; Dungeness Crabcakes; Scallops with Shiitakes; Brioche Bread Pudding

CYPRESS CLUB
500 Jackson St. at Montgomery / 296-8555
Lunch Mon-Fri, dinner daily, brunch Sun

Cypress Club may be the most visually extravagant restaurant in San Francisco. Beyond the impressive bronze front door, every inch of space is filled with organic forms. Nipple-shaped ceiling light fixtures dominate, and swollen urnlike pillars and rounded archways frame a continuous mural depicting Northern California. Chef Cory Schreiber's eclectic menu of elaborate dishes occasionally competes with Cypress Club's theatrical atmosphere — not an easy feat.
Specialties: Loin of Venison with Chanterelles; Leg of Rabbit with Carrots; Pan-seared Yellowfin

DELANCEY STREET RESTAURANT
600 Embarcadero St. at Brannan / 512-5179
Lunch Tues-Fri, dinner Tues-Sun, brunch Sat & Sun

An airy interior of wood and brass and expansive views of the bay give this restaurant an elegance that belies its origins. Staffed by the residents of San Francisco's venerable Delancey Street organization, the restaurant has flawless service and a simple menu, with ample portions and first-rate ingredients. The staff serves high tea from 3PM to 5:30PM Tuesdays through Sundays.
Specialties: Rosemary Garlic Chicken; Penne Arrabbiata; Pot Roast; Prawns in Brandy Cream Sauce; Peach Blueberry Crisp with Scoop of Ice Cream

EMBARKO
100 Brannan St. at The Embarcadero / 495-2021
Lunch Mon-Fri, dinner daily

This lively South-of-Market restaurant, with an upbeat decor, is the setting for a menu of updated ethnic American dishes.

THE FILLMORE GRILL
2301 Fillmore St. at Clay / 922-1444
Lunch Tues-Fri, dinner Tues-Sun, brunch Sat & Sun

If you're in the mood for basic meat-and-potatoes food and lots of hustle-bustle, join the young Pacific Heights crowd at the Fillmore Grill.

FLY TRAP
606 Folsom St. at 2nd / 243-0580
Lunch Mon-Fri, dinner Mon-Sat

Reminiscent of a turn-of-the-century bar and grill, the Fly Trap turns out classic San Francisco dishes. The food is straightforward and beautifully rendered.

FOURNOU'S OVENS
Stouffer Stanford Court Hotel
905 California St. at Powell / 989-1910
Breakfast & lunch Mon-Fri, dinner daily, brunch Sat & Sun

A Mediterranean-style room arranged around huge tiled ovens, Fournou's Ovens is just the place when you're in the mood for unusual, contemporary American cuisine. Chef Ercolino Crugnale presides over the award-winning kitchen, which highlights seasonal menus. The beautifully designed wine cellar displays an extensive corkage; the wine list is the recipient of *The Wine Spectator* Grand Award since 1991.
Specialties: *Oak-roasted Rack of Lamb; Roasted Meats; Fresh Seafood; Organic meats & vegetables whenever possible*

HAMBURGER MARY'S
1582 Folsom St. at 12th / 626-5767
Lunch & dinner Tues-Sun

A lively atmosphere prevails at Hamburger Mary's. A young mixed crowd munches juicy hamburgers acclaimed as among the best in the city, served by a wild-looking staff.

HARRY DENTON'S
161 Steuart St. at Harbor Court Hotel / 882-1333
Lunch Mon-Fri, dinner daily

Harry Denton and Bill Kimpton add to their impressive combined repertoire of victorious San Francisco restaurants with a lively grill/dance club on the waterfront. Their new venture conjures a turn-of-the-century saloon with antiques, ruby walls and rich drapery. Hearty sandwiches, seafood plates and desserts are the "real food" served on all three levels. For romance, there is bay-view dining and a dance floor.
Specialties: *Fresh Maine Lobster with Penne Pasta Gratin; Double-cut Grilled Housecured Pork Loin Chop with Apple Chutney; Grilled Filet Mignon with Applewood-smoked Bacon & Fries*

IRONWOOD CAFE
901 Cole St. at Carl / 664-0224
Lunch Mon-Fri, dinner Mon-Sat

A neighborhood eatery, the Ironwood Cafe has earned applause for its exciting, housemade American cuisine.

IVY'S
398 Hayes St. at Gough / 626-3930
Lunch Mon-Fri, dinner daily, brunch Sun

Just steps from the Civic Center, Ivy's is especially popular at lunch, when a lively crowd jams in for the large salads and light entrees.

JOHNNY LOVE'S
1500 Broadway at Polk / 931-6053
Dinner daily

Along with its reputation as San Francisco's liveliest bar, Johnny Love's has been hailed by critics for its exceptional food. As creative in the kitchen as Johnny "Love" Metheny is behind the bar, Chef Mark Hartman, a veteran of Stars and the Coyote Cafe in Santa Fe, turns out updated classics with a fresh California twist. The menu changes regularly, as does the music. You'll want to make a night of it!
Specialties: Crispy-fried Monterey Calamari; Individual Pizza; Grilled Ginger & Garlic Marinated Prawns; Grilled Dry-aged Cowboy-cut Rib Steak

JULIE'S SUPPER CLUB
1123 Folsom St. at 7th / 861-0707
Dinner Tues-Sat

Julie's Supper Club has '50s-style decor in Day-Glo colors, but '90s-style food that adds a lot of California whimsy to its American basics.

L'AVENUE
3854 Geary Blvd. at 3rd Ave. / 386-1555
Dinner daily

Owned by Chef Nancy Oakes, this is one of the most elegant bistros around. She turns out a huge repertoire of regularly changing dishes, many with a Provencal accent. This fall, the restaurant moves to a new address, 1 Mission Street at Steuart, adds a lunch service and takes on a new name — Boulevard.

LIVERPOOL LIL'S
2942 Lyon St. at Lombard / 921-6664
Lunch & dinner daily, brunch Sat & Sun

Liverpool Lil's has a great pub ambiance and surprisingly good food, from fish to pasta and salads.

MAX'S DINER
311 3rd St. at Folsom / 546-MAXS
Lunch & dinner daily

It's loud, it's trendy, it's crowded, and it's a lot of fun. Max's has huge portions of all-American diner fare.

MAX'S OPERA CAFE
601 Van Ness Ave. at Golden Gate / 771-7300
Lunch & dinner daily

This bright, light, always busy New York-style deli features singing waiters, a creative menu and late-night hours. The portions are so huge that one order easily satisfies two hungry people.

MAXFIELD'S
Sheraton Palace, 2 New Montgomery St. at Market
392-8600 / Lunch & dinner daily, breakfast Sun

The recently refurbished Sheraton Palace is dazzling, and Maxfield's shares its shine. Like an elegant men's club but with a contemporary open grill, it gives a gently innovative twist to American fare. Meat and seafood are grilled on mesquite and alderwood — a preparation unique to Maxfield's. On Monday, Wednesday and Friday, the restaurant offers Martini Madness, a jumbo martini served with caviar for $4. Maxfield's is a good choice for a leisurely lunch, business dinner or relaxed drinks at the Pied Piper Bar.
Specialties: Pasta; Steak; Fresh Seafood; Daily Specials

ONE MARKET
1 Market St. at Steuart / 777-5577
Lunch Mon-Fri, dinner daily, brunch Sun

Chef Bradley Ogden and his partner Michael Dellar have repeated their success with the Lark Creek Inn in Marin, opening one of San Francisco's hot new restaurants. It's large, fashionable and bustling, yet Ogden's creations remain as irresistible and bountiful as ever.

PARAGON BAR & CAFE
3251 Scott St. at Chestnut / 922-2456
Dinner daily

Known as a favorite Marina watering hole, the Paragon is also a great place to dine. Chef Kerry Heffernan brings to the kitchen her experience at the Cypress Club, Checkers and the Beverly Hills Hotel. The burgers are huge, the entrees tasty, and the warmth of the pub-like interior makes unwinding here easy. Add nightly piano (with live jazz or blues three times a

week) and a cozy fireplace, and you have a paragon of dining pleasure.

Specialties: Crab Cakes with Roasted Tomato-lemon Horseradish Sauce: Caesar Salad with Garlic Croutons; Paragon Burger with Bacon, Cheddar & Avocado; Maple-cured Double-cut Pork Chop with Fresh Yams & Homemade Applesauce

PARK GRILL

Park Hyatt Hotel, 333 Battery St. at Clay / 296-2933
Breakfast daily, lunch Mon-Fri, dinner daily,
brunch Sat & Sun

Under the direction of Chef Charles Lewis, Park Grill offers a wide variety of grilled specialties drawn from the international marketplace and uses only the freshest ingredients. A pianist entertains Tuesday through Saturday evenings, and a light fare is served throughout the day.

Specialties: Twin Filet Mignon Medallions with Cheese Polenta in a Sauce of Roasted Shallots & Truffles; Grilled Pacific Swordfish on a Bed of Braised Watercress in a Sweet Bell Pepper Sauce, Served with Wild Rice Flan

PERRY'S

1944 Union St. at Laguna / 922-9022
Breakfast Mon-Fri, lunch & dinner daily, brunch Sat & Sun

As enduringly popular as it is reliable, Perry's sets the standard for old-fashioned American food. Whether you're enjoying breakfast, dinner or a leisurely weekend brunch, you are assured of large portions, fresh ingredients and speedy service. Food is served until 11PM weeknights and midnight on weekends, and the friendly bar is always open until 2AM.

Specialties: Chinese Chicken Salad; Caesar Salad; Perry's Hamburger; Grilled Veal Chop; Apple Brown Betty

THE ROTUNDA AT NEIMAN MARCUS

150 Stockton St. on Union Square / 362-4777
Lunch Mon-Sat

Under the "Glass Ship," a stained-glass dome built in 1909, diners can enjoy lunch or afternoon tea in Beaux Arts splendor. Windows look out on the lively city scene around Union Square.

VINCE

395 Hayes St. at Gough / 864-4824
Lunch & dinner Wed-Mon

This casual new restaurant in the Civic Center has made a hit with theatregoers and neighborhood residents. The menu is inexpensive and zestfully prepared.

ASIAN

MANDALAY RESTAURANT

4348 California St. at 5th Ave. / 386-3895
Lunch & dinner daily

Polite waitresses in authentic Burmese costume greet you at Mandalay. The dishes at this delightful restaurant demonstrate the Chinese, Indian and Thai influences typical in Burmese cuisine. The dumplings, curries, soups and salads are especially good.

Specialties: Curried Beef & Potato Wontons with Chile Sauce & Cucumber Relish; Moo Hing Nga (Spicy Fish Soup with Coconut Milk, Roasted Lentils & Rice Noodles); Burmese Dish: Tea Leaf Salad (Tender Tea Leaves with Nuts, Shrimp Paste, Lemon Juice, Dressing)

SINGAPORE STRAITS CAFE

3300 Geary Blvd. at Parker / 668-1783
Lunch & dinner daily

Asian-food fanatics in search of new palate-pleasing discoveries will want to try the Straits Cafe. This simple, stylish family restaurant serves the cuisine of Singapore, which incorporates elements of Chinese, Malay, Indian and Indonesian cooking.

BRAZILIAN

BAHIA

41 Franklin St. at Oak / 626-3306
Lunch Mon-Fri, dinner daily

If you have never been to Brazil, you can get a taste of what you're missing. *San Francisco Focus Magazine* has voted Chef/owner Valmor Neto's Bahia the Bay Area's best Central and South American restaurant for two years in a row. When it comes to hot, lively and exciting, Bahia has it all. Brightly colored tropical decor and live Brazilian jazz set the stage for tempting Brazilian cuisine that mingles African, Spanish and Portuguese elements.

Specialties: Tossed Greens with Lobster & Crab; Fresh Prawns in Tomato & Coconut Sauce; Fejoida (Black Bean Stew with Mixed Meats); Thick Coconut Pudding

CALIFORNIA

ATRIUM

101 California St. at Front / 788-4101
Lunch Mon-Fri, dinner Mon-Sat

The Atrium restaurant, designed by Ron Nunn, is a composition in elegance, drama, light and spaciousness within a beautiful, two-level marble dining room. Says *Chronicle* food guru Patricia Unterman: "The food at the

Atrium sparkles. The menu represents a distillation of all the years of California cooking at its best." The exotic greenhouse extension adds lushness to David Mahler's warmhearted and sophisticated menu.

Specialties: Dungeness Crab Cakes with a Relish of Papaya, Tomato, Cucumber & Rice Wine Vinegar; Grilled Hawaiian Swordfish with Tobiko Caviar & Cucumber Relish; Lamb Tenderloin in Phyllo with Wild Mushrooms & Zinfandel Sauce

CAFE 53
Ana Hotel, 50 3rd St. at Market / 974-6400
Breakfast Mon-Sat, lunch & dinner daily

In the newly renovated Ana Hotel, Cafe 53 has a stylish decor. A marble entryway leads into the restaurant. Praised for its high quality, fresh ingredients and unfussy preparations, Cafe 53's menu is surprisingly reasonable for an international hotel. The restaurant is also a great choice for locals who want sophisticated dining. The menu, which features excellent appetizers and housemade desserts, includes a buffet at lunch. A lounge and bar area nearby encourage a stop after work.

Specialties: Warm Scallops with Chanterelles & Leeks Wrapped in Phyllo; Salmon-filled Ravioli; Tempura; Roasted Rack of Lamb; Meringue with Coffee Cream in a Vanilla & Caramel Sauce

CAFE MAJESTIC
1500 Sutter St. at Gough / 776-6400
Breakfast daily, lunch Tues-Fri, dinner daily, brunch Sat & Sun

When you step into the Cafe Majestic, you enter the era of gracious dining and romantic decor. Restored to its original 1902 splendor, the Cafe Majestic is a soothing interplay of apricot, soft grey-green, high ceilings and tall mirrors. In this rich Victorian ambiance, the innovative California cuisine comes as a pleasant surprise. Everything is fresh and appealing, light and beautifully presented. Best of all, the Parisian bistro bar is always open until midnight. Proprietor Tom Marshall, who renovated the cafe in 1985, is at the door to greet you and make you feel at home.

Specialties: Fresh Lobster Salad with Papaya Lime & Cilantro; Warm Wild Mushrooms with Crispy Potato Garnish; Roast Breast of Duck with Honey, Lemon & Cumin; Filet of Beef with Puree of Walnut, Pear & Roquefort

CAFE 222
Hotel Nikko San Francisco
222 Mason St. at O'Farrell / 394-1100
Breakfast, lunch & dinner daily

Located on the second floor of Hotel Nikko San Fran-

RESTAURANTS

cisco, Cafe 222 features an innovative blend of California freshness with Pacific Rim spices. The restaurant serves signature dishes such as specialty pastas and housemade desserts. Cafe 222 also serves Japanese breakfast and luncheon items seven days a week. Cafe 222's casual bistro style provides a perfect setting for any occasion.

Specialties: Fresh Dungeness Crab Cakes; Sauteed Pacific Salmon; Grilled Meats; Seafood

CAFFE ESPRIT

235 Sixteenth St. at Illinois / 777-5558
Lunch Mon-Sat

Caffe Esprit offers standbys such as pizzas, pasta, hamburgers and salads come with fresh California ingredients. The Esprit outlet next door has great bargains on Esprit's casual, colorful fashions.

CAVA 555

555 Second St. btwn. Brannan & Bryant / 543-2282
Lunch Mon-Fri, dinner Mon-Sat

By day, Cava 555 is a neighborhood cafe offering pastas, seasonal salads and soups, daily specials and tasty sandwiches on homemade focaccia. At night, the cafe turns into a dazzling supper club. The romantic ambiance of neon lights, murals and sprays of floating lights is enhanced by the popping of champagne corks and the rhythmic flow of live jazz. Chef Patrick Rice's eclectic menus featuring California cuisine complement the mood, as well as the extraordinary selection of Champagnes and sparkling wines — Cava 555 has more than 50 to choose from. Go for the food and atmosphere, stay for the live jazz.

Specialties: Smoked Norwegian Salmon with Crisp Potato Pancake; Lasagnette with Wild Mushrooms, Tomatoes, Spinach & Eggplant; Swordfish with Black Beans & Smoked Prawns; Banana Corn Bread with Ice Cream & Berries

CHEERS

127 Clement St. at 2nd Ave. / 387-6966
Breakfast, lunch & dinner daily

Cheers attracts a regular crowd that appreciates the fabulous breakfasts, homemade muffins and pastries, creative specialties and extended hours.

CITICOURT CAFE

1 Sansome St. at Sutter / 362-6297
Lunch Mon-Fri

Enjoy a relaxing lunch in Citicourt Cafe's bright, tree-filled atrium. The restaurant also offers a happy hour from 4PM to 7:30PM, with live music, cocktails, complimentary hors d'oeuvres and special drinks featured each weeknight. Citicourt Cafe is available for dinners and private parties.

Specialties: Homemade Pastas; Fresh Fish; Variety of Unique Salads; Meat & Poultry Specials; Stuffed Roast Chicken; Fresh Fruit Tart

CITYSCAPE

San Francisco Hilton, 333 O'Farrell St.
776-0215 / Dinner daily, brunch Sun

Panoramic views and seasonal California cuisine make dining here a treat. The atmosphere is both elegant and romantic. At night, there is entertainment and dancing under a retractable skylight, and Sunday brunch features an elaborate buffet, accompanied by live music. On the 46th floor of the San Francisco Hilton, Cityscape is also popular as a cocktail bar.

ENRICO'S

504 Broadway at Kearny / 982-6223
Lunch & dinner daily

For decades, Enrico's sidewalk tables have been crowded with San Francisco's thinkers and revelers, and the city mourned when it closed. Now it's open again, spruced up for the '90s and serving food as lively as the ambiance. The pizzas are out of this world, the hamburger is West Coast state-of-the-art, and the rest of the menu, which changes daily, is fresh and innovative. Best of all, you can dine until midnight, enjoy pizza until 1AM, and party until 2AM. The terrace is still a favorite, but the dining room, with its large windows and modern art exhibits, is cozy and upbeat, a great place to enjoy nightly jazz or Monday night opera.

Specialties: Deep-fried Calamari with Black Bean Sauce; Pizza Margherita; Niman-Schell Hamburger on Focaccia with Polenta Fries & Housemade Condiments; Grilled Swordfish with Roasted Beets, Arugula & Tarragon Aioli

FOG CITY DINER

1300 Battery St. at Embarcadero / 982-2000
Lunch & dinner daily

Even if you're too young to remember the '50s, the zany magic of the period is recaptured at Fog City Diner. While the decor reflects an earlier era with leather booths and polished mahogany walls, the menu emphasizes up-to-date adaptations of diner cuisine — and much more!

Specialties: Crabcakes; Cheeseburgers; Red Curry Mussel Stew; Sesame Chicken; Quesadilla; Hot Fudge Sundaes

GABBIANO'S

One Ferry Plaza / 391-8403
Lunch Mon-Sat, dinner Wed-Sun, brunch Sun

Located in an up-and-coming section of the city,

Gabbiano's Restaurant and Oyster Cafe doesn't disappoint. Upstairs the Bay Room overlooks Alcatraz Island, Treasure Island and the Bay Bridge, and the casual Oyster Cafe downstairs sights Bayside Promenade in its panoramic scope. The Financial District, a glamorous backdrop of lively lights after dark, is the focus of the City Lights Room, ideal for intimate dinner or cocktail parties. Doubling as a banquet facility, the restaurant has breathtaking views that make any event memorable.
Specialties: Red Snapper Baked in a Banana Leaf; Angel-hair Pasta with Manila Clams; Veal Piccata; Lobster in Puff Pastry

GORDON BIERSCH BREWERY RESTAURANT
2 Harrison St. at Steuart / 243-8246
Lunch & dinner daily

Always crowded, Gordon Biersch Brewery Restaurant serves a variety of pastas, beef, fish and chicken dishes to go with its highly acclaimed beers. A success since it opened last year, the restaurant offers California cuisine with a Mediterranean flair. The atmosphere is friendly and casual. Huge brewing tanks are visible behind large plate-glass windows, and guests can watch beer being made as they dine. Dan Gordon, a master brewer, uses the finest hops and yeast to produce unique beers according to strict German purity laws. His menu, selected from Southwestern, Mediterranean and Asian specialties, perfectly matches his beers and excellent selection of California wines.
Specialties: Antipasto Platter; Braised Lamb Shank with Red Wine, Leek-Onion Confit & Polenta; Grilled Rib Eye with Mole Verde, Goat Cheese Chile Relleno & Salsa Fresca; Wild Mushroom Risotto

LA SCENE CAFE AND BAR
490 Geary St. at Taylor / 292-6430
Breakfast daily, dinner Tues-Sat

La Scene's great location opposite the Curran Theatre makes it ideal for an early dinner before the show, especially if you take advantage of the very reasonable prix-fixe menu.

LEHR'S GREENHOUSE RESTAURANT
740 Sutter St. at Taylor / 474-6478
Breakfast, lunch & dinner daily, brunch Sun

Dine in a garden in full bloom. Here, you can enjoy Chef Randal Lehr's great steaks and prime rib with the accent on New American cuisine. With hundreds of hanging plants, the restaurant is an oasis just steps from Union Square. Lehr's Greenhouse, a local favorite, features certified Angus steaks and prime rib as well as fresh local seafood. Chef Lehr individually dry ages the beef strips

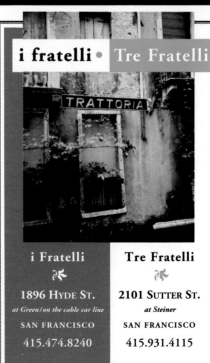
RESTAURANTS

in a special climate-controlled beef-aging locker to achieve the optimum in taste, texture and tenderness. The Ramos Fizz Sunday Buffet Brunch is magnificent and is served from 10AM until 2PM.

Specialties: Dry-aged New York Steak; Filet Mignon; Prime Rib; Petrale Sole Macadamia; Fresh Grilled Salmon; Rack of New Zealand Lamb

MASONS

950 Mason St. at California / 392-0113
Lunch Mon-Fri, dinner Mon-Sat

Designed with marble, contemporary bleached woods and pale leather, Masons is one of San Francisco's most glamorous restaurants, featuring reasonably priced California cuisine in a French style, with celebrated pianist Peter Mintun providing lively music to dine by. Private rooms, magnificently appointed for parties of up to 130 guests, excellent cuisine and an extensive wine cellar make for a first-class restaurant. Masons was selected for the prestigious AAA Four Diamond Award, one of the few San Francisco restaurants to earn this honor.

Specialties: Roasted Squab with Spinach Leaves, Caramelized Baby Onions & Juniper Berry Sauce; Free-range Chicken Marinated with Herbs & Lemon, Served with Couscous & Spiced Vegetables; Grilled Salmon on Greens with a Tomato Coulis Vinaigrette

MOOSE'S

1652 Stockton St. at Union / 989-7800
Lunch Mon-Sat, dinner daily, brunch Sun

Moose's is as warm and welcoming as owner Ed Moose himself, with straightforward, appealing cuisine that gives an Italian punch to a creative California menu.

NOB HILL RESTAURANT

Mark Hopkins Hotel, One Nob Hill / 392-3434
Breakfast, lunch & dinner daily

An atmosphere rich with wood paneling, luxurious chairs, impeccable linen tablecloths and soft candlelight makes for sumptuous dining on French and California cuisines. As cable cars climb Nob Hill outside the restaurant's grand windows, you will have an intimate and memorable special occasion.

Specialties: Roasted Rack of Lamb; Fresh Sonoma Duck Foie Gras; Creme Brulee

POSTRIO

545 Post St. at Mason / 776-7825
Breakfast, lunch & dinner daily, brunch Sat & Sun

Postrio is Los Angeles superstar Chef Wolfgang Puck's San Francisco culinary masterpiece. Contemporary lighting and modern artwork make a stylish setting for California cuisine with Mediterranean influences.

RITZ-CARLTON RESTAURANT

600 Stockton St. at California / 296-7465
Breakfast, lunch & dinner daily, brunch Sun

Inventive, California-style dishes served in one of the more opulent hotel dining rooms in town. An abundance of marble and rich fabric creates the glamour, and the talent of the chef provides the incentive for an equally mixed local and out-of-town crowd. Outdoor seating around the hotel courtyard is a popular feature on warm days.

Specialties: Crispy Cornmeal with Sesame-coated Oysters, Seasonal Greens & Tahini; Warm Scallop & Shrimp Salad with Spinach, Avocado, Mango & Ginger; Lamb Tenderloin Rolled in Mustard Seeds & Fennel

SILKS

222 Sansome St. at Pine / 986-2020
Breakfast daily, lunch Mon-Fri, dinner daily, brunch Sun

Located in the plush Mandarin Oriental Hotel, Silks has won nationwide accolades. Chef Michele Sampson combines California cooking with an Asian touch for a creative menu that emphasizes seafood and fresh seasonal produce.

Specialties: Asian Marinated Lamb with Crispy Potato Napoleon; Roasted Monkfish with Mirin Leeks, Horseradish & Smoked Salmon; Hawaiian Prawns Tempura with Rock Shrimp Salad

THE ST. FRANCIS GRILL

335 Powell St. btwn. Geary & Post, Westin St. Francis
774-0233 / Dinner daily

Turn-of-the-century elegance, up-to-the-minute culinary trends and a Union Square location make the St. Francis Grill a favorite among downtown shoppers, businesspeople and pre-theatre diners. Chef Bernd Liebergesell prepares traditional grill dishes that pair well with the restaurant's outstanding California wines.

Specialties: Grilled Seafood Specialties; New York Steak; Breast of Chicken with Soy Sauce, Ginger & Green Onions

STARS

150 Redwood Alley off Van Ness near Golden Gate
861-7827 / Lunch Mon-Fri, dinner daily

When the father of California cuisine, Jeremiah Tower, opened Stars in 1984, he created a dining legend. Nearly a decade later, the restaurant, with its glamorous, international clientele and innovative cuisine, is still San Francisco's trendsetter. Always packed and filled with energy, the restaurant also boasts the

RESTAURANTS

longest bar and best desserts in the city.

Specialties: Roast Squab with Potato Risotto & Grilled Tomatillo Sauce; Corn & Truffles Crepe with Wild Mushrooms; Grilled Double-cut Pork Chop with Braised Red Cabbage, Mushroom Duxelle & Whole Grain Mustard Sauce

STARS CAFE

555 Golden Gate Ave. at Van Ness / 861-4344
Lunch & dinner daily

Jeremiah Tower's more casual, relaxed, European-style cafe offers a menu of simpler, reasonably priced dishes, all made with the same quality and imagination as the cuisine of Stars. With its quick service, the cafe has become a mandatory pit-stop for opera, symphony and ballet attendees. Stars Cafe also offers take-out and early morning pastries and coffee.

Specialties: Steam Mussels with Lime; Spinach with Apricots & Pine Nuts; Polenta with Special Stews; Fried Fish & Chips; Garlic Shrimp; Linguine with Braised Leeks, Cherry Tomatoes, Spinach & Goat Cheese

VICTOR'S

The Westin St. Francis, 32nd floor
335 Powell St. at Geary / 956-7777
Dinner daily, brunch Sun

Victor's features fine California cuisine with an innovative dash of creativity and an outstanding wine list. The restaurant is named after the chef who ran its kitchen for several decades starting from the hotel's opening in 1904 and continuing for several decades. The restaurant's most renowned dish is Celery Victor: braised celery hearts marinated in a vinaigrette dressing, served with bay shrimp. Victor's panoramic view from the 32nd floor is unforgettable, and the service is excellent.

Specialties: Mesquite-smoked Rack of Lamb on Four-bean Ragout with Sweet Garlic Sauce; Maine Lobster Ragout on North Beach Pasta with Madeira Sauce; Napoleon of California Smoked Sturgeon in Pinot Noir Sauce

CAMBODIAN

ANGKOR BOREI

3471 Mission St. at 30th / 550-8417
Lunch & dinner daily

If you've never tried Cambodian food, start here. A little less hot than Thai food, Cambodian cuisine mixes many ingredients for haunting and sophisticated specialties.

ANGKOR PALACE

1769 Lombard St. at Octavia / 931-2830
Dinner daily

The busy dining room, filled with Cambodian art, has

an exotic ambiance. The curries are wonderful, as are the appetizers and soups. In fact, everything here is good.

ANGKOR WAT

4217 Geary Blvd. at 6th Ave. / 221-7887
Dinner Tues-Sun

The stone carvings of Angkor Wat are reproduced on the walls of this stylish restaurant, where the food is the highest cuisine Cambodia has to offer.

CARIBBEAN

THE CARIBBEAN ZONE

55 Natoma St. btwn. Mission & Howard at 1st
541-9465 / Lunch Mon-Fri, dinner daily

A corrugated metal shack behind Club DV8 is Dr. Winkie's latest brainchild, a restaurant that easily qualifies as San Francisco's most original. The Doobie Brothers' old tour plane crashed into a lush tropical garden where the drinks are plentiful, the food is exotic, and relaxation is inevitable.

Specialties: Chicken Poblano; Swordfish Hispaniola; Babaloo Ribeye Steak; Chunky Monkey Ice Cream

CHA CHA CHA

1801 Haight St. at Shrader / 386-5758
Lunch Mon-Fri, dinner daily, brunch Sat & Sun
No credit cards

A mixture of tempestuously flavored Cuban/Caribbean styles is served in a colorful, raucous atmosphere.

EL NUEVO FRUTILANDIA

3077 24th St. at Folsom / 648-2958
Lunch & dinner Tues-Sun

El Nuevo Frutilandia is the only restaurant in San Francisco that serves both Puerto Rican and Cuban cuisine. The 1940s jukebox plays salsa and Caribbean music to get you in the mood.

GEVA'S

482-A Hayes St. at Octavia / 863-1220
Dinner daily, brunch Sun

If you're looking for a new taste sensation, try Geva's. The Caribbean dishes, both traditional and updated, will please lovers of island cuisine and excite those who like spicy foods. An outdoor patio, reggae music and friendly service make dining at Geva's the next best thing to a trip to Jamaica. In addition to garden dining, Geva's offers catering to spice up your party or business function.

Specialties: Jerked Chicken; Black Bean Soup; Stamp & Go; Curried Goat Stew; Babyback Ribs

MISS PEARL'S JAM HOUSE
Phoenix Hotel, 601 Eddy St. at Larkin / 775-5267
Lunch Tues-Fri, dinner Tues-Sun, brunch Sun

Wacky Caribbean decor and a marvelously inventive menu focusing on small plates make this one of the most entertaining restaurants in town. The bar, made of old driftwood, corrugated steel and Plexiglas top covering a vista of sand and shells, is especially amusing. Live reggae Thursday through Saturday nights.
Specialties: Jerked Chicken; Jerked Pork Ribs; Housecured Salmon; Plantain Chips with Paw Paw Sauce; Ginger Scones

CHINESE

BRANDY HO'S ON BROADWAY
450-452 Broadway at Kearny / 362-6268
Lunch Mon-Fri, dinner daily

Brandy Ho designed his theatrical new restaurant to be "a total experience in both visual and culinary arts." With a bright red-and-white lacquer decor and dramatic neon columns styled after the palaces in the Forbidden City, the restaurant's award-winning facade lights up Broadway. As at the original Brandy Ho's at 217 Columbus Avenue (788-7527), Ho serves real Hunan cuisine without any MSG.
Specialties: Smoked Ham with Cloves of Garlic; Gon-Pou Chicken Hunan; Brandy's Spareribs with Sweet & Sour Sauce; Steamed Fish with Ginger & Green Onions

CHINA MOON CAFE
639 Post St. at Jones / 775-4789
Lunch Mon-Sat, dinner daily

Owner/chef Barbara Tropp interprets Chinese cooking with a personal Western touch that never fails to surprise and satisfy.

EMPRESS OF CHINA
838 Grant Ave. at Clay / 434-1345
Lunch & dinner daily

The Empress is a sixth-floor retreat featuring the cuisine of all China. Its interior reflects the beauty, color and architectural form of the Han dynasty.

FORTUNE RESTAURANT
675 Broadway at Stockton / 421-8130
Lunch & dinner daily

Chao Zhou cuisine is the specialty here, emphasizing fresh seafood and clay-pot dishes.

FOUNTAIN COURT
354 Clement St. at 5th Ave. / 668-1100
Lunch & dinner daily

The cuisine of Shanghai is rich with garlic, sauces and deep, braised flavors. Refined in looks and service, the Fountain Court executes these specialties perfectly.

GOLD MOUNTAIN
644 Broadway at Columbus / 296-7733
Breakfast, lunch & dinner daily

A very large restaurant on two floors, Gold Mountain's cosmopolitan Hong Kong style is hugely popular, with excellent seafood and wonderful dim sum.

HAPPY FAMILY
3809 Geary Blvd. near 3rd Ave. / 221-5095
Lunch Mon-Fri, dinner daily

Northern Chinese-style noodles are pulled by hand and served in a variety of delicious forms. If you love potstickers the ones here will make your day.

HARBOR VILLAGE
Embarcadero Four, lobby level / 781-8833
Lunch & dinner daily

Dim sum remains a luncheon favorite here, but the wide range of classical Chinese dishes for dinner and banquets also has a large and appreciative audience.

HONG KONG FLOWER LOUNGE
5322 Geary Blvd. near 17th Ave. / 668-8998
Lunch & dinner daily

An outpost of the famous Millbrae original, the Flower Lounge has the style and spirit of its namesake restaurant in Hong Kong. The room is attractive, and the food quality is high. Try the spareribs, the roast chicken and the outstanding Peking duck.
Specialties: Seafood Combination Appetizers; Pan-fried Fresh Scallop & Shrimp with Chef's Sauce; Smoked Black Cod Fish; Crab with Green Onion & Ginger; Spicy Indonesian-style Crab; Wok-charred Baby Ribs with Chinese Five Spices

HOUSE OF NANKING
919 Kearny St. near Columbus / 421-1429
Lunch & dinner daily / No credit cards

What's fun about this tiny, nondescript restaurant is that you can witness chef/owner Peter Fong cooking at top speed in the open kitchen. Fabulous describes the food he turns out.

RESTAURANTS

IMPERIAL PALACE
919 Grant Ave. at Washington / 982-4440
Lunch & dinner daily

One of the best restaurants in the city, Imperial Palace is famous throughout the world for its lavish interior and award-winning cuisine. The walls are papered with gold foil panels, and Chinese art and antiques add to the sumptuous decor. Owner Tommy Toy has welcomed guests to the Imperial Palace for more than three decades. His attention to detail has made it one of the most refined restaurants in Chinatown. Classic Cantonese dishes beautifully presented on lovely china, excellent service and a good wine list guarantee a memorable meal.

Specialties: Squab Imperial; Lichee Chicken; Peking Duck; Emperor's Gourmet; Tossed Chicken Imperial (Baked Clams, Shredded Scallop Soup, Lobster Imperial, Lichee Chicken, Four Seasons Rice Prepared at Tableside)

KAN'S
708 Grant Ave. at Sacramento / 982-2388
Lunch Mon-Sat, dinner daily

From the Cantonese fish rolls to the Peking Duck dinner, Kan's offers an ultimate Chinese dining experience.

KIRIN
6135 Geary Blvd. at 25th Ave. / 752-2412
Lunch & dinner Tues-Sun

Are you a noodle lover? Then you'll adore Kirin where hand-pulled, tender noodles are a specialty along with Mandarin Chinese food.

THE MANDARIN
900 North Point, Ghirardelli Square / 673-8812
Lunch & dinner daily

Decor opulent as an emperor's palace provides a setting for exquisite fare from all the major cuisines of China. For more than 20 years, proprietor Julian Mao has offered the very finest Chinese food — hundreds of authentic Szechuan, Hunan and Mandarin selections superbly prepared by Chef Chao Lee Sing.

Specialties: Peking Duck; Beggar's Chicken; Prawns Szechuan; Ginger Crab

NORTH CHINA RESTAURANT
2315 Van Ness Ave. at Vallejo / 673-8201
Lunch & dinner Mon-Sat

Just when you despair of ever finding an inexpensive

dining establishment on what is fast becoming Restaurant Row, up comes North China. This Mandarin eatery is a real find, but make reservations — many others have already found it. Highly acclaimed by *Gourmet Magazine*, kung pao shrimp is a popular choice among its seafood dishes.

Specialties: Variety of Potstickers; Smoked Tea Duck; North China Dry Braised Beef; Mu Shu Dishes

R & G LOUNGE
631 Kearny St. at Clay / 982-7877
Lunch & dinner Mon-Sat

Although you might have to share a table in this tiny Chinatown basement restaurant, the exceptional Cantonese food is worth it.

TOMMY TOY'S HAUTE CUISINE CHINOISE
655 Montgomery St. at Washington / 397-4888
Lunch Mon-Fri, dinner daily

The cooking style at Tommy Toy's is a unique blend of Cantonese cuisine and French inspiration. This is one of the only Chinese restaurants where you can order peach mousse for dessert. Cream tablecloths, flowers, handcrafted lanterns and imported Chinese antiques lend romance and elegance to the setting. The opulent decor includes hand-carved antique wood archways and ancient Chinese paintings framed in sandalwood. In addition to a la carte selections, Tommy Toy's offers a prix-fixe lunch and dinner menu. The restaurant's beautiful Jade Room is available for private parties.

Specialties: Fresh Maine Lobster with Garlic Chives on Peppercorn Sauce; Vanilla Prawns & Raisins with Melon; Szechuan Lamb with Marinated Spinach; Wok-charred Medallions of Beef with Garlic, Wine & Tea Leaves in a Plum Wine Sauce

WU KONG
One Rincon Center, 101 Spear St. at Mission
957-9300 / Lunch & dinner daily

Wu Kong presents the vibrant culinary blends of China's Yangtse Kiang Valley and Northern Plain.

YET WAH
2140 Clement St. at 23rd Ave. / 387-8040
Lunch & dinner daily

The most popular Chinese food in San Francisco can be found at Yet Wah restaurants. The others are at Pier 39 and Diamond Heights.

YUET LEE
1300 Stockton St. at Broadway / 982-6020
Lunch & dinner Wed-Mon

It's very plain, very noisy, and very crowded, but Yuet Lee has the very best fresh seafood. The noodle dishes are also excellent. Best of all, it's open until 3AM.

CONTINENTAL

THE BIG FOUR
Huntington Hotel
1075 California St. at Taylor / 771-1142
Breakfast daily, lunch Mon-Fri, dinner daily

Named after San Francisco's four famed railroad tycoons, the Big Four is an elegant yet comfortable restaurant. Contemporary Continental cuisine prepared by Chef Gloria Ciccarone-Nehls has helped earn this restaurant several awards.

CARNELIAN ROOM
555 California St. at Kearny / 433-7500
Dinner daily, brunch Sun

The sumptuous Carnelian Room commands one of the best views in town from its perch atop the 52nd story of the marble-glazed Bank of America building.

GARDEN COURT
Sheraton Palace, 2 New Montgomery St. at Market
392-8600 / Breakfast Mon-Sat, lunch & dinner daily,
brunch Sun

Recognized as one of the world's most beautiful dining rooms with its spectacular, stained-glass dome and exquisite chandeliers, the Garden Court is back. Refurbished with the rest of the landmark Palace Hotel, the restaurant features innovative California cuisine for lunch and a classic menu for dinner. Whether it's breakfast, lunch, dinner or afternoon tea, a meal here is an event to remember.

Specialties: Phoenix & Dragon Noodle Soup of Shrimp, Scallops, Crab & Chicken with Oyster & Green Onion Broth; Petite Beef Filet on Potato Pancake with Hodge-Podge of Mushrooms; Trout "En Croute," Served with Scallop Mousse on Angelhair Pasta

JACK'S
615 Sacramento St. at Montgomery / 421-7355
Lunch & dinner Mon-Sat

An unofficial club for the city's business elite, Jack's has been in business since Lincoln was president. Private dining facilities are available.

RESTAURANTS

PORTICO RESTAURANT
246 McAllister St. at Hyde / 861-2939
Breakfast daily, lunch & dinner Tues-Sat

Located in the Abigail Hotel just minutes from the opera, ballet and symphony, Portico is charmingly housed in a former carriage house. A European ambiance prevails in the patio-style restaurant, with an eclectic international menu that includes superlative fondues just right for sharing before a performance — or anytime at all. Portico is also available for private parties.
Specialties: Exotic Fondues; Smoked Chicken & Wild Mushroom Risotto; Squash & Leek Ravioli; Mediterranean Lamb Stew; Tiramisu

TUBA GARDEN
3634 Sacramento St. at Locust / 921-8822
Lunch Mon-Fri, brunch Sat & Sun

Located in a lovingly restored Victorian with a secluded courtyard, Tuba Garden — open only until 2:30PM — is a place to keep in mind while shopping on busy Sacramento Street.

WASHINGTON SQUARE BAR & GRILL
1707 Powell St. at Union / 982-8123
Lunch & dinner Mon-Sat

Popular with the media crowd and local politicians, the cuisine and jazz pianists at the "Washbag" are equally famed. The dishes are Continental, with a strong Italian influence. The bar is always crowded, but it's a great place to make friends.

CREOLE/CAJUN

ELITE CAFE
2049 Fillmore St. at California / 346-8668
Dinner daily, brunch Sun

The Elite serves delicious Cajun food, especially seafood. A festive bar and a separate oyster bar take the pain out of waiting for a table in this busy restaurant. The Elite also offers a Southern-style Sunday brunch.

EAST/WEST

CRUSTACEAN
1475 California St. at Polk / 776-2722
Dinner daily

Known for roasted crab, Crustacean serves fine "Euro-Asian" cuisine in a fantasy underwater setting. Although seafood is the specialty here, savory meat, poultry and vegetarian dishes expand the menu.

RESTAURANTS

MA TANTE SUMI
4243 18th St. at Diamond / 626-7864
Dinner daily
[icons]

Tante (French for aunt) Sumi is the clever Japanese woman who launched this creative bistro where the cuisines of Japan, France and California meet.

ORITALIA
1915 Fillmore St. at Pine / 346-1333
Dinner daily
[icons]

Serving an intriguing amalgam of Asian and Italian cuisines, Oritalia is the perfect place for a light dinner. Its interior is contemporary and cozy, accented by warm woods, with a huge copper hood over an open kitchen. Dishes are served in small portions, dim sum- and tapas-style. For lunch as well as dinner, try Cafe Oritalia at Ghirardelli Square.

Specialties: Fried Shrimp & Pork Dumplings with Cilantro-Mint Sauce; Spicy Mabo-Tofu Pasta with Shiitakes & Sun-dried Tomatoes

PACIFIC GRILL
500 Post St., Pan Pacific Hotel / 771-8600
Breakfast daily, lunch Mon-Sat, dinner daily, brunch Sun
[icons]

Exuding an exotic international air, the bistro setting inspires thoughts of places far away. A quiet piano, Pacific/Asian cuisine and location in Pan Pacific's sumptuous lobby define the restaurant's style.

FRENCH

AIOLI
Hotel Triton, 469 Bush St. at Grant / 249-0900
Lunch & dinner daily
[icons]

Jean-Claude Lair and Giorgio Allegro, the owners of the popular Brasserie Chambord, teamed up for a new venture last year. Aioli has a relaxed, comfortable atmosphere that makes a meal pleasurable. Warm lighting, big colorful canvases and ochre-and-umber textured walls set the mood. The menu is the creation of Chef Sebastien Urbain, known here for his cooking at the Pierre in the former Meridien hotel. Born on the island of Reunion and classically trained in France, Urbain is honing Aioli's menu to reflect a more Franco-Californian palate.

Specialties: Roasted Monkfish Filet with Bacon, Mushrooms & Spring Onions; Salmon with Capers, Bell Peppers & Italian Parsley; Braised Lamb Shanks with Couscous & Vegetables; Sauteed Duck Breast with Sour Cherries, in a Provencal Crust

AMELIO'S
1630 Powell St. at Union / 397-4339
Dinner Wed-Sun
[icons]

A cozy setting for fine dining has been provided at Amelio's. Generations of San Franciscans have experienced the excellent cuisine, gracious service and old-world atmosphere. Known for his creativity and beautiful presentation, Chef Jacky Robert offers a prix-fixe menu, as well as dishes a la carte. For more casual dining, there is L'Entree des Artistes next door. Chef Robert's bistro has been a hit since it opened last year.

Specialties: Woven Pasta with Hawaiian Prawns; Crispy Quail in a Nest of Snow Peas; Grand Marnier Souffle Baked in Orange Shells

BISTRO CLOVIS
1596 Market St. at Franklin / 864-0231
Lunch & dinner Mon-Sat
[icons]

Many so-called bistros don't have the low prices and little-known French wines true to the idea, but Bistro Clovis definitely lives up to its name. The bistro spirit is further captured with a blackboard menu, wide plank floors, small black tables and chef/owner Max Boureille's very generous food portions. Bistro Clovis also has a popular wine bar with a different tasting each day.

Specialties: Boned Chicken Breast Stuffed with Goat Cheese, Tarragon, Chervil & Parsley; Baby Vegetable Salad with Salmon; Veal Sweetbreads with Red Vinegar Butter Sauce

BISTRO ROTI
Hotel Griffon
155 Steuart St. near Mission / 495-6500
Lunch Mon-Sat, dinner daily, brunch Sun
[icons]

Chef/owner Cindy Pawlcyn and partners have opened an extremely popular, clubby restaurant that specializes in French country cooking. The lively space stars an open hearth and a rotisserie, where a variety of meat and fowl are tantalizingly roasted.

Specialties: Roast Duck; Roast Chicken; Pommes Frites; Onion Rings

BRASSERIE CHAMBORD
152 Kearny St. at Sutter / 434-3688
Breakfast daily, lunch & dinner Mon-Sat
[icons]

This favorite lunch spot for Financial District executives doubles as a romantic dinner house. Part of the Galleria Park Hotel, the award-winning Brasserie Chambord serves regional specialties, daily specials, and what may be the best foie gras in town. Banquet rooms and outside catering are available. At lunch, the lively ambiance brings to mind a Parisian bistro, with quick, efficient service for the business crowd.

Specialties: *Chambord Homecured Prosciutto with Cantaloupe; Filet of Red Snapper in Basquaise Sauce; Filet Mignon with Five Peppercorn Sauce; Rib Steak Bordelaise Sauce*

BRASSERIE SAVOY
Savoy Hotel, 580 Geary St. at Jones / 474-8686
Breakfast & dinner daily

Chef Tony Najiola deftly blends the cooking style of a Parisian brasserie with local seafood and American produce. The result is some of the most inspired fare this side of the City of Light.

CAFE CLAUDE
7 Claude Lane off Bush / 392-3505
Breakfast, lunch & dinner Mon-Sat

Small, bustling and bohemian, Cafe Claude meets all expectations of what a French bistro should be. Authenticity carries over to the popular cafe latte in a bowl. On weekdays, there's outdoor seating, when historic Claude Lane is closed to traffic.

CITY OF PARIS
101 Shannon Alley btwn. Geary & Post / 441-4442
Breakfast, lunch & dinner daily

Remarkably well-priced for the quality, the cuisine at City of Paris recalls French bistro flavors with delectable fries and such seldom-found specialties as an open-faced sandwich of pork *rillettes* or *raclette,* melted cheese with new potatoes and cornichons. Comfortable and casual, City of Paris is open until midnight, which makes it ideal for after-theatre dining. Or, you can dine first, then come back later for drinks or dessert. The wine list is excellent, and just as affordable as the food. Lunch here is speedily delivered, a plus for busy shoppers and office workers.

Specialties: *Onion-fennel Soup Gratinee; Seared Yellowfin with Warm Tomato Vinaigrette; Half Herb-roasted Chicken with Fries; Duck Confit with Rosemary-garlic Home Fries; Gite-gite, Spicy Skirt Steak with Harissa & Fries*

ERNIE'S
847 Montgomery St. at Pacific / 397-5969
Lunch Tues-Fri, dinner daily

Opened in 1934, legendary Ernie's is noted for its excellent wine list, impeccable service and innovative creations.

RESTAURANTS

FLEUR DE LYS
777 Sutter St. at Jones / 673-7779
Dinner Mon-Sat

The sumptuous, tented decor of the intimate Fleur de Lys is a fine setting for a romantic dinner before the theatre or any time at all. With Hubert Keller as chef, it is one of San Francisco's finest dining experiences. Chef Keller trained under some of the world's best chefs including Paul Bocuse, Roger Verge and Gaston Lenotre. His award-winning cuisine combines a California influence with respect for the French classical tradition. The private dining rooms at Fleur de Lys are perfect for parties of up to 25.
Specialties: Pan-fried Sturgeon with Mashed Potatoes & Roasted Peppers; Boneless Squab in a Port Wine Sauce; Veal Chop with Onion Persillade, Zucchini, Eggplant & Tomato Pie; Oven-roasted Lamb Loin with Parsnip Flan & Mustard Seed Sage Sauce

FLYING SAUCER
1000 Guerrero St. at 22nd / 641-9955
Dinner Tues-Sat

Yes, this place with only eight tables is out of this world — foodwise and otherwise. Sheet metal table tops, mismatched utensils, heavy silver plates and odd wines make the Flying Saucer one of the most eccentric eateries around.

FRENCH ROOM
Four Seasons Clift Hotel, Geary St. at Taylor / 775-4700
Breakfast, lunch & dinner daily, brunch Sun

Since 1917, the French Room has featured classical French cuisine with a California touch. The elegant appointments of this five-star, five-diamond hotel enhance any special occasion. Peek into the adjoining Redwood Room, where guests enjoy a drink before or after dinner in an equally stunning environment.
Specialties: Prime Rib; Veal & Seafood

FRINGALE
570 Fourth St. near Brannan / 543-0573
Lunch Mon-Fri, dinner Mon-Sat

A soothing interior, an elegant semi-circular bar and an upbeat ambiance make a strong first impression when you enter this bistro. The prices are reasonable for French food, and the Southern French cuisine is traditional without being boring. Fringale is a good choice for relaxing with friends in a friendly atmosphere.
Specialties: Basque Corn Galette with Prosciutto; Mashed

Potatoes & Duck Confit Patties with Black Truffle Vinaigrette; Medallions of Venison with Seasonal Fruits & Black Pepper; Hazelnut Mousse Cake

JANOT'S
44 Campton Place btwn. Stockton & Grant
392-5373 / Lunch & dinner Mon-Sat

A sunny bistro located off Union Square, Janot's offers unpretentious, delicious French food. The small brick room with skylights and floral canopies gives the feeling of a sunny garden.

JULIUS' CASTLE
1541 Montgomery St., north of Union / 362-3042
Dinner daily

A San Francisco tradition since 1922, Julius' Castle is indisputedly one of the top five romantic restaurants in Northern California. Perched atop Telegraph Hill, the restaurant serves splendid cuisine in an environment that makes you feel like royalty. Two intimate dining rooms, lit by candlelight, are appointed with the finest china and linen, and the service is formal and unobtrusive. A third-floor dining room, featuring a fireplace and an outdoor deck, is available for private parties and special-occasion events.
Specialties: Magret of Smoked Duck; Lobster Topped with Caviar; Medallions of Veal with Wild Mushrooms & Prosciutto; Chateaubriand

LA BRASSERIE FRANCAISE
3 Embarcadero, podium level / 981-5530
Lunch Mon-Fri, dinner Mon-Sat

Hailed by *Bon Appetit* as "one of the best and most affordable French restaurants in San Francisco," La Brasserie Francaise marries cuisine Parisienne with Nouvelle California, yet remains distinctly San Franciscan. The house specialty is a three-course set menu for $18. Chef/owner Eric Branger's first-course selections include a fresh salmon tarte served with sweet basil dressing, and the entrees feature many delicious choices, also available a la carte. You can lunch outdoors in the sun or dine beside the restaurant's large open fire. To complement the varied bistro menu, the select wine list offers California and French wines by the glass. Every Friday and Saturday evening, you can enjoy live jazz by well-known local artists in La Brasserie Francaise's full-service cocktail lounge.
Specialties: Escargot in Pastry with Shallots & Cabernet Sauvignon; Filet of Salmon, Eggplant & Tomato Gratin with Fennel Seed Oil; Australian Rack of Lamb with Gratin Provencal; Creme Brulee a l'Espresso

RESTAURANTS

A Little Bit of France
In Downtown San Francisco

BREAKFAST, LUNCH & DINNER

BANQUET FACILITIES FOR UP TO 150

PARKING AVAILABLE

BRASSERIE
Chambord

152 KEARNY STREET AT SUTTER

434-3688

LA FOLIE

2316 Polk St. at Green / 776-5577
Dinner Mon-Sat

$$$ ☎ 🖥 ❢ ◑

La Folie is a relaxed, cheery little place with a peach-and-yellow country print decor and a cloud-dotted blue sky for a ceiling. A gleaming copper hood marks the entrance to the kitchen, where Chef Roland Passot creates unusual, delicious, and beautifully presented dishes, which change continually. A less expensive three-course menu, served Monday through Thursday, draws a neighborhood crowd. Chef Passot, a French native, was recently awarded the title Maitre Cuisinier de France. In 1991 Julia Child named La Folie one of her favorite restaurants in *Food Arts Magazine*.

Specialties: *Atlantic Salmon & John Dory with Crust of Horseradish & Celery Root; Ravioli of Foie Gras; Cannelloni of Fresh Crab & Lobster; Parsley & Garlic Soup with Ragout of Snails & Shiitakes; Roti of Quail & Squab Wrapped in Crispy Potato Strings with Truffles*

LA MARMITE

2415 Clement St. at 25th Ave. / 666-3781
Dinner Mon-Sat

$$ ☎ ╫

On one of San Francisco's cold windy nights, La Marmite beckons like a lighthouse in the fog. This is a restaurant where you'll be treated like a regular client, perhaps because the owners are so sure you'll return. Once you've feasted on the rich stews and other traditional French specials with a Provencal influence, basked in the warmth of the Parisian bistro ambiance and enjoyed a bottle of well-priced French wine, you'll be hooked.

Specialties: *Lamb Stew with Spring Vegetables; Coq au Vin; Sauteed Prawns with Garlic, Herbs & Tomatoes; Boneless Chicken Breast with Champagne Cream Sauce & Mushrooms; Riz de Veau with Madeira*

L'ENTRECOTE DE PARIS

2032 Union St. at Buchanan / 931-5006
Lunch & dinner daily, brunch Sat & Sun

$$ ☎ 🖥 ❢ ◑ ♪

A glass-enclosed sidewalk terrace provides Parisian charm at L'Entrecote. Inside, the cozy restaurant is filled with the mouth-watering aroma of their unique steak sauce, a blend of 12 ingredients, created at the renowned Cafe de Paris in Geneva. The restaurant also has a full seafood menu, a weekend brunch and live entertainment on Friday and Saturday .

Specialties: *Entrecote; Duck with Raspberry Sauce; Grilled Baby Chicken; Dover Sole Meuniere*

L'OLIVIER
465 Davis Court at Jackson / 981-7824
Lunch Mon-Fri, dinner Mon-Sat

A romantic, charmingly decorated restaurant located near the Financial District, L'Olivier specializes in traditional French cuisine, with a contemporary California accent. It is well worth seeking out this award-winner, set in the courtyard of the Golden Gateway Center. Elegant but casual, the restaurant's main dining room opens onto a greenhouse. L'Olivier is a member of the Charte de la Bouillabaisse of Marseille. The restaurant is available for banquets, and a private dining room may be reserved for special occasions.
Specialties: Bouillabaisse; Roasted Rouelles of Sonoma Rabbit; Breast of Pheasant with Seared Spinach & Morels; Creme Brulee

LE CASTEL
3235 Sacramento St. at Presidio / 921-7115
Dinner Tues-Sun

A romantic hideaway in a converted townhouse, Le Castel combines gracious service with an exciting menu. This is a very French, special-occasion restaurant where meticulous attention is paid to every detail.

LE CENTRAL
453 Bush St. at Grant / 391-2233
Lunch & dinner Mon-Sat

A trendy place, popular with business executives, Union Square shoppers and the social set, Le Central features Country French dishes. The restaurant is known for authenticity and ambiance since its 1974 inception as San Francisco's original French bistro brasserie. The intimate decor featuring posters, blackboard menus and specials handwritten on the mirrors will evoke the warmth of a brasserie in Paris.
Specialties: Fresh Celery Remoulade; Leeks Vinaigrette; Cassoulet Le Central; Choucroute Alsacienne; Poached Salmon with Beurre Nantais; Paillard of Chicken with Pasta; Filet Mignon with Pepper

LE ST. TROPEZ
126 Clement St. at 2nd Ave. / 387-0408
Dinner Tues-Sun

A cozy, romantic dining room, with a warming fireplace and candlelit tables, sets the scene for comfortable French dining. In addition to a la carte selections, Le St. Tropez has a *dégustation* menu. This summer, Le St. Tropez reopens under the ownership of Chef Alain Rondelli, formerly of Ernie's.

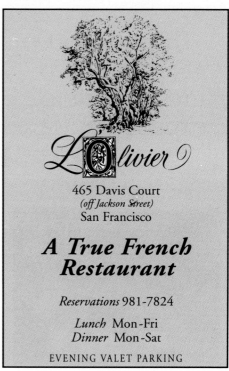

RESTAURANTS

LE TROU
1007 Guerrero St. at 22nd / 550-8169
Dinner Tues-Sat

A labor of love for cooking teacher Robert Reynolds, Le Trou is a small, comfortable restaurant. The menu of regional specialties changes weekly.

THE MANSIONS
2220 Sacramento St. at Laguna / 929-9444
Dinner Tues-Sat

If you love French food but find most restaurants a tad predictable, try the Mansions for a change. On weekends, the dinner is preceded by a world-class magic show, and accompanied by invisible pianist Claudia the Ghost the rest of the week. This entertainment adds a zany touch to the sumptuous restaurant. Described as "elegance to the nth degree" by the *San Francisco Examiner*, the Mansions is housed in a registered historic landmark. Its Victorian decor features a multimillion-dollar collection of fine arts. The excellent menu is a la carte on weekdays and prix-fixe on weekends.
Specialties: Fresh Lobster Bisque; Roast Duckling with Root Vegetables & Orange Sauce; Veal Chop Beethoven; Freshly Baked Breads

MASA'S
648 Bush St. at Stockton / 989-7154
Dinner Tues-Sat

Masa's is the ultimate in dining. Make your reservation well in advance and anticipate a delightful experience. Chef Julian Serrano creates classic French cuisine, delicious to taste and beautiful to admire.

RITZ-CARLTON DINING ROOM
600 Stockton St. at California / 296-7465
Breakfast, lunch & dinner daily, brunch Sun

From the moment you enter the lobby of the new Ritz-Carlton, the pampering begins. The Dining Room's highly attentive staff doesn't let up on service for one moment during dinner, while the kitchen serves some of the most elaborate dishes in the city. Emmanuel Kemiji, one of 23 Master Sommeliers in America, complements the chef's efforts with supreme food and wine pairing guidance.
Specialties: Daily Five-Course Tasting Menu; Warm Quail Salad with Soft Polenta, Arugula & Goat Cheese Croutons; Roast Lobster with Asparagus, Blood Oranges & Tarragon; Pan-roasted Squab with Leeks, Wild Mushrooms & Pine Nuts; Baked Chocolate Souffle with Two Sauces

RUE LEPIC
900 Pine St. at Mason / 474-6070
Lunch Mon-Fri, dinner daily

A small bistro with high ceilings and big windows, Rue Lepic draws a loyal clientele. The uncontrived menu is first-rate. In addition to a la carte selections, the menu includes a five-course chef's special.

THE SHADOWS RESTAURANT
1349 Montgomery St. at Union / 982-5536
Dinner Sat & by appointment

Romantic and pretty, The Shadows serves contemporary French cuisine in an airy, beautiful dining room. Add a prime location on Telegraph Hill with sweeping bay views, and you have a perfect evening.

SOUTH PARK CAFE
108 South Park (btwn. 2nd & 3rd, Brannan & Bryant)
495-7275 / Breakfast & lunch Mon-Fri, dinner Mon-Sat

With a warm European look, South Park Cafe is a great place to enjoy an uncomplicated lunch, an afternoon drink with tapas, or a leisurely dinner.

GERMAN

SCHROEDER'S RESTAURANT
240 Front St. near California / 421-4778
Lunch Mon-Fri, dinner Mon-Sat

Looking much as it did at the turn of the century, the eatery's shelves are lined with beer steins stacked below life-sized murals and portraits of long-ago customers.

SPECKMANN'S
1550 Church St. at Duncan / 282-6850
Lunch & dinner daily

Modeled on a German beer garden, Speckmann's is upbeat and authentic, with wonderful sausages, veal and potatoes and a good selection of beer on tap.

GREEK

ASIMAKOPOULOS CAFE & DELI
288 Connecticut St. at 18th / 552-8789
Lunch Mon-Fri, dinner daily

Award-winning Asimakopoulos Cafe, perched atop Potrero Hill, has become a San Francisco landmark for authentic Greek specialties. The cafe's home-style traditional Greek fare is prepared with the finest, freshest ingredients available. You can enjoy your meal in a

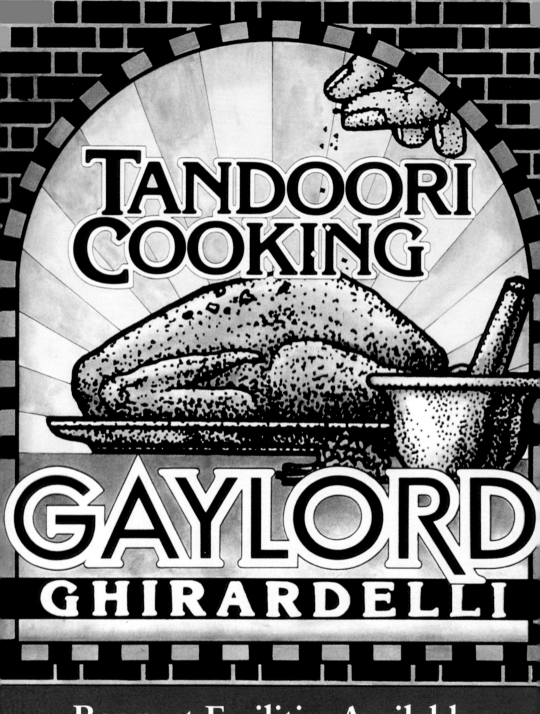

light and airy atmosphere — and then take a Greek treat home with you by stopping by Kali Orexi, the restaurant's nooksize deli around the corner.
Specialties: Moussaka; Goulbasi (Braised Lamb); Kota Lemoni (Grilled Chicken)

ATHENS BY NIGHT
811 Valencia St. at 19th / 647-3744
Dinner Mon-Sat

A taverna with live music and a warm ambiance, Athens by Night serves all the Greek favorites, plus quite a few dishes not seen on run-of-the-mill Greek menus.

SALONIKA
2237 Polk St. near Green / 771-2077
Dinner Tues-Sun

For many years Salonika has been serving authentic Greek fare to those who appreciate the real thing.

STOYANOF'S
1240 9th Ave. at Lincoln / 664-3664
Lunch & dinner Tues-Sun

Casual, noisy and bright, Stoyanof's is a place to seek out when you feel like eating traditional Greek food. Everything, including desserts, is made in-house.

INDIAN

GAYLORD INDIA RESTAURANT
900 North Point, Ghirardelli Square / 771-8822
Embarcadero One, podium level / 397-7775
Lunch Mon-Sat, dinner daily

Gaylord's is a beautifully decorated restaurant where diners are treated to a panoramic view of the bay. Specializing in tandoori barbecue cooking, the restaurant has an authentic Indian menu. The exquisite tandoori dishes are complemented by well-prepared curries and meatless specialties for vegetarians. Be sure to try Gaylord's delicious breads, including the garlic nan and the onion kulcha.
Specialties: Lamb Booti Kabob; Bara Kabob; Bengan Bartha; Chicken Tikka Masala; Tandoori Prawns & Saffron Pillau Rice

INDIA HOUSE
350 Jackson St. at Sansome / 392-0744
Lunch Mon-Fri, dinner Mon-Sat

Established in 1947 and located on fashionable Jackson Street, India House is the country's oldest Indian restaurant. This is where the legendary drink Pimm's Cup was

first introduced on the West Coast. Patricia Unterman, food critic for the *San Francisco Chronicle*, praises the cuisine, saying it has upheld Indian tradition for more than 45 years.
Specialties: Khorma; Tandoori Chicken Tikka; Curries

INDIAN OVEN
237 Fillmore St. near Haight / 626-1628
Dinner daily

In the heart of the Haight, Indian Oven serves traditional and creative variations of South Indian fare, thoughtfully paired with selected wines.

MAHARANI
1122 Post St. near Polk / 775-1988
Lunch & dinner daily

Maharani updates traditional Indian cuisine. Meat and fowl, cooked in the tandoori oven to retain their juices and full flavor, are served with raw vegetable garnishes and unusual chutneys. On the weekends, a flutist entertains in the restaurant's Indian-style dining room, with floor seating in separate alcoves.
Specialties: Tandoori Chicken; Boti Kabob; Lamb Khorma; Dal Makhni; Murgh Makhni; Chicken Tikka Masala

NEW DELHI RESTAURANT
160 Ellis St. at Cyril Magnin / 397-8470
Lunch & dinner Mon-Sat

From Calcutta and New Delhi to Hong Kong and now San Francisco, owner Ranjan Dey has maintained a passion for the restaurant business. In the process, he has perfected his culinary interpretations of North Indian fare, including strong Persian influences. In 1992, the restaurant was voted the top Indian restaurant in the country by *The New York Times*. Because of its food and popularity with the Indian community, New Delhi was selected by Bill Clinton last year as the site to meet the state's Indian leaders.
Specialties: Kofta Shah Jahani (Stuffed Meatballs & Kashmiri Spices); Murg Akbari (Chicken with Dried Fruits & Homemade Cheese); Tandoori Chicken

NORTH INDIA RESTAURANT
3131 Webster St. at Lombard / 931-1556
Lunch Mon-Fri, dinner daily

North India Restaurant has been voted the top Indian restaurant each year since 1987 by the *Zagat Restaurant Survey*. In 1989, it received the *San Francisco Focus* Gold Award, presented by Chef Paul Bocuse. This North Indian restaurant serves reasonably priced, authentic cuisine. Tandoori seafood, lamb and poultry and the finest curries are beautifully prepared. Banquet facilities are available, and there is also a very inexpensive prix-fixe menu.

Specialties: Mesquite Tandoori; Curries; Vegetarian & Non-vegetarian Preparations; Freshly Baked Bread & Desserts; Daily Specials

ITALIAN

ACQUERELLO
1722 Sacramento St. near Van Ness / 567-5432
Dinner Tues-Sun

Chef Suzette Gresham has an expertise in Italian cooking that encompasses the best of regional cuisines. Co-owner Giancarlo Paterlini is the wine expert, and together they reign over a softly lit, elegant restaurant.

ALBONA RISTORANTE ISTRIANO
545 Francisco St. at Mason / 441-1040
Dinner Tues-Sat

Originally from Albona on the Istrian peninsula, the Viscovi family has created a warm ambiance conducive to excellent dining and good conversation. The only Istrian restaurant on the West Coast, Albona's cozy dining room is a place to linger and sample a unique cuisine at reasonable prices. This captivating little North Beach restaurant specializes in cooking that reflects the influences of Venetian, Austrian and Slavic flavors. The combination produces some of the most distinctive dishes in the city.
Specialties: Crafi Albonesi (Ravioli with Three Cheeses, Pine Nuts & Sirloin-Cumin Sauce); Lamb Filet with Pomegranate Glaze; Homemade Pastas; Pappardelle with Rabbit Saute in Tokai White Wine

ALLEGRO RISTORANTE ITALIANO
1701 Jones St. at Broadway / 928-4002
Dinner daily

A friendly place where regulars are all greeted by name, Allegro has a lively repertoire that puts the limelight on freshness and simplicity.

BASTA PASTA
1268 Grant St. at Vallejo / 434-2248
Lunch & dinner daily

In the heart of North Beach, Basta Pasta offers Italian specialties late into the night. You can get fresh pastas, homecured prosciutto and pizzas from the wood-burning oven up to 1:45AM. With affordable prices and prompt service, Basta Pasta is great for lunch or for late dining after a movie or the theatre. A wine cellar is available for intimate private parties and a sky room

can accommodate up to 30 guests.
Specialties: Fresh Pacific Seafood; Homemade Pastas; Pizza; Osso Buco; Linguine with Clams; Petrale Portofino with Lemon White Wine Sauce; Penne with Porcini

BELLAVOCE
Fairmont Hotel
950 Mason St. at California / 772-5199
Breakfast daily, lunch Mon-Sat, dinner daily, brunch Sun

Touted as one of the most creative Italian restaurants in San Francisco for its cuisine and "La Scala" atmosphere. Dinner is served by professionally trained opera singers who pause for an occasional aria or Broadway selection. BellaVoce is also open for breakfast and lunch. The prix-fixe lunch menu is $9.95. At dinner, the prix-fixe menu is $12.95-$14.95.
Specialties: Fresh Seafood; Pizza; Osso Buco; Linguine with Clams

THE BLUE FOX
659 Merchant St. at Montgomery / 981-1177
Dinner Mon-Sat

Gianni Fassio brought new meaning to Italian dining when he purchased The Blue Fox in 1988. Since then the restaurant has come to epitomize fine dining with its attentive service, soft sumptuous decor and creative Italian dishes. Located near the TransAmerica Pyramid in the heart of the Financial District, it is a short cab ride from major hotels.
Specialties: Veal & Beef Carpaccio; Risotto with Fontina & White Truffles; Grilled Ahi Tuna with Herb-infused Olive Oil; Veal Chop with Porcini; Tortellini in Panna; Tiramisu

BONTA
2223 Union St. at Fillmore / 929-0407
Dinner Tues-Sun

A tiny, lively Roman-style restaurant where every meal is a celebration, Bonta turns out delectable pastas, risotto and other specialties.

BUCA GIOVANNI
800 Greenwich St. at Columbus / 776-7766
Dinner Mon-Sat

Giovanni Leoni has been cooking in San Francisco for nearly 40 years and his expertise in traditional and contemporary Italian cuisine has earned him many awards. His brick-walled underground dining room is typical of those in his native Italy.
Specialties: Veal-filled Ravioli in Ricotta & Walnut Sauce; Veal Medallions with Porcini; Rabbit with Grappa & Oyster Mushrooms; Roasted Lamb; Tiramisu

CAFE ADRIANO
3347 Fillmore St. at Chestnut / 474-4180
Dinner Tues-Sun

$$ ☎

Owners Adriano and Deborah Paganini designed this charming Italian bistro in the Marina. Dedicated to serving moderately priced seasonal Italian dishes, they offer a daily menu complimented by an ample Italian wine list. California wines are also available. Cafe Adriano is casual and friendly, and the gracious service will make dining here enjoyable.
Specialties: Antipasti; Tagliatelle Pasta with Artichokes & Fresh Herbs; Saffron Risotto with Wild Mushrooms; Pan-fried Filet of Beef with Gorgonzola, Polenta & Red Wine Sauce; Strawberry Sfogliatina

CAFE PESCATORE
2455 Mason St. at North Point / 561-1111
Breakfast daily, lunch Mon-Fri, dinner daily, brunch Sat & Sun

$$ ☎ 🍸 🙂

Cafe Pescatore is a friendly, open-air neighborhood cafe featuring housemade pastas, fresh seafood, gourmet pizzas baked in a wood-burning oven and daily antipasti selections. This classic Italian trattoria, ideally located near Fisherman's Wharf, is a favorite of San Franciscans and visitors alike.
Specialties: Linguine Pescatore (Fresh Seafood with Lin-guine, Tossed with Spicy Tomato Sauce); Tuna Saltimbocca (Fresh Tuna Seared with a Red Wine Demiglaze & Garlic Mashed Potatoes)

CAFE RIGGIO
4112 Geary Blvd. at 5th Ave. / 221-2114
Lunch Fri, dinner daily

$$ 🍸

The liveliest crowd in the avenues is usually found gathered here. The warm atmosphere complements well-prepared Italian dishes and daily specials.

CAFFE SPORT
574 Green St. at Columbus / 981-1251
Lunch & dinner Tues-Sat

$$ 🙂

A lively, crowded place with a character all its own, Caffe Sport serves Italian family-style meals in the heart of North Beach. There are three seatings each evening: 6:30, 8:30 and 10:30PM.

CALZONE'S
430 Columbus Ave. at Vallejo / 397-3600
Lunch & dinner daily

$ ☎ 🍸 🙂

Calzone's, located on the site of an old-fashioned North Beach grocery store, is a fun-filled restaurant serving con-

RESTAURANTS

temporary Italian cuisine. Seasonal fresh produce that is often organically grown and a delicious variety of pizzas from a wood-burning oven make meals here memorable. Pasta is homemade and portions are like "Mama's."

Specialties: Tricolor Polenta with White Beans, Red & Green Onions & Smoked Mozzarella; Potato & Three-cheese-filled Ravioli with Pesto Cream Sauce; Angelhair Pasta with Smoked Salmon & Asparagus in a Tomato Cream Sauce

CAPP'S CORNER
1600 Powell St. at Green / 989-2589
Lunch Mon-Fri, dinner daily

Recipient of The Critic's Choice for best Italian family-style restaurant in the Bay Area, Capp's Corner gives an enormous amount of great food for incredibly little.

CIAO
230 Jackson St. at Battery / 982-9500
Lunch Mon-Sat, dinner daily

The dazzling decor and authentic Northern Italian food have made Ciao one of the most wonderful trattorias in town, frequented by a young, affluent crowd.

CIRCOLO RESTAURANT & CHAMPAGNERIA
161 Sutter St., Crocker Galleria / 362-0404
Lunch Mon-Fri, dinner Mon-Sat

Circolo serves contemporary Italian cuisine, featuring fresh pastas, grilled meats and wood-baked pizzas, in a setting that manages to be elegant yet unostentatious.

DONATELLO RISTORANTE
Donatello Hotel, 501 Post St. at Mason / 441-7182
Breakfast & dinner daily

The most elegant Italian restaurant in town, Donatello Ristorante is decorated with sumptuous furnishings and wall hangings. Known for its inventive and unique dishes, this special-occasion restaurant has been an award-winner for many years. Now under the direction of Chef Patrizio Sacchetto, the kitchen is as up to date as the best restaurants in Italy.

Specialties: Risotto Daily Specials; Sauteed Salmon Served with Creamed Yellow Bell Pepper; Grilled Veal Chop in a Barolo Wine Sauce; Spaghetti with Braised Duck Ragout; Grilled Filet of Beef with Cabbage & Beans

E'ANGELO
2234 Chestnut St. at Pierce / 567-6164
Dinner Tues-Sun

Northern Italian food and a warm, casual ambiance attract a hungry crowd eager to sample the homemade pastas and pizzas E'Angelo is justly famous for. You can count on

honest cooking and prices in this friendly restaurant; it's a great place to relax with friends and family.

Specialties: Lasagna Bolognese; Eggplant Parmigiana; Homemade Tortellini; Homemade Ravioli di Ricotta

EMPORIO ARMANI EXPRESS
One Grant Ave. at O'Farrell / 677-9010
Lunch & dinner daily

A stylish restaurant on the mezzanine of Armani's retail store, this is a great place for pasta and people-watching. The food is authentically Italian.

ETRUSCA
121 Spear St., Rincon Center / 777-0330
Lunch Mon-Fri, dinner daily

The breathtaking dining room with amber, onyx and white marble accents is filled with hand-painted frescoes. Earthy dishes and a varied Italian wine list are true to the restaurant's heritage.

FINO
Andrews Hotel
One Cosmo Place near Taylor / 928-2080
Dinner daily

Fino has an understated urbanity that fosters conversation and romance. The menu features plenty of pasta, pizza, seafood and meat.

FIOR D'ITALIA
601 Union St. at Stockton / 986-1886
Lunch & dinner daily

Established more than a century ago, Fior d'Italia is America's oldest Italian restaurant. Overlooking Washington Square, the restaurant's beautiful setting and traditional cuisine reflect its North Beach history. Award-winning Chef Gianni Audieri prepares such classic dishes as saltimbocca, fresh pastas and osso buco. Four banquet rooms, seating up to 80 guests, include a room dedicated to Tony Bennett. Old world service and excellent Northern Italian cuisine have made this landmark famous. To celebrate its history, the Fior offers a special four-course dinner for $18.86 — to mark when it was founded in 1886.

Specialties: Caesar Salad for Two; Fried Calamari; Lamb Carpaccio; Gnocchi in a Piemontese Tomato Sauce; Scalloppine Sauteed with Prosciutto & Mushrooms

FRASCATI
1901 Hyde St. at Green / 928-1406
Dinner daily

Overlooking the Hyde Street cable car that climbs Russian

Hill, Frascati is a sophisticated, yet relaxed neighborhood restaurant devoted to fine food and fun — with a dash of the romance of Rome. The modern, breezy interior and open kitchen create an ideal backdrop for this eatery's innovative pastas and desserts complemented by some of the best wine values in town. Warm, indulgent service is an invitation to linger.

Specialties: *Fresh Seafood; Grilled Meat & Poultry Dishes; Capellini alla Rughetta (Homemade Angelhair Pasta with Arugula & Sundried Tomatoes, Garlic & White Wine)*

GIRA POLLI
659 Union St. btwn. Powell & Columbus / 434-4472
Dinner daily

Rock-bottom prices and terrific chicken from the rotisserie keep neighborhood fans coming back to Gira Polli.

HYDE STREET BISTRO
1521 Hyde St. at Pacific / 441-7778
Dinner daily

Hyde Street Bistro is a good neighborhood spot for unpretentious food. Northern Italian and Austrian dishes reflect the owner's Tyrolean background.

I FRATELLI
1896 Hyde St. at Green / 474-8603
Dinner daily

A longtime neighborhood favorite, I Fratelli is known for its wide range of pastas, seafood, antipasti, veal and bruschetta. This popular, family-owned trattoria on Russian Hill also features an excellent selection of Italian and California wines in its bar overlooking the Hyde Street cable cars. If you are in the Fillmore Street neighborhood, you can stop at the owners' other restaurant, Tre Fratelli, at 2101 Sutter Street (931-4115), serving the same great Italian food.

Specialties: *Fettuccine with Seafood; Insalata Testarossa (A Variety of Lettuces with Walnuts & Gorgonzola); Veal Saltimbocca; Rigatoni Amatriciana; Ravioli ai Gamberetti (Ravioli with Shrimp); Caesar Salad with Radicchio*

IL FORNAIO
1265 Battery St. in Levi Plaza / 986-0100
Lunch Mon-Fri, dinner daily, brunch Sat & Sun

High-tech lighting and marble evoke a sophisticated Italian restaurant. There's a delicatessen, grill and bakery, and outdoor seating in view of leafy Levi Plaza.

RESTAURANTS

JACKSON FILLMORE TRATTORIA
2506 Fillmore St. at Jackson / 346-5288
Dinner daily
$$ ☎ ☺

Pacific Heights' most unpretentious restaurant, Jackson Fillmore is a neighborhood hangout where the food is plentiful and the noise level high. Italian cuisine in the style of Rome and Tuscany is remarkably consistent and authentic. You can choose from a plentiful selection of appetizers, pasta dishes, salads and specials such as radicchio wrapped in pancetta and large squares of homemade pasta stuffed with asparagus and prosciutto. *Specialties: Branzino Fra Diavolo (Sea Bass in spicy Tomato Sauce); Chicken with Olives, Onions & Anchovies; Linguine with Prawns; Tuscan Soup*

KULETO'S
221 Powell St. at Geary / 397-7720
Breakfast, lunch & dinner daily
$$ ☎ ♈ ☺

Marble floors and high ceilings, a large exhibition kitchen, and a long bar with tasty antipasti on the counter and strings of garlic and peppers overhead make Kuleto's a San Francisco favorite for Italian food. Downstairs, the Machiavelli Room reflects the charm of an Italian trattoria, accommodating up to 50 guests for private dinners. The Machiavelli Room is also available for receptions. *Specialties: Breast of Chicken Stuffed with Ricotta & Herbs; Saffron Risotto with Prawns, Scallops & Sundried Tomatoes; Grilled Radicchio Wrapped in Pancetta with Basil Vinaigrette*

LA FIAMMETTA
1701 Octavia St. at Bush / 474-5077
Dinner Tues-Sat
$ ☎ ⅲ ♈ ☺

Off the beaten track on the edge of Pacific Heights, La Fiammetta is a pleasant cafe that's comfortable and tranquil even when it's packed. The neighborhood hideaway serves classic Italian country dishes. The menu, mostly Tuscan and Roman, changes monthly. Try the unusual *zuppa imaginativa* — soups you create yourself from an assortment of ingredients and prepared to order for you in the kitchen. *Specialties: Grilled Italian Mushrooms; Mixed Grill; Grilled Veal Rack with Oyster Mushrooms; Vegetarian & Seafood Pastas; Chocolate Torte; Tiramisu*

LA PERGOLA
2060 Chestnut St. at Steiner / 563-4500
Dinner daily
$$ ☎ ☺

Everything about La Pergola is convivial — the atmosphere, the service and the indulgent attention of owners Sandra and Giancarlo Bortolotti. Even a short wait for a table is fun, whether sipping a pre-dinner glass of wine at the compact bar or watching diners enjoy the house specialties. The food is La Pergola's main attraction. Authentic Northern Italian dishes emphasize herbs, grilling and homemade pasta. Uncompromised regional recipes are perfected months in advance, and unusual vintages from the mostly Italian wine cellar make the most of every course. *Specialties: Mezzaluna: Squash-filled Pasta with Browned Butter & Sage; Marinated Rabbit Served with Roasted Juniper & Grappa Sauce; Sauteed Seasonal Mushrooms with Soft Polenta; Sonoma Lamb Chop in a Balsamic Vinegar Sauce*

LA TRAVIATA
2854 Mission St. at 24th / 282-0500
Dinner daily
$$ ☎ ☺

Dedicated to the opera, La Traviata is filled with photos of opera stars and sounds of their greatest recordings.

LAGHI
1801 Clement St. at 19th Ave. / 386-6266
Dinner Tues-Sun
$$ ☎

Named for chef/owner Gino Laghi, this is the culinary statement of a talented man with firm ideas. The authentic, housemade menu changes daily.

LITTLE CITY ANTIPASTI BAR
673 Union St. at Powell / 434-2900
Lunch & dinner daily
$$ ♈ ☺

If you like Italian appetizers and enjoy making a meal of several small plates, you'll love the selection of dishes at Little City.

L'OTTAVO RISTORANTE
692 Sutter St. at Taylor / 922-3944
Dinner daily
$$ ☎ 🚗

The owners of Pietro's Ristorante moved from their Union Street location, lightened their menu, created a more intimate decor and reopened last year as L'Ottavo. The restaurant still presents traditional dishes at moderate prices, offering cuisines from different regions of Italy, but with an emphasis on healthier specialties. An antipasti bar at the entrance reflects this new commitment. The walls are pastel and decorated with paintings, and the fragrant aroma of homemade pasta and sauces whets your appetite. *Specialties: Antipasti; Osso Buco alla Milanese; Scaloppine alla Corsara; Seafood Pasta; Fettuccine All'Uovo; Insalate Speciali; Grilled & Marinated Vegetables*

THE MAGIC FLUTE
3673 Sacramento St. at Spruce / 922-1225
Lunch Mon-Fri, dinner Mon-Sat

Often selected as one of San Francisco's most romantic restaurants, The Magic Flute has a charming south-facing garden, great for sunny lunches and private parties. The menu has lots of Tuscan dishes, including a memorable polenta lasagna with Muscovy duck.

MARBLE WORKS
555 North Point at Taylor
Hyatt at Fisherman's Wharf / 749-6161
Breakfast & dinner daily

Housed in the old stone-cutting facility of The Joseph Musto Marble Works Company, the restaurant specializes in Northern Italian and fresh seafood dishes.

MARINA CAFE
2417 Lombard St. at Scott / 929-7241
Dinner Tues-Sun, brunch Sun

Located in San Francisco's finest district, The Marina Cafe is popular with locals. The restaurant offers gracious, well-paced service and fresh seafood served with an Italian touch. As the *San Francisco Examiner* says, "The Marina Cafe has done very well since it opened in 1980 and for several reasons. The main reason is a double one: the food is very good and at prices 30 to 40 percent below its competitors for the same items." Four private dining rooms are available for parties.
Specialties: Milk-fed White Veal; Sauteed Prawns & Fresh Eastern Scallops; Mesquite-broiled Fresh Fish; Choice Aged New York Steak; Full Pasta Selection

MILANO JOE'S
1175 Folsom St. at 8th / 861-2815
Lunch Mon-Fri, dinner daily

Milano Joe's is a handsome eatery in the booming SOMA restaurant scene, serving excellent homemade pasta, veal and seafood.

MODELLA RISTORANTE
7 Spring St. at California / 362-1990
Lunch Mon-Fri, dinner daily

An intimate, elegant restaurant, Modella Ristorante showcases the intensely flavorful Northern Italian creations of Chef Loretta Rampone.

RESTAURANTS

NEW JOE'S
347 Geary St. at Powell / 989-6733
Lunch & dinner daily

Right off Union Square, traditional-style New Joe's serves hearty food in generous portions to customers at "front row" counter seats. Those who prefer dining in comfortable booths will find plenty.
Specialties: Housemade Pastas; Grilled & Roasted Meats, Game, Poultry & Seafood

NORTH BEACH RESTAURANT
1512 Stockton St. at Green / 392-1700
Lunch & dinner daily

Located in the heart of North Beach, the restaurant specializes in authentic Northern Italian cuisine. Home-cured prosciutto, homemade pasta, fresh seafood dishes and generously prepared dishes make North Beach Restaurant a traditional San Francisco favorite. Its wine list was chosen as one of the top 100 outstanding wine lists by *The Wine Spectator*. The restaurant has several private rooms, available for groups up to 75 guests.
Specialties: Calamari Vinaigrette; Spaghetti Smirnoff; Abalone Dore Mugnaia; Chicken Toscana; Veal Scalloppine alla Sorrento; Lamb with Barolo Sauce; Pepper Steak with Grappa Sauce; Torta di Gelato

OLIVE'S GOURMET PIZZA
3249 Scott St. btwn. Lombard & Chestnut / 567-4488
Lunch & dinner daily

Olive's gourmet pizzas are among the best in town. Its most famous has a crunchy cornmeal and imported olive oil crust. Premium toppings, such as mushroom, eggplant, roasted garlic and fennel sausage, are selected daily. At Olive's, you can get a whole pie, or you can order by the slice. This friendly Italian restaurant in the Marina serves pizzas and fresh pasta dishes every day, with late-night hours on Friday and Saturday. Olive's takes reservations for parties of six or more.
Specialties: Wild Mushroom Pizza with Sun-dried Tomato Pesto; Smoked Chicken Pizza with Sweet Corn Salsa; Venetian Sausage Pizza with Tricolor Pepperonata; Mixed Grilled Vegetable Pizza with Fresh Herbs

ORIGINAL JOE'S #2
2001 Chestnut St. at Fillmore / 346-4000
Lunch & dinner daily, brunch Sun

Located in the scenic Marina district, Original Joe's #2 attracts a crowd. With an all-new look, the restaurant has an exhibition kitchen and a bar that is popular with the area's young professionals. The contemporary Italian-style cuisine features daily specials, antipasti, salads, hearty entrees, gourmet pizzas and a variety of Italian desserts.
Specialties: Saltimbocca; Broiled Pork Tenderloin with Mushrooms & Balsamic Vinegar; Grilled Scampi with Tomato, Basil, Garlic & Rice; Veal Piccata; Rotisserie Chicken with Garlic & Parsley

PALIO D'ASTI
640 Sacramento St. at Montgomery / 395-9800
Dinner Mon-Sat

Il palio, a bareback horse race held in Asti since the 13th century, is the theme of owner Gianni Fassio's latest Northern Italian restaurant. Medieval colors, bright banners and a bar curved like a racetrack set the mood, and the open kitchen's traditional dishes create the magic. Don't overlook the custom-made antipasti cart, or *carrello*, which contains more than a dozen different trays of delicacies.
Specialties: Mezzaluna Stuffed with Fontina, Almonds & White Truffles; Quails with Garlic & Fennel Stuffing & Blueberry Sauce with Soft Polenta; Pizza with Mozzarella, Artichoke Hearts, Olives, Capers & Prosciutto; Risotto with Wild Mushrooms

PANE E VINO
3011 Steiner St. at Union / 346-2111
Dinner daily

Small and warm, with tile floors and a long wooden table laden with good things, Pane e Vino draws a neighborhood crowd.

PIZZERIA UNO
2200 Lombard St. at Steiner / 563-3144
2323 Powell St. at Bay / 788-4055
Two Embarcadero Center, podium level / 397-8667
Lunch & dinner daily

The pizzas are cooked and served in the pan. Chronicle Books voted Pizzeria Uno's Chicago deep-dish pizza the best pizza in San Francisco. The restaurant also serves thin-crust gourmet pizzas, pastas, salads, sandwiches and desserts. Nothing on the menu is fried, and dishes are prepared with fresh ingredients daily. A full bar and lunch specials are offered at all three locations Monday through Friday. The Pizzeria Uno on Lombard Street is open until 1AM on Friday and Saturday and until midnight the rest of the week. Validated parking, for an hour and a half, is available at Powell Street and after 5PM and on weekends at Embarcadero Center.
Specialties: Deep-dish Pizza with Fresh Eggplant, Marinated Artichoke, Roasted Red Pepper, Mozzarella & Feta Cheese; Chicago Classic Pizza with Crisp Crust, Tomato, Extra Sausage & Extra Cheese; Fettuccine Alfredo

PREGO
2000 Union St. at Buchanan / 563-3305
Lunch & dinner daily

The stylish restaurant on Union Street is so popular that even with a reservation you may have to wait. However, the bar scene is lively and friendly and the food is worth waiting for, particularly from the rotisserie. If you like pizza, be sure to try one from Prego's oak-burning oven.

RISTORANTE GRIFONE
1609 Powell St. at Green / 397-8458
Dinner Tues-Sun

This little restaurant attracts a loyal following eager to enjoy authentic Northern Italian specialties. Ristorante Grifone is always satisfying, with large portions and an intimate ambiance.

RISTORANTE MILANO
1448 Pacific Ave. at Larkin / 673-2961
Dinner Tues-Sun

Ristorante Milano is a friendly, intimate restaurant

serving authentic, delicious Milanese specialties. The crowded, upbeat atmosphere is delightfully urban.

RISTORANTE PARMA
3314 Steiner St. at Lombard / 567-0500
Dinner Mon-Sat

A trattoria in style and spirit, Parma is ruled by owner Pietro Elia, who has a friendly word for everyone. The walls are brick, the room is small and lively, and the food, says Pietro, "is just like being in Italy." No wonder so many of Pietro's customers are devoted regulars.
Specialties: Linguine alle Vongole; Fettuccine Amatriciana; Bocconcini de Casa (Veal with Mushrooms, Spinach & Cheese)

THE STINKING ROSE
325 Columbus Ave. at Broadway / 781-ROSE
Lunch & dinner daily, brunch Sat & Sun

It's hard to find a North Beach restaurant that is more fun than The Stinking Rose. If the whacky murals and little garlic train and factory above the bar aren't entertainment enough, there's always the crowd, a lively bunch reveling in their shared passion for garlic. Luckily, they are never let down by a Cal-Italian cuisine with

a Gilroyan gusto for garlic in everything from pasta to pizza to — no kidding — ice cream. Come with a crowd and expect to have a stinking good time. (P.S. Fanatics love the weekend Garlic Brunch.)

Specialties: Bagna Calda; 40-Clove Garlic Chicken; Braised Lamb Shank with Garlic Mashed Potatoes; Garlic-roasted Whole Dungeness Crab

TRATTORIA CONTADINA
1800 Mason St. at Union / 982-5728
Dinner daily
$$ ☎

This old-style restaurant continues to be a favorite with San Franciscans who savor North Beach atmosphere with their pasta. Veal, chicken and seafood dishes are served with produce from the owner's ranch.

TRE FRATELLI
2101 Sutter St. at Steiner / 931-4115
Lunch Mon-Fri, dinner daily
$$ ☎ ☺

This bustling family-owned neighborhood trattoria, like its popular brother I Fratelli, specializes in pasta with fresh seafood, grilled meats and fish, and sparkling salads. The restaurant's full cellar of California and Italian wines includes special selections from Toscana and Veneto. Tre Fratelli is one block from the Kabuki Theatre and all the lively shopping on Fillmore Street.

Specialties: Linguine with Shrimp & Scallops; Rigatoni with Prosciutto & Vegetables; Bruschetta; Veal Saltimbocca; Fettuccine Carbonara

UMBERTO'S
141 Steuart St. at Mission / 543-8021
Lunch Mon-Fri, dinner Mon-Sat
$$ ☎ Y ☺ ♫

Low ceilings and Mediterranean tiles give Umberto's a Tuscan flavor. Entertainment includes a lively jazz combo on Saturday nights.

UNDICI
374 11th St. at Harrison / 431-3337
Dinner Mon-Sat
$$ ☎ Y ⅱⅱ

Located in San Francisco's avant-garde South-of-Market area, Undici draws a young, trendy crowd. A lovely space made to look like ancient Italy makes dining here a pure pleasure. Antiqued walls and dramatic loft-style ceiling set the stage for Chef Donna Nicoletti's boldly flavored Southern Italian cuisine.

Specialties: Neapolitan-style Zuppa di Pesce with Tomatoes; Grilled Baby Octopus; Roasted Chicken Vesuvio with Roasted Potatoes, Garlic & Oregano; Gnocco Sardo with Roasted Veal

VANESSI'S RESTAURANT
1177 California St. at Jones / 771-2422
Lunch Mon-Fri, dinner daily
$$ ☎ Y ⅱⅱ ☺

Now located on Nob Hill, this North Beach classic was one of the first restaurants with an exhibition kitchen. Under the direction of the original owner's daughter, Vanessi's upholds its reputation in comfortable modern quarters. A broad menu includes fresh local fish, grilled meats and poultry, veal dishes, a variety of homemade pastas and the best zabaglione in town.

Specialties: Homemade Pastas; Veal; Fresh Fish; Breast of Chicken Parmigiana; Veal Scalloppine; Chicken Saute Vanessi; Seafood Pasta

VENTICELLO RISTORANTE
1257 Taylor St. at Washington / 922-2545
Dinner daily
$$ ☎ ◎ Y ⅱⅱ

Venticello's pizzas have thin light crusts with varied toppings. A rustic setting is the perfect backdrop for the restaurant's full menu of Northern Italian fare.

VINOTECA JACKSON FILLMORE
586 Bush St. / 983-6200
Breakfast daily, lunch Tues-Fri, dinner daily
$ ☎ Y

Next to the Hotel Juliana, Vinoteca perches above the Stockton Tunnel. Casual and down-to-earth, the restaurant feels like a congenial Roman trattoria, complete with checkered tablecloths and white-aproned waiters. Very Southern Italian, anchovies and artichokes play leading roles at the table, as do the cellar's red and white wines from that region. There is a good selection of meat and fish entrees, including a savory mixed seafood dish, steamed and served in a Fra Diavolo sauce.

Specialties: Deep-fried Artichokes Tossed with Garlic & Parmesan; Chicken Contadino; Grilled Choice Lamb Chop with Garlic, Herbs & Spears of Asparagus

VIVANDE PORTA VIA
2125 Fillmore St. at California / 346-4430
Lunch daily
$$

Marvelous pastas, Italian cheeses and luscious desserts can be found at this popular takeout shop.

JAPANESE

BENKAY
Hotel Nikko San Francisco
222 Mason St. at O'Farrell / 394-1105
Dinner Tues-Sat
$$$ ☎ 🚗 ◎ Y 🅥

Atop the 25th floor of Hotel Nikko, Benkay provides

sweeping views of San Francisco from its sushi bar, Western-style dining room and five private tatami rooms. Benkay serves exquisitely prepared Japanese cuisine from an a la carte menu, including selections from the sushi bar. The restaurant also offers prix-fixe dinners. Traditional kaiseki dinners are prepared with advance notice.
Specialties: Kaiseki; Yosenabe; Shabu-Shabu; Sushi; Sashimi

CHO-CHO JAPANESE RESTAURANT
1020 Kearny St. at Broadway / 397-3066
Lunch Mon-Fri, dinner Mon-Sat

Step inside Cho-Cho and experience a bit of authentic Japan. The interior has been recreated as an old farmhouse with traditional Japanese folk art and antiques.
Specialties: Shabu-Shabu; Sukiyaki; Beef Bara-Yaki; Tempura

EBISU RESTAURANT
1283 9th Ave. at Irving / 566-1770
Lunch & dinner Mon-Sat

A restaurant and sushi bar, Ebisu is a popular spot on Ninth Avenue's restaurant row.
Specialties: Sushi; Sukiyaki; Yosenabe; Tempura

FUJIYA RESTAURANT
Embarcadero One, lobby level / 398-1151
Lunch Mon-Fri, dinner Mon-Sat

With a new shabu-shabu bar added to its sushi bar, Fujiya features an assortment of Japanese cuisine, including teppan dishes. Professionals in the Financial District often meet here for lunch, dinner or for cocktails from Fujiya's full bar.
Specialties: Teppan Steaks & Seafood; Sushi; Shabu-Shabu; Tempura; Yakitori

FUKU-SUSHI
1581 Webster St.
Japan Center, West Building / 346-3030
Lunch & dinner Wed-Mon

The very freshest sushi is prepared by some of the fastest sushi makers in town at Fuku-Sushi. You'll also find a regular menu of Japanese favorites.
Specialties: Sushi; Tempura; Sukiyaki; Yosenabe

ICHIRIN
330 Mason St. at O'Farrell / 956-6085
Dinner daily

Western seating is available here, but ask to sit in the lovely Japanese-style dining room upstairs, or in one of

RESTAURANTS

several private tatami rooms. You'll enjoy fresh sushi and a wide variety of Japanese dishes.
Specialties: Sushi; Yakitori; Tempura

ISOBUNE
1737 Post St. at Webster
Japan Center, upper floor / 563-1030
Lunch & dinner daily

A perfect place to introduce friends — or children — to sushi, Isobune is famous for its floating sushi bar. Little boats go by and you take what appeals to you. They figure out your bill by counting up the plates. Service couldn't be faster or better! Isobune is open continually from 11:30AM to 10PM, seven days a week. (There's another Isobune in Burlingame near the airport. For information, call 344-8433.)
Specialties: Sushi of all Kinds

IZUMI
317 Sanchez St. at 17th / 552-8070
Dinner Wed-Mon

Chef/owner Yoshio has created a tiny gem of a restaurant. The exquisite, inexpensive specialties range from sushi to cooked delicacies. You can order a Chef's Special Meal created to taste, if you phone a day in advance.
Specialties: Kimchee Roll; Agenasu (Deep-fried Eggplant with Bean Paste Sauce); Broiled Oysters with Spinach

KABUTO SUSHI
5116 Geary Blvd. at 15th Ave. / 752-5652
Dinner Tues-Sun

From far and wide people flock to Kabuto to witness the fastest sushi maker in town. Using only the freshest fish, Sachio has entertained customers with his extraordinary dexterity for years.
Specialties: Fresh Fish; Sushi; Daily Specials

KANSAI
325 Sacramento St. at Front / 392-2657
Lunch & dinner Mon-Fri

The former chef for the Japanese embassy in Washington turns out beautiful, authentic dishes often not found here. You can try an elaborate kaiseki dinner or choose from a lengthy menu, perfectly rendered.
Specialties: Kaiseki; Sushi; Sashimi; Tempura; Yosenabe

KIKU OF TOKYO
333 O'Farrell St. at Mason / 441-5458
Lunch Mon-Fri, dinner daily

In the San Francisco Hilton Hotel, this downtown

restaurant is a favorite with Japanese tourists.
Specialties: Sashimi; Tempura Combinations

KINOKO
San Francisco Marriott, 55 4th St. at Market
896-1600 / Dinner daily

At Kinoko, in the San Francisco Marriott, diners can watch the chefs prepare breast of chicken and assorted seafood teppanyaki style — the food is sliced and cooked on a steel-top surface right at your table. There is also a sushi bar.
Specialties: Seafood Tempura; Shabu-Shabu; Kinoko Shrimp; Sushi; Sea Scallops; Filet Mignon & Chicken Breast Shabu-Shabu; Tempura Combination

KYO-YA
Sheraton Palace Hotel
2 New Montgomery St. at Market / 392-8600
Lunch & dinner Mon-Fri

Hailed as an "emissary for the best of Japanese culture" by the *San Francisco Chronicle*, Kyo-ya has critics raving about its superb, jewel-like sushi and traditional cuisine. Kyo-ya's world-class service and elegant setting complete this unique dining experience.
Specialties: Shabu-Shabu; Tempura Combination; Sushi; Salmon Teriyaki

MIFUNE
1737 Post St. at Buchanan / 922-0337
Lunch & dinner daily

The best Japanese noodles in the city can be found right in the heart of Japantown. Whether you like them hot or cold, white or wheat, with meat or without, the choice is yours at Mifune. As any fan will attest, nothing warms and satisfies as well as a steaming bowl of delicious udon or soba.
Specialties: Tenzaru Soba; Tempura Udon; Nabeyaki Udon

OSOME RESTAURANT
1923 Fillmore St. at Pine / 346-2311
Dinner daily

Osome is a moderately priced restaurant serving authentic Japanese cuisine. You can sample a delicious variety of sushi and hot food without waiting in line for hours. Individual tatami rooms are available at Osome's other location, 3145 Fillmore Street at Greenwich. It is open for dinner daily and for lunch during the week (931-8898).
Specialties: Fresh Fish; Sushi; Sashimi

SANPPO RESTAURANT
1702 Post St. at Buchanan / 346-3486
Lunch Tues-Sat, dinner Tues-Sun

$$ 🚗

In business for 19 years, Sanppo has developed a fine reputation for Japanese cuisine. Their large menu lists many inexpensive dishes.
Specialties: *Tempura; Gyoza; Nabemono; Sushi*

SUSHI A
1737 Buchanan St. btwn. Post & Sutter / 931-4685
Lunch & dinner Wed-Mon

$$ ☎

A traditional-style Japanese restaurant on the Buchanan Mall in Japantown, Sushi A is best known for its excellent sushi and sashimi. Just as good are its numerous other dishes, including daily specials. Choose between the sushi bar, Western tables or the restaurant's peaceful tatami room.
Specialties: *Sushi; Sashimi; Salmon Teriyaki; Fried Oysters; Calamari Tempura*

TOKYO SUKIYAKI
225 Jefferson St. at Taylor / 775-9030
Lunch Sat & Sun, dinner Mon-Fri

$$ ☎ 🚗 🍸

Japanese locals feel instantly at home upon entering this Fisherman's Wharf restaurant. Items of decor have been imported directly from the homeland and many of the dishes are prepared at tableside.
Specialties: *Sukiyaki; Sashimi; Sushi; Butteryaki*

TORAYA
1914 Fillmore St. at Bush / 931-9455
Dinner Tues-Sun

$$

An updated version of a sushi house, Toraya boasts a granite bar and a variety of menus, from cold seafood and sushi to robata grill and traditional Japanese.
Specialties: *Fresh Salmon Sushi; Spider Rolls with Soft Shell Crabs; Toraya Rolls; Shiitake Robata-Yaki; Beef Rolls with Green Onion Teriyaki; Rainbow Rolls*

YAMATO RESTAURANT & SUSHI BAR
717 California St. at Grant / 397-3456
Lunch Tues-Fri, dinner Tues-Sun

$$ ☎

Yamato is as popular today as it was in 1946. Kimono-clad waitresses serve imaginative dishes and sauces at Western tables and low Japanese tables with leg wells. Yamato is a Travel/Holiday Award winner. There is no extra charge for Japanese tatami rooms. Yamato Restaurant also offers catering and banquets for up to 300 guests.
Specialties: *Shrimp Tempura; Steak Teriyaki; Sukiyaki; Salmon Teriyaki; Yakitori; Kaiseki*

Yoshida-ya

A Different Japanese Restaurant

Upstairs Japanese Style Room

Yakitori Bar (The Only One in Town)

- Over 60 Appetizers (Yakitori, Kushi-Katsu, Sushi, etc.)
- Holiday Award Winner
- Special Vegetarian Dinner (Advance Reservation Required)
- Traditional & Original Creation Dishes (Seafood Fantasia, "Prawn-Lovers" Special, Filet Mignon, "Leave-It-Up-To-The-Chef" Dinner)

**2909 Webster St.
(at Union St.)
346-3431
Open 7 Days for Dinner**

YOSHIDA-YA
2909 Webster St. at Union / 346-3431
Lunch Mon-Fri, dinner daily

Gourmet cuisine is served in a setting of Japanese tranquility a few steps from busy Union Street. A Holiday Award Winner since 1979, Yoshida-Ya has been chosen by many Bay Area restaurateurs as one of their favorites. You'll never get a bad meal here, and you'll want to come back. It's an attractive restaurant, with a sushi bar downstairs and a dining room with low tables and leg wells upstairs. Yoshida-Ya also has the best yakitori bar in town, where little savory meat and vegetable tidbits are grilled, then served with a portable brazier for reheating at your table.
Specialties: *Assorted Sushi; Kushi-Katsu; Teba-Saki; Shabu-Shabu*

KOREAN

BROTHER'S WOODEN CHARCOAL BARBECUE RESTAURANT
4128 Geary Blvd. at 6th Ave. / 387-7991
Lunch & dinner daily

Braziers of glowing hot charcoal are brought to your table. Now you're ready to cook your dinner to order before wrapping it in lettuce leaf and adding rice or any of a dozen condiments.

KOREAN HOUSE
1640 Post St. at Buchanan / 563-1388
Lunch & dinner daily

One of San Francisco's original Korean restaurants, Korea House is well known for hibachi cooking and hearty fish and meat soups served late into the night.

NEW KOREA HOUSE
1620 Post St. at Buchanan / 931-7834
Lunch Mon-Fri, dinner daily

New Korea House, across the street from the Japan Center, offers terrific broiled meats that come wrapped in nori seaweed with rice and chile sauce.

LATIN

ALEJANDRO'S
1840 Clement St. at 20th Ave. / 668-1184
Dinner daily

Some of the best Spanish, Mexican and Peruvian food in the city is served in this friendly, popular restaurant in the Richmond. The tiny bar has the most authentic tapas in town.

EL CUZCATLECO
1500 South Van Ness at 26th / 648-0911
Lunch & dinner daily / No credit cards

This unpretentious restaurant offers good Salvadorean and Mexican standards, and unusual specials unavailable anywhere else in the Bay Area.

EL OSO
1153 Valencia St. at 23rd / 550-0601
Lunch Tues-Sun, dinner daily

Nothing in the decor matches, but it all works together. Colorful paintings, stained glass and live music accompany marvelous Spanish food fragrant with garlic. Try the tapas at the lively bar.

FINA ESTAMPA
2374 Mission St. at 20th / 824-4437
Lunch & dinner Tues-Sun

An unassuming decor belies the excellence of the Peruvian cuisine. The specialties are authentic, with outstanding appetizers and seafood dishes.

LAS PALMERAS
2723 Mission St. at 23rd / 285-7796
Lunch & dinner daily

Salvadorean food is the draw here, a spicy Latin cuisine with excellent shrimp and pork dishes. Start your meal with *pupusas*, savory stuffed pancakes.

NICARAGUA RESTAURANT
3015 Mission St. at 23rd / 826-3672
Lunch & dinner daily

Small and crowded, Nicaragua Restaurant serves abundant, inexpensive food. The tamales are lighter than the Mexican version, and the cooked bananas are delicious.

SOL Y LUNA
475 Sacramento St. at Battery / 296-8191
Lunch Mon-Fri, dinner Mon-Sat

A stark, cubist interior is the stage for provocative interpretations of Iberian and other Latin dishes that shape a new international cuisine. Served to a live flamenco, rhumba and salsa beat, Sol y Luna's food revolves around tapas. Be prepared to mix with a chic crowd at the red neon-lit bar while indulging in them.
Specialties: *Paella Suprema; Housemade Empanadas; Tamales; Grilled Marinated Lamb Chops with Jerez Sherry; Grilled Peppered Steak with Grilled Vegetables & Chimi Churri Sauce*

MEDITERRANEAN

GEORDY'S

One Tillman Place, off Grant Ave. at Sutter / 362-3175
Lunch & dinner Mon-Sat

$$ ☎ 🍸 🍴

One of San Francisco's most acclaimed newcomers, Geordy's deserves its popularity for the inspired cuisine of Chef Charles Solomon and the expert coordination of owner Geordy Murphy, who formerly managed both Kuleto's and Postrio. Solomon is a veteran of New York's number-one restaurant, Bouley, and his Provencal style of cooking is as sophisticated as it is earthy. The reasonable prices are a delightful surprise (especially in contrast to the city's other top spots), making Geordy's more than a special-occasion restaurant. With a convenient downtown location perfect for a business lunch or a leisurely dinner after work, Geordy's is a restaurant you'll always enjoy.
Specialties: Vegetable Pot au Feu; Spinach Risotto with Fresh Maine Sweet Shrimp; Monkfish Tails with Ricotta Gnocchi; Roasted Chicken with Brioche Stuffing & Fricasse of Wild Mushrooms; Roasted Rack of Lamb & Curried Grits

LASCAUX

248 Sutter St. at Kearny / 391-1555
Lunch Mon-Fri, dinner daily

$$ ☎ 🍽 🍸 🎵

Frescoes like those of the prehistoric Lascaux caves adorn the walls of this modern-age cavern. Hearty Mediterranean dishes are served, with delicious appetizers, spit-roasted meats, grilled fish and pasta.

RENDEZVOUS DU MONDE

431 Bush St. at Grant / 392-3332
Breakfast Mon-Fri, dinner Fri, brunch Sat

$ 🎨

This warm, friendly cafe in the heart of the French quarter recalls a rustic bistro. Family run, it features fresh organic produce and seasonal menus, with a special Friday night dinner menu every week. In the kitchen is Sam Mogannam, who trained in one of Switzerland's top-rated two-star Michelin restaurants, with Mom alongside creating the desserts. There are always vegetarian offerings, and the prices are so right that in 1991 *San Francisco Focus* called Rendezvous du Monde the "best deal in little Paris."
Specialties: Warm Goat Cheese Salad with Roasted Tomatoes & Moroccan Olives; Housemade Sausages; Polenta Lasagna with Grilled Eggplant, Spinach, Ricotta & Basil; Grilled Fish Specials; Espresso Pots de Creme

RESTAURANT LULU

816 Folsom St. at Fourth / 495-5775
Lunch Mon-Sat, dinner daily

$$ ☎ 🍸 🎨

South of Market is bustling with new activity this year,

RESTAURANTS

much of it centered on LuLu's. This energetic newcomer is the creation of Chef Reed Hearon and Louise (Lulu) Clement. Their partnership guarantees fantastic food and country wines at great prices, with a fun, casual welcome that's as fitting for a late-night nibble with friends as it is for a family-style feast. The restaurant's wood-burning oven and rotisserie create a warmth and drama new to San Francisco.

Specialties: Rosemary-scented Roast Chicken with Warm Potato & Winter Lettuce Salad; Pork Loin with Fennel, Garlic & Olive Oil Mashed Potatoes; Local Petrale Sole with Salsa Verde

ROSMARINO
3665 Sacramento St. at Spruce / 931-7710
Lunch Mon-Sat, dinner Tues-Sat, brunch Sun

Rosmarino, secluded in a courtyard garden, has offbeat artwork and a chef willing to take culinary chances, inspired by Italian and Country French cuisines.

SPLENDIDO MEDITERRANEAN RESTAURANT
Embarcadero Four, podium level / 986-3222
Lunch Mon-Fri, dinner daily

Owner Bill Kimpton and restaurant designer Pat Kuleto teamed up to create Splendido's classic Mediterranean look. The restaurant's 200-year-old doors, made from olive wood, open onto a sumptuous environment. Hand-hewn beams, stone walls, Italian marble table-tops and a live grape arbor hanging above the 40-foot pewter bar evoke a rustic Mediterranean inn. Chef Chris Majer, formerly at New York's Quilted Giraffe and Gotham Bar and Grill, emphasizes freshness and creativity in his preparations. All of Splendido's breads, pastas and desserts are made fresh daily in the restaurant's display bakery.

Specialties: Ravioli with Prosciutto & Mascarpone; Pizza with Smoked Chicken, Feta Cheese & Roasted Tomatoes; Seared Peppered Tuna with Chive Potatoes

SQUARE ONE RESTAURANT
190 Pacific Ave. at Front / 788-1110
Lunch Mon-Fri, dinner daily

The name implies fresh beginnings every day using seasonal, locally procured foods. Breads, pastries, pastas, chutney, preserves, ice cream — even ketchup — are freshly made. Chef Joyce Goldstein's varied international menu, primarily Mediterranean, changes daily. Square One is informal yet elegant, with a friendly atmosphere and a great bar.

Specialties: Paella; Moroccan Mixed Grill; Bouillabaisse; Provencal Duck with Lavender Honey & Thyme

ZUNI CAFE
1658 Market St. at Franklin / 552-2522
Lunch & dinner Tues-Sun

Zuni offers fresh oysters, a late-night bar menu, outdoor seating, and sensational food, influenced by Italian and Southern French cooking.

MEXICAN

BAJA CANTINA
3154 Fillmore St. at Greenwich / 885-2252
Lunch & dinner daily

The best dishes come from the menu of daily specials. The Mexican dishes are perfectly complemented by the restaurant's margaritas.

BORDER CAFE & CANTINA
1192 Folsom St. at 8th / 626-6043
Lunch Mon-Fri, dinner Mon-Sat

A bright Tex-Mex decor gives a South-of-the-border flavor to this South of Market restaurant. The portions are generous and reasonably priced.

CADILLAC BAR & RESTAURANT
325 Minna St., near Mission btwn. 4th & 5th
543-8226 / Lunch & dinner daily

Seek out the Cadillac when you're looking for a good time along with tasty Mexican food and margaritas.

CASA AGUILA
1240 Noriega St. at 19th Ave. / 661-5593
Lunch & dinner daily

Everything in this colorful, happy restaurant is cooked to order. The chicken mole is outstanding, the fish is fresh and the variety of dishes is amazing for such a small place.

CHEVYS
150 4th St. at Howard / 543-8060
Embarcadero Two, podium level / 391-2323
Lunch & dinner daily

Chevys makes its own tortillas and uses only the freshest ingredients to create light, authentic Mexican dishes.

CORONA BAR & GRILL
88 Cyril Magnin St. at Ellis / 392-5500
Lunch Mon-Sat, dinner daily

In a warm, rosy setting reminiscent of a South-of-the-border sunset, the Corona Bar & Grill redefines Mexican cuisine with its fresh approach to traditional favorites. The menu consists of quesadillas, burritos and entrees with California twists; imaginative fillings include duck, shiitake mushrooms and crab.

Specialties: Dungeness Crab Fritters; Paella Valenciana; Petaluma Duck Burrito; Crab & Shrimp Enchilada; Wood-grilled Seafood

LA CUMBRE
515 Valencia St. near 17th / 863-8205
Lunch & dinner daily

It's not much more than a cheerful taqueria, but people drive for miles for La Cumbre's steak burritos. They're state of the art.

LA RONDALLA
901 Valencia St. at 20th / 647-7474
Lunch & dinner Tues-Sun / No credit cards

La Rondalla is a visual fiesta of Christmas tinsel lights. Hearty meals are served into the wee hours, and mariachi singers perform Wednesday through Sunday.

LOS JARRITOS
901 South Van Ness at 20th / 648-8383
Lunch & dinner daily / No credit cards

Jarritos are tiny, earthenware cups used in Mexico. You'll see hundreds of them hanging everywhere in this restaurant where the food is rich in flavor and character.

MUCHACHA'S
4238 18th St. off Collingwood / 861-8234
Dinner Tues-Sun, brunch Sun

The amusing, colorful Aztec decor complements an intriguing menu at this restaurant in the Castro.

TORTOLA
3640 Sacramento St. at Locust / 929-8181
Lunch Tues-Sat, dinner Tues-Sun

Tortola's unique menu offers Southwestern and updated Mexican cuisine made with fresh produce.

MIDDLE EASTERN

YAYA CUISINE
1220 Ninth Ave. at Lincoln / 566-6966
Dinner Tues-Sun

This lovely space of arches and soft lights is a fitting showcase for savory stuffed chickens, stews and kabobs.

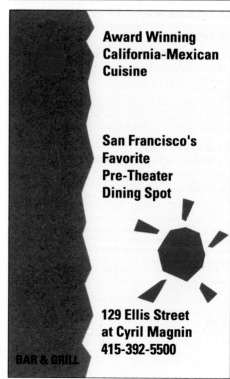

MOROCCAN

CITRUS CAFE & GRILL
2373 Chestnut St. at Divisadero / 563-7720
Lunch & dinner Tues-Sat, brunch Sun

Citrus Cafe serves aromatic North African dishes. The bright yellow lemons and orange kumquats in the Moroccan cooking palette inspired the name Citrus and its lively interior.

MARRAKESH
419 O'Farrell St. at Taylor / 776-6717
Dinner daily

Marrakesh is a treat, with plush pillow seating, authentic Morrocan dishes you eat with your fingers and nightly belly dancing.

PASHA
1516 Broadway at Polk / 885-4477
Dinner Tues-Sun

A sumptuous supper club with belly dancers, Pasha is decorated like an ornate desert tent — Persian rugs, hand-worked brass, huge pillows and ceilings draped with colorful fabric.

PERSIAN

KASRA
349 Clement St. at 5th Ave. / 752-1101
Lunch Fri-Sun, dinner daily

Iranian cuisine, preferably called Persian by natives, is the focus. Kasra offers wonderful lamb, stews and kabobs.

MAYKADEH
470 Green St. at Grant / 362-8286
Lunch Mon-Fri, dinner daily

A sophisticated restaurant, Maykadeh is worthy of any occasion. The kabobs, marinated in yogurt, lime and mysterious spices then grilled over hot coals, are of the highest quality.

RUSSIAN

LITTLE RUSSIA
5217 Geary Blvd. at 16th Ave. / 751-9661
Lunch & dinner daily

Intimate and friendly, Little Russia on Geary Boulevard is a great introduction to Russian cuisine. Insiders know it as a source of authentic Russian food — borscht, thick rye bread and delicious piroshki — where the Richmond's many Soviet emigres converge. At night, there's live Russian music.

SEAFOOD

A. SABELLA'S RESTAURANT
2766 Taylor St. at Jefferson / 771-4416
Lunch & dinner daily

A. Sabella's has been a landmark on Fisherman's Wharf since the early 1920s. Enjoy fresh seafood, pasta or veal with a panoramic view of the surrounding wharf while relaxing to the sounds of a quiet piano. Service in the attractive, elegant dining room is excellent, and servers answer truthfully to the question, "Is it fresh?" A. Sabella's earned the 1992 Wine List Award from *The Wine Spectator* and *Hospitality Magazine*.
Specialties: *Fresh Monterey Abalone; Fresh Maine Lobster; Cioppino; Sand Dabs; Linguine with Crab Alfredo*

ALIOTO'S
#8 Taylor St. at Jefferson / 673-0183
Lunch & dinner daily

Since the roaring '20s, the Alioto family has been preparing delicious Italian-style seafood in their comfortable, traditional-style restaurant at Fisherman's Wharf. A lovely view of the bay and free two-hour validated parking add to Alioto's allure.
Specialties: *Rex Sole; Sand Dabs; Calamari Saute; Abalone; Fresh Housemade Pasta; Fresh Seafood; Sicilian Regional Specialties*

AQUA
252 California St. at Front / 956-9662
Lunch Mon-Fri, dinner Mon-Sat

San Francisco Focus gave Aqua the Best Newcomer and the Best Seafood awards for 1991-1992. Spectacular mirrors, banquettes covered with a deep, rich fabric, commissioned artworks and enormous floral bouquets set off the elegant menu. Young chef/owner George Morrone worked at the Bel Air Hotel in Los Angeles before opening Aqua. Voted among the rising star chefs in 1992, he combines traditional French technique with contemporary American tastes. The result is daring but never frivolous. He pairs tuna with foie gras, swordfish with duck and pike with morels — and all of it works. The dishes are prepared with fresh, seasonal ingredients, and finished off with show-stopping desserts.

Specialties: Foie Gras Sauteed with Apples, Calvados & Sauternes Jelly; Dungeness Crab Cakes with Saffron Vinaigrette; Abalone with Black-Olive Fettuccine, Pine Nuts & Sweet Peppers; Alaskan Halibut in a Potato Crust with a Salad of Bacon & Morels; Sea Scallops with Couscous & Dried Fruit

BENTLEY'S SEAFOOD GRILL
185 Sutter St. at Kearny / 989-6895
Lunch Mon-Sat, dinner daily

🍴 🍷 ☕ 🎵

The best oyster bar in San Francisco keeps getting better. Bentley's Seafood Grill also features the freshest fish and the finest quality lamb and steaks. The restaurant's pastas are delicious and imaginative. Bentley's serves a great Bloody Mary, which you can enjoy at the airy, spacious bar while listening to live jazz.
Specialties: Broiled Salmon with Citrus Glaze; Stuffed Roasted Swordfish with Tequila-Lime Sauce; Seared Ahi Tuna with Deep-fried Ginger

THE CLIFF HOUSE
1090 Point Lobos / 386-3330
Breakfast, lunch & dinner daily, brunch Sun

🍴 🚗 📷 🍷 🍽

The original Cliff House was built in 1850 and has since experienced four reincarnations on its present site. Directly adjacent are the ruins of Sutro Baths, built in 1894 and consumed by fire in 1966. All rooms offer a view of famed Seal Rock amid the Pacific's crashing waves. The main dining area specializes in fresh seafood. California-style fare is featured in the dining room above, known as Upstairs at the Cliff House.
Specialties: Stuffed Filet of Sole with Crab & Shrimp; Seafood Platter: Oysters, Shrimp, Sole, Clams & Prawns

ELKA
1611 Post St., Miyako Hotel / 922-7788
Breakfast, lunch & dinner daily

🍴 🍷 🍽

Since opening her restaurant in 1992, Elka Gilmore has been winning over both critics and gourmets with fresh, Japanese-inspired California cuisine. Named one of the top 28 new restaurants in the country by *Esquire* magazine, Elka has been lauded by *Gourmet* as well as myriad local publications. Seafood is king here, but every ingredient, from meat to asparagus, is treated with equal respect, and every plate shines with simple beauty. The two-story dining room is colorful and airy, cheerful by day, gently lit by night through paper-shaded lamps.
Specialties: Coriander-crusted Tuna with Lemongrass in a Galingale Consomme; Roasted Sea Scallops with Whipped Potatoes & Black Truffles; Crispy Whole Catfish

RESTAURANTS

HAYES STREET GRILL
320 Hayes St. at Franklin / 863-5545
Lunch Mon-Fri, dinner daily

Located a block from the Symphony Hall and Opera House, the grill is extremely popular with local residents and pre-theatre diners. Hayes Street Grill serves only the freshest seafood, prepared to perfection on a wood-fired grill. The menu also includes interesting appetizers, which change daily, as well as salads with fresh and unusual ingredients. The housemade desserts are irresistible. Reservations are advised, and may be made seven days in advance.
Specialties: Grilled Fresh Fish & Meats; Shellfish Salads & Appetizers Change Daily

LA ROCA
4288 24th St. at Douglass / 821-7652
Dinner Tues-Sun

Bill Mandel, noted *San Francisco Examiner* columnist, calls it "the best seafood restaurant in the Bay Area." Spanish-style seafood, including an outstanding paella, is the house specialty. Rich and deeply flavored, the paella comes in large portions, and everything is as fresh as can be.

MCCORMICK & KULETO'S SEAFOOD RESTAURANT
900 North Point, Ghirardelli Square / 929-1730
Lunch & dinner daily

Dream of renowned restaurant designer Pat Kuleto and partners Bill McCormick and Doug Schmick, this new restaurant was created to please locals in a tourist location that doesn't always. Really two restaurants in one — a fun food and take-out area called The Crab Cake Lounge, and classic maritime dining room reminiscent of an East Coast fish house — McCormick & Kuleto's offers 35 fresh catches daily. Designer Kuleto's talent for lighting is articulated with a variety of romantic table lamps and impressive chandeliers. And every diner is guaranteed a fantastic view.
Specialties: Crabcakes; Seafood Pizzas; Seafood Chowder; Pacific Seafood Stew; Dungeness Crab; Oyster Bar

NICK'S LIGHTHOUSE
#5 Fisherman's Wharf / 929-1300
Lunch & dinner daily

Overlooking Fisherman's Wharf, Nick's Lighthouse specializes in fresh seafood. Daily specials feature several kinds of fish, and you can also choose from a wide selection of dishes prepared with prawn, shrimp, shellfish,

crab or lobster. For pasta lovers, there are many seafood and pasta combination plates.
Specialties: Boston Clam Chowder; Prawns Julius Sauteed with Garlic, Wine & Herbs; Shrimp Napoletana Sauteed in Tomatoes, White Wine, Capers & Olives; Fettuccine with Shrimp, Scallops & Seafood Broth; Cannelloni with Cheese, Crab & Shrimp

PJ'S OYSTER BED
737 Irving St. near 9th Ave. / 566-7775
Lunch Mon-Fri, dinner daily, brunch Sat & Sun

This modest little storefront has excellent chowder, fresh oysters, live Maine lobsters and skillfully grilled fish. PJ's serves Cajun seafood three nights a week from March to June.

SAM'S GRILL & SEAFOOD RESTAURANT
374 Bush St. at Kearny / 421-0594
Lunch & dinner Mon-Fri

A simple decor accented by tuxedoed waiters is similar to its food — straightforward, yet first-class. If you want a taste of old San Francisco, Sam's is the place to go.

SCOTT'S SEAFOOD GRILL & BAR
2400 Lombard St. at Scott / 563-8988
Lunch & dinner daily, brunch Sun

Scott's was a success the moment it opened in 1976. Well known for fresh seafood, it has maintained its popularity to this day. Traditional seafood dishes are prepared with light, modern sauces. Owner Lloyd Wiborg and his partner, Chef Uffe Gustafsson, oversee the bustling restaurant, served by a bright and a cheerful staff. There's often a wait for tables, but only if you don't have a reservation.
Specialties: Seafood Saute; Scallops with Wine, Garlic & Lemon Butter; Pacific Salmon; Petrale Sole; Fried Calamari

TADICH GRILL
240 California St. at Battery / 391-2373
Lunch & dinner Mon-Sat

San Franciscans have loved this classic restaurant for its innovative skill with seafood since 1849. Dining at Tadich is a real San Francisco experience.

THE WATERFRONT
Pier 7, The Embarcadero / 391-2696
Lunch Mon-Fri, dinner daily, brunch Sun

The Waterfront has huge windows on San Francisco Bay

and an extensive menu of fish, shellfish and oysters. Eighteen varieties of seafood are available in season, as entrees or in pastas, soups or salads. The decor is understated, with tables set on several levels so you can have views from every seat. The Sunday brunch is considered one of the best in town.

Specialties: Waterfront Cocktail (Marinated Calamari, Shrimp & Bay Scallops); Scampi; Abalone Grenobloise (Abalone with Capers); Grilled Fish; Seafood Salads; Whole Dungeness Cracked Crab

SOUTH PACIFIC

TONGA ROOM
Fairmont Hotel
950 Mason St. at California / 772-5278
Dinner daily

A landmark San Francisco restaurant known for its Polynesian atmosphere including indoor rainstorms and a live band performing on a floating platform. The Tonga Room offers Pacific Rim cuisine, exotic drinks and dancing to a live band. A happy hour buffet and drink specials are served Monday through Friday 5PM to 7PM. Prix-fixe menus are available.

TRADER VIC'S
20 Cosmo Place at Jones / 776-2232
Dinner daily

Trader Vic Bergeron turns out trademark Chinese, American, Indian and Polynesian dishes. Trader Vic's is a San Francisco institution where local luminaries flock to see and be seen.

STEAK HOUSE

ALFRED'S
886 Broadway at Mason / 781-7058
Lunch Thurs, dinner daily

Mesquite charcoal from Mexico burns clean and hot under the restaurant's grills to seal in the juices and flavors of the restaurant's Midwestern corn-fed beef.

HARRIS' RESTAURANT
2100 Van Ness Ave. at Pacific / 673-1888
Lunch & dinner daily

Voted eight years in a row as having the best steaks in San Francisco, Harris' also offers fresh seafood, chicken and lamb. Elegant "Old San Francisco" decor, high ceilings, tall palms, and spacious booth seating make this one of the city's most handsome restaurants. Don't

RESTAURANTS

miss Chef Goetz Boje's delicious pate, which, like the dry-aged beef, is available to go from Harris's retail meat counter.

Specialties: Mesquite-grilled Steaks; Prime Rib; Fresh Maine Lobster; Fresh Catch of the Day

HOUSE OF PRIME RIB
1906 Van Ness Ave. at Washington / 885-4605
Dinner daily

For more than 40 years, this establishment has concentrated on preparing and serving one dish to perfection, and it has succeeded. Loyal patrons return again and again to savor the prime rib, carved to order at tableside. If you still have room, second helpings are complimentary.

Specialties: Prime Rib; Yorkshire Pudding & Vegetables; Fresh Fish of the Day

IZZY'S STEAK & CHOP HOUSE
3345 Steiner St. at Lombard / 563-0487
Dinner daily

Izzy's memorializes Izzy Gomez, San Francisco's legendary Barbary Coast saloonkeeper.

RUTH'S CHRIS STEAK HOUSE
1700 California St. at Van Ness / 673-0557
Dinner daily

This is the San Francisco franchise of the successful chain of top-notch steakhouses.

SWISS

THE MATTERHORN SWISS RESTAURANT
2323 Van Ness Ave. at Vallejo / 885-6116
Dinner Wed-Sun

Rich, old-fashioned food celebrates Swiss cuisine, including dishes from Valais, the owner's native canton.

OLD SWISS HOUSE
Pier 39, 2nd level / 434-0432
Lunch & dinner daily

The menu offers authentic Swiss entrees and elaborate desserts. The bay view is dramatic.

THAI

KHAN TOKE THAI HOUSE
5937 Geary Blvd. at 24th Ave. / 668-6654
Dinner daily

Some of the best Thai cuisine in town is served at Khan Toke. Waitresses dress in traditional costume, and there is Thai dancing Sunday nights.

MANORA'S THAI CUISINE
1600 Folsom St. at 12th / 861-6224
Lunch Mon-Fri, dinner daily

Thai paintings and scrollwork adorn Manora's, a restaurant well worth seeking out for its flavorful, beautifully presented food and prompt, attentive service. The menu features an abundance of appetizers and seafood dishes, all seasoned thoroughly yet delicately with exotic herbs, spices and chiles.

MARNEE THAI
2225 Irving St. at 24th Ave. / 665-9500
Lunch & dinner Wed-Mon

The decor here is simple; the food complex. Marnee offers some of the best Thai barbecue in town. Unlike western-style barbecue, the delicious, crisp-grilled meats are marinated in herbs and spices rather than sauced.

NARAI RESTAURANT
2229 Clement St. at 23rd Ave. / 751-6363
Lunch & dinner Tues-Sun

One of the most popular restaurants in the Richmond District, Narai increasingly attracts patrons from all over the Bay Area.

PLOY THAI
1770 Haight St. at Cole / 387-9224
Dinner daily

This sparkling family restaurant features outstanding curries made from scratch, as well as excellent dishes you won't find on a typical Thai menu.

SAMUI
2414 Lombard St. at Scott / 563-4405
Lunch Mon-Sat, dinner daily

Samui serves southern Thai dishes influenced by Malaysian cooking. The specialties, including great appetizers and curries, are spectacular.

SWATDEE THAI CUISINE
4166 24th St. at Castro / 824-8070
Lunch Mon-Sat, dinner daily

All the comforts of a family-operated restaurant make Swatdee a genuine treat. Complex sauces enrich a wide variety of Thai standards.

THEP PHANOM
400 Waller St. at Fillmore / 431-2526
Dinner daily

How a restaurant in this offbeat spot (more middle Haight than upper) could attract such a large following can have only one answer: the food is fabulous.

THEPIN THAI
298 Gough St. at Fell / 863-9335
Lunch Mon-Fri, dinner daily

Thep Phanom's elegant offspring brings the same great food to the Civic Center.

VEGETARIAN

GREENS
Building A, Fort Mason, Marina & Buchanan
771-6222 / Lunch & dinner Tues-Sat, brunch Sun

Greens is highly praised by vegetarians and meat eaters alike, and its Tassajara bakery is famous for breads. For dinner, be sure to reserve ahead as Greens is packed almost every night.

VIETNAMESE

GOLDEN TURTLE
2211 Van Ness Ave. at Broadway / 441-4419
Lunch & dinner Tues-Sun

Family-owned, the restaurant has soft lighting and friendly service, with some of the best Vietnamese food in the Bay Area — light, fresh, and exotically spiced.

KIM'S
508 Presidio Ave. at California / 923-1500
Lunch & dinner Mon-Sat

A friendly, cozy cafe, Kim's has excellent, homey food, including a wonderful filet mignon salad. Customers tend to become regulars in no time.

MAI'S
316 Clement St. btwn. 4th & 5th / 221-3046
Lunch & dinner daily

This celebrated restaurant is a little out of the way but worth the visit. The imperial rolls, la-lot beef and other Vietnamese standards are that much more appreciated when you get them.

RESTAURANTS

QUICK PICKS

*W*hether you're planning a Sunday brunch, looking for the best pizza in town or trying to find food at midnight, our quick picks will come in handy.

BREAKFAST

CAMPTON PLACE RESTAURANT
Campton Place Hotel Kempinski
340 Stockton St. at Sutter / 955-5555

Start a day on the town with lemon-poppyseed French toast, corned beef hash with poached eggs, and rich hot chocolate with bitter chocolate cream.

DOIDGE'S
2217 Union St. at Fillmore / 921-2149

One of the most popular breakfasts in town: eggs Benedict, French toast with fresh berries, eggs Florentine and a breakfast casserole are favorites.

ELLA'S
500 Presidio Ave. at California / 441-5669

Breakfasts and brunches here are old-fashioned good, with mouth-watering baked breads and muffins, superb pancakes and thick home fries.

IL FORNAIO
1265 Battery St., Levi Plaza / 986-0100

A San Francisco favorite for Italian baked goods, Il Fornaio offers weekend brunches and full breakfasts during the week. Try their pancakes, vegetable omelettes and French toast.

LOUIS' RESTAURANT
902 Point Lobos / 387-6330

A real American diner with a glorious view of the Pacific. The eggs come any way you want, the bacon is crisp, and the pancakes are stacked high.

POSTRIO
545 Post St. at Mason / 776-7825

Wolfgang Puck's restaurant serves breakfast from simple to sumptuous.

SEARS FINE FOODS
439 Powell St. at Post / 986-1160

Sears has been serving its popular breakfast for longer than most of us can remember. The egg dishes and Swedish pancakes are specialties.

BRUNCH

CARNELIAN ROOM
Bank of America Bldg., 555 California St. at Kearny
52nd floor / 433-7500

The Carnelian Room commands one of the best views in town. The Sunday brunch is just as spectacular: soup, omelettes, eggs Benedict, roasted meat, fish and dessert courses accompanied by Champagne and coffee.

CITYSCAPE
San Francisco Hilton & Tower, 333 O'Farrell St.
46th floor / 771-1400

Boasting a huge buffet table serving fresh, seasonal cuisine, Cityscape's Sunday brunch — with sensational views 46 stories above downtown — is unforgettable.

THE CLIFF HOUSE
1090 Point Lobos / 386-3330

Everyone loves the view of the Pacific and Seal Rock and the two weekend brunch menus here: hearty American favorites downstairs; a choice of 30 omelettes upstairs.

THE FRENCH ROOM
Four Seasons Clift Hotel, 495 Geary St. / 775-4700

Muraled walls, rich draperies, needlepoint chairs, 17th century Austrian crystal chandeliers and large potted palms set the scene for an elegant Sunday brunch buffet.

THE GARDEN COURT
Sheraton Palace Hotel
2 New Montgomery St. / 392-8600

The Garden Court presents a Champagne brunch buffet on Sundays in a dazzling room, with beautiful chandeliers suspended under a soaring stained-glass dome.

RESTAURANTS

GOLDEN GATE GRILL
3200 Fillmore St. at Greenwich / 931-4600

Weekend brunch in the Marina is a tradition and a treat at this lively restaurant.

GREENS
Fort Mason, Building A / 771-6222

Great bay views compete with vegetarian specialties at Sunday brunch: omelettes, pancakes, open-face sandwiches, salads and breads from the Tassajara Bakery.

DIM SUM

CANTON TEA HOUSE
1108 Stockton St. at Jackson / 982-1030

Dim sum can be pastries filled with meat, shrimp and other delicacies, or can be any savory tidbit such as tiny pork spareribs or chicken "lollipops." You can try dim sum at the Canton Tea House, a large tea house in the heart of Chinatown.

CELADON
881 Clay St. at Stockton / 982-1168

An elegant Cantonese restaurant at night, Celadon also serves many varieties of dim sum for lunch.

HANG AH TEA ROOM
One Pagoda St. off Sacramento / 982-5686

The first tea house in San Francisco, Hang Ah has an authentic old-time atmosphere. Bay Area writer Amy Tan features the restaurant in *The Joy Luck Club*.

HARBOR VILLAGE RESTAURANT
Embarcadero Four, lobby level / 781-8833

A dim sum lunch spot favored by Financial District executives.

THE NEW ASIA
772 Pacific Ave. btwn. Grant & Stockton / 391-6666

More than 60 varieties of dim sum attract a loyal following.

ROYAL HAWAII CHINESE RESTAURANT
835 Pacific Ave. at Stockton / 391-6365

A Chinatown favorite serving dozens of dim sum varieties.

WU KONG
101 Spear St. at Mission / 957-9300

Modern and attractive, Wu Kong has a huge dim sum selection in addition to its regular menu.

YANK SING
427 Battery St. at Clay / 362-1640

An elegant setting and gracious service as well as the best dim sum make Yank Sing very popular.

AFTERNOON TEA

THE BREAD & HONEY TEA ROOM
King George Hotel, 334 Mason St. / 781-5050

The homey Bread & Honey offers a full range of tea service, from a single scone to the King George High Tea of finger sandwiches, crumpets and trifle.

COMPASS ROSE
Westin St. Francis Hotel, 335 Powell St. / 774-0167

A stately meeting place for the city's elite since the turn of the century. Enjoy crumpets, scones, tea sandwiches, berries with Grand Marnier cream, dessert and your choice of teas.

FOUR SEASONS CLIFT HOTEL
495 Geary St. at Taylor / 775-4700

High tea service in the lobby bar includes tea sandwiches, toasted scone, fresh berries or pastry and a selection of teas.

THE GARDEN COURT
Sheraton Palace Hotel
2 New Montgomery St. / 392-8600

A dazzling room, with beautiful chandeliers suspended under a soaring stained-glass dome, sets the scene for elegant teas. The Garden Court serves tea sandwiches, pastries, scones and a selection of teas daily from 2:30PM to 5PM.

MANDARIN LOUNGE
Mandarin Oriental Hotel
222 Sansome St. at Pine / 885-0999

Piano music sets a luxurious tone, with an extensive selection of tea sandwiches, brown sugar scones, tea pastries and fresh fruit tarts. Tea is served Monday through Friday from 3PM to 5PM.

THE RITZ-CARLTON
600 Stockton St. at California / 296-7465

Sink into a comfortable chair in the Lobby Lounge any day between 2:30PM and 5PM and listen to a soothing classical trio as you enjoy scones, muffins, finger sandwiches and pastries with your tea.

THE ROTUNDA
Neiman-Marcus
150 Stockton St. at Geary / 362-4777

Sit below a shining stained-glass dome as you sip freshly brewed tea and sample petite sandwiches, delicious scones and ginger muffins.

THE STOUFFER STANFORD COURT
905 California St. at Powell / 989-3500

Teas from John Harney & Sons, ports, sherries and sparkling wines accompany tea sandwiches, scones and a variety of pastries. The Stouffer Stanford Court's tea service is available every day from 2:30PM to 5PM.

SWEET SHOPS

THE CANDY JAR
210 Grant Ave. near Post / 391-5508

Owner Maria Stacho makes wonderful truffles and chocolates, based on recipes from her native Hungary.

CONFETTI LE CHOCOLATIER
Four Embarcadero Center, lobby level / 362-1706

Confetti imports Gartner and Manon chocolates from Belgium.

ETHEL M. CHOCOLATES
San Francisco Shopping Centre / 227-0875

Ethel M. has two other outlets in San Francisco: at One Embarcadero Center and at the Stonestown Galleria.

GHIRARDELLI CHOCOLATE
900 North Point, Ghirardelli Square / 771-4903

Ghirardelli's brick building, where the chocolates used to be made, now houses a shop and a soda fountain where you can sample their delicious chocolates.

GODIVA CHOCOLATIER
Crocker Galleria, 50 Post St. / 982-6798

Godiva Chocolates, hand-dipped in Belgium, has another location at the Stonestown Galleria.

JOSEPH SCHMIDT CONFECTIONS
3489 16th St. at Sanchez / 861-8682

Known nationwide for its innovative chocolate bowls and its 26 flavors of egg-shaped truffles, Joseph Schmidt Confections produces delicious works of art.

LA NOUVELLE PATISSERIE
2184 Union St. at Fillmore / 931-7655

While you are staring at the incredible edibles in the windows of La Nouvelle Patisserie, the creator, Jean-Yves Duperret, is in the back kitchen blending the finest ingredients from recipes that have been in his family for three generations. Other locations: Ghirardelli Square and San Francisco Shopping Centre.

SEE'S CANDIES
Three Embarcadero Center, street level / 391-1622

The California confectioners have been making outstanding chocolates and candies since 1921, available at numerous outlets around town.

TEUSCHER CHOCOLATES OF SWITZERLAND
255 Grant Ave. at Sutter / 398-2700

Teuscher's incomparable chocolates — rated the best in the world — are flown in from Zurich every week.

ICE CREAM SHOPS

BEN & JERRY'S
1480 Haight St. at Ashbury / 249-4685

The Vermont company's only San Francisco outlet is a favorite on Haight Street.

DOUBLE RAINBOW
519 Powell St. at Sutter / 982-3097

The award-winning San Francisco ice cream company now has franchises throughout the state. For other locations, call 861-5858.

GELATO CLASSICO
448 Post St. at Powell / 989-5884

Now famous all over the country, Gelato Classico started in San Francisco in 1976, introducing dense, all-natural Italian-style ice cream to the Bay Area. The company has more than a dozen local franchises.

LATIN FREEZE
3338 24th St. near Mission / 282-5033

Delicious frozen fruit bars, made from such exotic fruit as mango and tamarind. You can also get strawberry, pineapple, coconut and many other flavors.

SWENSEN'S ICE CREAM
1999 Hyde St. at Union / 775-6818

Swensen's serves excellent ice cream and soda fountain items. There is another Swensen's at 350 Bay Street, near Fisherman's Wharf.

BAKERIES

BOUDIN SOURDOUGH BAKERY
156 Jefferson St. at Fisherman's Wharf / 928-1849

Through large picture windows you can view how Boudin bakes its famous sourdough bread, judged the best in San Francisco.

COCORICO
1 Market Plaza, Plaza level / 541-4948

Cocorico is a French patisserie specializing in good-looking sweets that taste even better — triple chocolate layer cake goes from dark to white chocolate in one delicious mouthful.

IL FORNAIO
2298 Union St. at Steiner / 563-3400

Il Fornaio's Italian breads and pastries are a city favorite. Other locations include 1265 Battery St. at Levi Plaza.

JUST DESSERTS
3735 Buchanan St. at Marina / 922-8675

In a cozy cafe atmosphere, savor a cappuccino with a

rich dessert — everything from a morning Danish to the thickest chocolate cake around. Other locations: Embarcadero Three, 248 Church Street and 836 Irving Street.

LA NOUVELLE PATISSERIE
2184 Union St. at Fillmore / 931-7655

Jean-Yves Duperret's elegant fresh fruit tarts, light mousse cakes, croissants, small pastries, truffles and chocolates beckon. Other locations: Ghirardelli Square and San Francisco Shopping Centre.

TASSAJARA BAKERY
1000 Cole St. at Parnassus / 664-8947

Tassajara is a Cole Valley fixture. On weekend mornings the line spills onto the street as people from all over town come to buy their famous bread and pastries.

VICTORIA PASTRY COMPANY
1362 Stockton St. at Vallejo / 781-2015

Rum custard cakes, chocolate rum cakes, cookies and the pastry shop's luscious St. Honore (a napoleon layered with three kinds of cream) draw a crowd.

OYSTER BARS

BENTLEY'S SEAFOOD GRILL & OYSTER BAR
Galleria Park Hotel, Sutter & Kearny / 989-6895

Order oysters singly from a choice of at least 12 varieties to create a personal oyster tasting.

ELITE CAFE
2049 Fillmore St. at California / 346-8668

Only two varieties of oysters are served each night, sometimes three or four, but unless you're a purist, you won't mind adding the cafe's spiced shrimp or mussels to your tasting menu.

PACIFIC HEIGHTS BAR & GRILL
2001 Fillmore St. at Pine / 567-3337

With so many oyster choices — 12 or more a night — you'll never be disappointed.

STARS
150 Redwood Alley off Van Ness / 861-7827

The choice on their menu is small — only one variety — but the oysters are always perfect.

SWAN OYSTER DEPOT
1517 Polk St. at California / 673-1101

San Franciscans have been enjoying oysters at the long marble counter here since 1912.

ZUNI CAFE
1658 Market St. at Gough / 552-2522

Fresh oysters, sometimes as many as 14 varieties, are kept cool in ice-filled vats, Parisian-style.

PIZZERIAS

CALZONE'S
430 Columbus Ave. at Vallejo / 397-3600

A lively North Beach spot serving a variety of pizzas from a wood-burning oven.

GOAT HILL
300 Connecticut St. at 18th / 641-1440

A Potrero Hill favorite — crispy crust, abundant toppings and super salads on the side.

NORTH BEACH PIZZA
1499 Grant Ave. at Union / 433-2444

Voted the best pizza in San Francisco at the SF County Fair, North Beach's version is a consistent winner.

OLIVE'S GOURMET PIZZA
3249 Scott St. near Chestnut / 567-4488

Olive's gourmet pizzas are among the best in town. Its most famous has a crunchy cornmeal and imported olive oil crust. Premium toppings, such as eggplant, roasted garlic and fennel sausage, are selected daily.

PAULINE'S
260 Valencia St. at 14th / 552-2050

Always packed, Pauline's is famous for its thin-crusted pesto pizza.

PAZZIA CAFFE & PIZZERIA
337 3rd St. at Folsom / 512-1693

Thin crust, a great tomato sauce and traditional toppings spell super pizza in a very friendly restaurant.

PIZZERIA UNO
2200 Lombard St. at Steiner / 563-3144
2323 Powell St. at Bay / 788-4055
Two Embarcadero Center, podium level / 397-8667

The pizzas are cooked and served in the pan. Chronicle Books voted Pizzeria Uno's Chicago deep-dish pizza the best pizza in San Francisco. The restaurant also serves thin-crust gourmet pizzas.

POSTRIO
545 Post St. at Mason / 776-7825

Postrio serves the pizza creations of Wolfgang Puck, the man who put the "gourmet" in gourmet pizza.

PREGO
2000 Union St. at Buchanan / 563-3305

Popular and stylish, Prego bakes authentic Italian pizzas in an oak-burning oven.

RUBY'S
489 Third St. at Bryant / 541-0795

When South of Market, don't miss Ruby's famous pizzas made with cornmeal and olive oil.

RESTAURANTS

SPUNTINO ITALIAN EXPRESS
524 Van Ness Ave. at McAllister / 861-7772

Before the opera, or after a long morning at the library, a pizza at Spuntino is just right.

TOMMASO'S FAMOUS PIZZERIA
1042 Kearny St. at Broadway / 398-9696

Years of pizza-making means people-pleasing pies, with lots of thin, crisp crust. Tommaso's is open only for dinner, Tuesday through Sunday.

VENTICELLO
1257 Taylor St. at Washington / 922-2545

A wood-burning oven, thin light crusts and fresh toppings add up to delectable pizzas.

VICOLO
201 Ivy St. at Franklin / 863-2382

Trendy Vicolo's offers deep-dish gourmet pizzas with cornmeal crusts and fresh seasonal toppings.

BARBECUE JOINTS

BIG NATE'S BARBECUE
1665 Folsom St. at 13th / 861-4242

Owned by ex-basketball star Nate Thurmond, Big Nate's has great ribs, cooked over wood and fragrant with barbecue sauce — hot, hotter and hottest.

BLACKBURN'S
1338 Ocean Ave. at Plymouth / 239-7115

A funky, tiny place with excellent barbecued meats served up in huge portions with coleslaw, potato salad, baked beans and corn muffins.

SAN FRANCISCO BARBECUE
1328 18th St. at Texas / 431-8956

For a change of pace, try Thai-style barbecue. The chicken here is especially good. Take out some spicy noodles while you're at it.

MIDNIGHT BITE

OPEN 'TIL MIDNIGHT

ACT IV
333 Fulton St. at Franklin / 553-8100
Performance nights only

After the kitchen closes, Inn at the Opera's romantic restaurant serves a light cafe menu and cocktails to cap an evening at the theatre.

BIX
56 Gold St. at Montgomery / 433-6300
Friday & Saturday only

The Jazz Age supper club serves reinterpreted American favorites and deftly prepared cocktails.

CADILLAC BAR
325 Minna St. near Mission / 543-8226
Friday & Saturday only

The decibel level at the Cadillac is probably the highest in town, but you'll love the fantastic Mexican food here.

CIAO
230 Jackson St. at Battery / 982-9500
Friday & Saturday only

Bright white decor with splashes of red in a chic setting. Northern Italian cuisine. Grilled meat and fish, homemade pasta, takeout service.

CITY OF PARIS
101 Shannon Alley btwn. Geary & Post / 441-4442

Comfortable and casual, this bistro is a great stop after the theatre. Or, you can dine first, then come back later for drinks or dessert.

DAVID'S DELICATESSEN
474 Geary St. at Taylor / 771-1600

Craving a pastrami on rye? San Francisco's only true Jewish deli keeps late hours, too.

ENRICO'S
504 Broadway at Kearny / 982-6223
Monday through Saturday

You can get great hamburgers, out-of this-world pizzas and creative California specialties at this legendary spot.

FOG CITY DINER
1300 Battery St. at Embarcadero / 982-2000
Friday & Saturday only

Try updated American classics and California cuisine in the place that started the neo-diner trend.

HARD ROCK CAFE
1699 Van Ness Ave. at Sacramento / 885-1699
Friday & Saturday only

Burgers, shakes and fries accompanied by rock 'n' roll, with a young, lively crowd.

IL FORNAIO
1265 Battery St., Levi Plaza / 986-0100
Friday & Saturday only

Great Northern Italian cuisine in a warm, sophisticated setting just right for socializing.

KABUTO SUSHI
5116 Geary Blvd. at 15th Ave. / 752-5652

Great sushi prepared with eye-boggling speed by Sachio.

LA SCENE CAFE & BAR
490 Geary St. at Taylor / 292-6430
Tuesday through Saturday

Located in the Warwick Regis Hotel in the theatre district, La Scene serves California cuisine.

MAX'S DINER
311 3rd St. at Folsom / 546-MAXS
Friday & Saturday only

All-American diner food in huge portions. Don't miss their pastrami Reuben sandwich!

PERRY'S
1944 Union St. at Laguna / 922-9022
Friday & Saturday only

Straightforward American grilled food, pasta and salads. Lively bar scene, two dining rooms.

PREGO
2000 Union St. at Buchanan / 563-3305

Chic, popular Italian restaurant and bar with homemade pasta, grilled fish.

SPUNTINO
524 Van Ness Ave. at McAllister / 861-7772
Friday & Saturday only

Order a sandwich, small gourmet pizza or wonderful pastries at the counter of this casual, very Italian eatery.

STARS
150 Redwood Alley off Van Ness / 861-7827
Tuesday through Saturday

Stars features an inexpensive "bar menu" — oysters, brochettes, individual pizzas and hamburgers.

ZUNI CAFE
1658 Market St. at Franklin / 552-2522
Tuesday through Saturday

Zuni's fantastic house menu, including appetizers, sandwiches, salads and a large oyster selection, is served late into the night.

OPEN 'TIL 1AM

MAX'S OPERA CAFE
601 Van Ness Ave. at Golden Gate / 771-7300
Friday & Saturday only

New York deli in Opera Plaza features singing waiters along with sandwiches, salads and large desserts.

POSTRIO
545 Post St. at Mason / 776-7825

Trendy Postrio's late-night bar menu offers outstanding pizzas, sandwiches and salads.

OPEN 'TIL 1:30AM

CAVA 555
555 Second St. near Brannan / 543-2282
Monday through Saturday

Cava 555 serves up jazz and a dazzling selection of Champagnes and sparkling wines. The restaurant also offers an appetizing menu of California specialties, created by Chef Patrick Rice.

OPEN 'TIL 1:45AM

BASTA PASTA
1268 Grant Ave. at Vallejo / 434-2248

Three convivial floors at North Beach offering fresh seafood, pizza from a wood-burning oven and pasta with fresh mussels a specialty.

OPEN 'TIL 2AM

HAMBURGER MARY'S
1582 Folsom St. at 12th / 626-5767
Friday & Saturday only

A crowded, jovial hangout famous for giant hamburgers.

OPEN 'TIL 3 AM

MEL'S DRIVE-IN
2165 Lombard St. at Fillmore / 921-3039
3355 Geary Blvd. near Arguello / 387-2244
Friday & Saturday only

The all-American diner with jukeboxes at every table serves classic burgers, chicken potpie, blue plate specials; breakfast available any time.

OPEN 'TIL 4 AM

EL ZOCALO
3230 Mission St. near Valencia / 282-2572
Friday & Saturday only

When you get the Mexican munchies, come here for their South-of-the-Border staples — tacos, burritos, enchiladas and more.

OPEN 24 HOURS

BIG HEART 24-HOUR VIDEO CAFE
5700 Geary Blvd. at 21st Ave. / 668-2919

Munch on sandwiches and burgers as you watch video movies.

LORI'S DINER
336 Mason St. near O'Farrell / 392-8646

Cheeseburgers, milkshakes, cherry cokes, fries and great jukeboxes.

MIDNIGHT CAFE
2550 Van Ness Ave. near Union / 673-0144

Seafood, steaks, pasta and eggs are served day and night in this lighted "beacon" on Van Ness.

SPARKY'S DINER
242 Church St. near Market / 621-6001

The trendy, bleary-eyed and hungry turn up here for diner-style burgers, omelettes, salads and desserts.

EAST BAY

BAY WOLF RESTAURANT
3853 Piedmont Ave., Oakland / 510-655-6004
Lunch Mon-Fri, dinner daily

CALIFORNIA/MEDITERRANEAN

The Bay Wolf is located in a house with a deck that's especially popular on warm days. The restaurant serves a spontaneous cuisine appropriate to the season and occasion.

BETTE'S OCEAN VIEW DINER
1807 4th St., Berkeley / 510-644-3230
Breakfast & lunch daily

AMERICAN

There's no ocean view, but the cheerful, slick design of this lively diner and the wonderful homemade food more than make up for it.

BLACKHAWK GRILLE
3540 Blackhawk Plaza Circle
Blackhawk Plaza, Danville / 510-736-4295
Lunch & dinner daily, brunch Sun

MEDITERRANEAN

Someone parked a vintage car inside sleek Blackhawk Grille — a clever idea, given its location near the Behring Auto Museum. Towering windows overlook dramatic waterfalls, and a 3,000-bottle display cellar showcases California's premium wines.

BUCCI'S
6121 Hollis St., Emeryville / 510-547-4725
Breakfast & lunch Mon-Fri, dinner Mon-Sat

MEDITERRANEAN

Artists, writers and other interesting characters from booming Emeryville hang out in colorful, airy Bucci's. The savory food celebrates Italian and Southern European cuisines.

CHEF PAUL'S
4179 Piedmont Ave., Oakland / 510-547-2175
Dinner Tues-Sun

FRENCH/CALIFORNIA

Oakland's only Grand Master Chef, Paul Grutter imbues French cooking with California spirit. The menu features five superb prix-fixe menus, which change nightly.

CHEZ PANISSE
1517 Shattuck Ave., Berkeley / 510-548-5525
Lunch & dinner Mon-Sat

INTERNATIONAL

Alice Waters seats you at 6, 6:30, 8:30 and 9:15PM by reservations made one calendar month in advance for her five-course prix-fixe dinners. The celebrated restaurant's exciting Mediterranean-influenced cuisine is created with seasonal, local ingredients.

CAFE AT CHEZ PANISSE: Located upstairs, the informal cafe is open throughout the day and evening.

DUCK CLUB RESTAURANT
3287 Mt. Diablo Blvd., Lafayette / 510-283-7108
Lunch Mon-Fri, dinner daily, brunch Sun

AMERICAN

Located in the elegant Lafayette Park Hotel, the Duck Club is a favorite in the East Bay. Intimate and relaxing, the restaurant offers a menu that encompasses the innovative and the traditional. Distinctive pastas, impeccably fresh fish, meat and fowl dishes, including an outstanding duck à l' orange, are some of the specialties. Sunday brunches feature expansive appetizers and dessert buffets, along with made-to-order entrees and free-flowing champagne.

Specialties: Caesar Salad; French Onion Soup; New York Steak with a Brandy Peppercorn Sauce; Duck à l'Orange

KIRALA
2100 Ward St. at Shattuck, Berkeley / 510-549-3486
Lunch Tues-Fri, dinner daily

JAPANESE

Popular and rightly so, Kirala delivers what some consider the best Japanese food in the Bay Area. The restaurant's robata grill is responsible for sensational specialties, including seafood, vegetable and several chicken variations. Don't miss the *negima*, an outstanding chicken dish. Kirala's sushi bar is also the scene for arresting taste sensations.

Specialties: Freshwater Eel in a Sake-based Sauce over Rice; Japanese Fish Stew; Salmon Teriyaki; Ginger Pork on a Bed of Shredded Vegetables; Sushi; Sashimi

LALIME'S
1329 Gilman St., Berkeley / 510-527-9838
Dinner daily

MEDITERRANEAN

Lalime's is a lively bistro, with light salmon-colored walls, wooden tables and booths and big picture windows. The food is good and the wine list noteworthy.

LE MARQUIS
3524B Mt. Diablo Blvd., Lafayette / 510-284-4422
Dinner Tues-Sat

FRENCH

Chef/owner Robert Guerguy offers an innovative seasonal menu to complement the contemporary decor of his elegant dining room and bar. The menu has an excellent selection of hot and cold appetizers, including smoked duck ravioli with ginger in a honey Cabernet sauce and eggplant cannelloni with a vegetable compote, served with slices of roasted loin of lamb. Le Marquis is available for group luncheons and special events. Customized catering services are also featured.

Specialties: Flat Salmon with Tomato & Tarragon Beurre Blanc; Medallions of Veal with Wild Mushrooms; Roasted Tenderloin of Pork with Fried Shallots on Bed of Mashed Potatoes; Kahlua Iced Souffle

NAN YANG RESTAURANT
301 Eighth St. at Harrison, Oakland / 510-465-6924
6048 College Ave., Oakland / 510-655-3298
Lunch & dinner Tues-Sun

BURMESE

Acclaimed by many California publications as the top eatery of its kind in the Bay Area, Nan Yang boasts a rare collection of dishes that are the best of Burma. The ginger salad alone is a culinary sensation that has attracted disciples since 1983, and they all think their find is a secret worth keeping. Since the original Nan Yang on Eighth Street was so well received, Owner Philip Chu has opened a second restaurant with a greatly expanded menu in the Rockridge area.

Specialties: Ginger Salad with Dried Shrimp, Coconut, Cabbage, Onion, Beans, Garlic, Hot Pepper Chili & Lemon; Vegetarian Dishes; Garlic Noodles; Lamb Curry; Seafood & Vegetable Dishes

O CHAME
1830 Fourth St., Berkeley / 510-841-8783
Lunch & dinner Mon-Sat

JAPANESE

This excellent Japanese restaurant has many fans who think it a rare find. What began as a tea shop and tea-cake factory has blossomed into a serene restaurant. Simple dishes that mix Japanese and Western cooking philosophies are inspiredby the seasons, and an extensive hot and cold sake menu lends authenticity. O Chame is also known for its impeccable sashimi.

Specialties: Grilled River Eel with Endive, Chayote & Pecans; Soba & Udon Noodle Dishes; Sashimi; Fish & Meats Roasted in Wood-burning Oven

OLIVETO
5655 College Ave., Oakland / 510-547-5356
Lunch Mon-Fri, dinner daily

ITALIAN

Oliveto is a favorite with those who know authentic Tuscan cuisine when they taste it. Slowly simmered risottos, rich seafood and meat stews, pastas and grilled

seafood and meats will please your palate, as will the extensive wine list.

Specialties: Risotto with Calamari; Paella; Osso Buco; Fresh Pappardelle Pasta with Duck & Thyme; Tiramisu

PASTORAL
2160 University Ave., Berkeley / 510-540-7514
Lunch & dinner Mon-Sat

CALIFORNIA/KOREAN/FRENCH/ITALIAN

This spacious restaurant, designed with a warm, eclectic decor, has earned a well-deserved reputation for its imaginative cuisine.

PLEARN THAI CUISINE
2050 University Ave., Berkeley / 510-841-2148
Lunch & dinner daily

THAI

Many critics have named Plearn the best Thai restaurant in the Bay Area.

TOURELLE RESTAURANT
3565 Mt. Diablo Blvd., Lafayette / 510-284-3565
Lunch Mon-Fri, dinner daily, brunch Sun

EUROPEAN COUNTRY

In a lovely, vine-covered brick building, Tourelle was re-decorated by Pat Kuleto, the famous Northern Californian restaurateur. The elegant and relaxing decor features a glass-enclosed courtyard, open exhibition kitchen and private dining rooms. The new decor is a fit setting for Tourelle's award-winning cuisine. Chef Stephen Silva's innovative menu changes seasonally.

Specialties: Rotisserie & Grilled Meats & Fish; Wood-burning Pizza Oven; Pastas; Pappardelle with Rabbit Ragout & Spinach; Sauteed Muscovy Duck Breast with Coriander, Green Olive & Orange Zest; Grilled Salmon with Beurre Rouge & Braised Endive

SOUTH BAY

BACCARAT AT HOTEL SOFITEL
223 Twin Dolphin Dr., Redwood City / 415-598-9000
Lunch Mon-Fri, dinner Mon-Sat, brunch Sun

FRENCH

Overlooking a tranquil lagoon, the elegantly appointed Baccarat Restaurant offers an exciting array of award-winning California French cuisine. Chef Laurent Dallot and Maitre d' Philippe Basselet await each guest's arrival with an attention to detail found only in restaurants of exceptional caliber.

Specialties: Tuna Tartare; Garlic Brie Soup; Rabbit Mint Ravioli; Stuffed Chicken with Goat Cheese & Sundried Tomato; Grilled Prawns on an Artichoke Ragout

RESTAURANTS

BARBAROSSA RESTAURANT
3003 El Camino Real, Redwood City / 415-369-2626
Lunch Tues-Fri, dinner Mon-Sat

$$ 🚗 📷 🍸 🍴 ⛵

ITALIAN/FRENCH

Awarded four stars by the Mobil Guide, Barbarossa is well established on the Peninsula. Elegant table settings complement the candlelit interior and gracious service.

BELLA VISTA
13451 Skyline Blvd., Woodside / 415-851-1229
Dinner Mon-Sat

$$$ 🚗 📷 🍸 🍴

CONTINENTAL

Dine among the redwoods overlooking the bay at Bella Vista. Built in 1927, the restaurant provides a romantic panorama of sparkling lights below.

BIT OF RHYTHM
1741 El Camino Real, Millbrae / 415-588-6151
Lunch Mon-Fri

$ 🚗 🍸 😊

AMERICAN

This hole-in-the-wall is a real find. Unpretentious and friendly, Bit of Rhythm serves wholesome back-to-basics cooking. Fresh fish, meat, and locally grown produce are the finest quality available and are offered in generous portions. In addition to its weekly lunch service, Bit of Rhythm has Sunday night dinners twice a month. Advance reservations are recommended for these special events.

Specialties: Marinated Lamb & Pork Chops; Grilled Salmon; Clam Bordelaise; Cobb Salad; Fresh Fish; Tomato-stuffed Tuna Salad

CHEF CHU'S
1067 N. San Antonio Rd., Los Altos / 415-948-2696
Lunch & dinner daily

$ 🚗 🍸

CHINESE

Owner/chef Lawrence Chu established his successful restaurant on the Peninsula years ago, serving reasonably priced cuisine from four regions of China.

DAL BAFFO
878 Santa Cruz Ave., Menlo Park / 415-325-1588
Lunch Mon-Fri, dinner Mon-Sat

$$$ 🚗 🍸 🍴 ⛵

CONTINENTAL

Dal Baffo is an elegant restaurant with the friendly family touch of owner Vincenzo Lo Grasso. The menu combines Genoese, French and California influences in an emphatically fresh style of cooking.

EMILE'S
545 South 2nd St., San Jose / 408-289-1960
Lunch Fri, dinner Tues-Sat

$$ 🚗 📧 🍸 😊

FRENCH

Chef/proprietor Emile Mooser, trained in classic French cooking in Lausanne, is noted for his attention to the seasoning, color and presentation of his dishes and for the texture of his sauces. He changes the menu every month, using the best of seasonal harvests. Emile's provides an intimate setting for lunch and dinner.

FLOWER LOUNGE
51 Millbrae Ave., Millbrae / 415-692-6666
1671 El Camino, Millbrae / 415-588-9972
Lunch & dinner daily

$$ 🚗 📧 🍸 😊

CHINESE

Critics rave about this elegant Peninsula restaurant for its consistently outstanding, sophisticated food, and rightly so. You'll find Cantonese specialties as well as dishes from other provinces, with an emphasis on subtly spiced seafood, all prepared with the freshest ingredients and carefully presented. Expect a crowd, even at lunch, at both locations.

Specialties: Winter Melon Soup; Whole Braised Duck; Squab with Mango; Hunan-style Lobster; Prawns with Walnuts in Special Sauce

LE MOUTON NOIR
14560 Big Basin Way, Saratoga / 408-867-7017
Lunch Tues-Sat, dinner daily

$$ 🚗 📧

FRENCH

Centered in the charming village of Saratoga, "The Black Sheep" is a delightful discovery for Bay Area gourmets. French cuisine with California overtones is prepared with care; the light and airy decor is replete with fresh flowers and Laura Ashley prints.

LE PAPILLON
410 Saratoga Ave., San Jose / 408-296-3730
Lunch Mon-Fri, dinner daily

$$$ 🚗 📧 🍸 🍴

FRENCH

Recognized for close to two decades as a distinctive dining establishment in San Jose, award-winning Le Papillon offers a peaceful interlude for lunch and dinner. Both classic and contemporary French cuisine are served in a formal dining room.

Specialties: Grilled Venison Chops with Shallots & Chanterelles; Poached Salmon with Port Wine & Ruby Grapefruit; Roasted Pheasant with Sour Cherry Sauce

RESTAURANTS

NOUVEAU TRATTORIA
541 Bryant St., Palo Alto / 415-327-0132
Lunch Tues-Fri, dinner Tues-Sun

FRENCH/ITALIAN

Nouveau Trattoria serves a wide variety of French and Italian entrees. Especially popular are the large plates of homemade pastas, offered for $8.50-$10.50. At night, the restaurant presents live jazz. Reservations are recommended at this lively South Bay restaurant with Carmel-like charm. Nouveau Trattoria also features facilities for private parties for lunch and dinner.
Specialties: *Salmon with Beurre Blanc; Rack of Lamb with Garlic Butter; Steak au Poivre; Ravioli Alfredo with Porcini; Cannelloni Romano*

PAOLO'S RESTAURANT
333 W. San Carlos St., San Jose / 408-294-2558
Lunch Mon-Fri, dinner Mon-Sat

ITALIAN

Paolo's is highly acclaimed nationwide for its exceptional contemporary adaptation of classic regional Italian cuisine as well as for its award-winning wine list and excellent service. In its new location at Riverpark, Paolo's boasts the city's most exciting view and atmosphere, incorporating warm, rich tones, dramatic touches and European style.
Specialties: *Filet of Seabass Poached in Broth with Prunes, Capers, Pine Nuts, Olives, Clams & Tomato; Quill-shaped Pasta in Tomato & Vodka Sauce*

RISTORANTE CAPELLINI
310 Baldwin at "B" St., San Mateo / 415-348-2296
Lunch Mon-Fri, dinner daily

ITALIAN

Renowned designer Pat Kuleto has done it again. Like his successful San Francisco restaurants Kuleto's and Kuleto's & McCormick, Ristorante Capellini has just the right mix of style and elegance.

SPORT CITY CAFE
10745 N. De Anza Blvd., Cupertino / 408-253-2233
Lunch Mon-Fri, dinner daily, brunch Sun

CALIFORNIA

A popular restaurant on the Peninsula, Sport City Cafe is owned by members of the 49ers football team. Sports photos on the walls add to the upbeat mood.

FOR RESTAURANTS IN MARIN COUNTY, PLEASE SEE THE MARIN SECTION ON THE AM SIDE, PAGE 103.

RESTAURANTS

The Master Sommeliers'
Guide To
California's Best Wines

by Evan Goldstein
MASTER SOMMELIER, DIRECTOR OF THE STERLING VINEYARDS
SCHOOL OF SERVICE AND HOSPITALITY

OVER THE YEARS, CALIFORNIA AND QUALITY WINES HAVE BECOME SYNONYMOUS. And for good reason: our winemakers and grape growers produce some of the world's finest wines.

While many of California's best wineries are right here in Northern California, there are more than 700 wineries and estates statewide from Mendocino in the north to Temecula in the south. In this wine guide, we will introduce you to some of the state's finest offerings.

About the Selections

In many a wine guide, the selection is either purely subjective or driven by hidden motives. We chose the democratic method. A ballot of California's finest wines in a variety of categories was mailed to more than 120 of the Bay Area's restaurant and hotel wine buyers. Not only does such a group know California wines, but it is also in tune with the preferences of the wine drinking public at large.

We asked the voters to choose the best wines in each category. We tabulated the votes and selected the top wines for our tasting. Then, we gave the wines to a tasting panel for their assessment. Their notes follow each wine.

What makes this effort so exciting is that California is now riding high on a wave of very good to excellent vintages. With that said, let's dive into the glory of the grape!

What is a Master Sommelier?

Our panel was made up of nine of the Bay Area's Master Sommeliers, unarguably among the finest wine evaluators in the world.

All successfully completed the Master Sommelier course in wine theory, service and tasting evaluation. In the United States, there are 23 Master Sommeliers, with a total of 48 active worldwide.

The standards are set by the Court of Master Sommeliers, which was established to improve the level of wine service in hotels and restaurants. The first Master Sommelier examination was held in the United Kingdom in 1969. By April 1977, the Court of Master Sommeliers was the premier international examining body for the hospitality industry. Within the next ten years, the Court perfected its qualifications, which are recognized by the National Restaurant Association as the top wine education and training program for the United States.

WINE-TASTING PANEL

Nunzio Alioto
Proprietor, Alioto's, San Francisco

Michael Bonaccorsi
Wine Consultant, San Francisco

Fred Dame
Director of National Accounts & Far East Exports, The Seagram Classics Wine Company, San Mateo

Timothy Gaiser
Educator & Consultant, The Julliard-Alpha Co.

Evan Goldstein
Director, The Sterling Vineyards School of Service & Hospitality, Calistoga

Peter Granoff
Wine Director, Square One Restaurant, San Francisco

Emmanuel Kemiji
Wine Director, The Ritz-Carlton, San Francisco

Steve Morey
Wine Director, Ernie's Restaurant, San Francisco

David O'Connor
Wine Director, The Westin St. Francis, San Francisco

RED WINE VARIETALS

CABERNET SAUVIGNON

The red king to Chardonnay's white queen, Cabernet Sauvignon has long been one of California's most successful wines. Like red Bordeaux in France, its combination of full body, stunning complexity and ability to age have contributed to its popularity. In contemporary California versions, Cabernet Sauvignon may be blended with related varietals to enhance its flavor profile, adding spice, herb and earth tastes to its intrinsically succulent flavors of cassis and small red berry fruit.

We will focus not only on the best Cabernet Sauvignons from several regions, but also highlight some of the state's finest single vineyards and reserve offerings.

MERITAGE & PROPRIETARY WINES

Meritage is coined from the words merit and heritage. Only recently an official category, Meritage refers to blended wines based on traditional Bordeaux examples, both red and white. In order for an American wine to carry a grape's name, it must be at least 75% pure. For example, a Cabernet Sauvignon must be made mostly from Cabernet Sauvignon grapes. Many wineries feel this rule stifles their creativity. So, to make the best possible wine they can, they suspend the rules and select and blend different grapes together to make a more complete wine, which they label with a proprietary name. Classically, this "formula" is native to Bordeaux, although many Rhone wines also fit this mold. Bordeaux reds are often combinations of Cabernet Sauvignon, Merlot, Cabernet Franc and other grapes. The Bordeaux whites meld Sauvignon Blanc with Semillon and Muscadelle de Bordelais.

MERLOT

Cabernet Sauvignon's kissing cousin is as prolific in California as it is in France's Bordeaux, specifically in its Pomerol district. Merlot has only recently stood alone as a varietal wine; the first examples date from the early 1970s, with the real growth happening only in the latter half of the decade. Merlot offers a flavor profile similar to Cabernet Sauvignon, but it has softer tannin so the wine is more approachable in its youth. Although an herbal, minty or eucalyptus flavor is typical of many Merlots, almost all explode with generous berry flavors and sweet earth tones.

ZINFANDEL

Our gift to the world of fine wine, Zinfandel is thought to be native to California, though some think the grape originated in Italy. Today, Zinfandel grows in neighboring states and even as far away as Australia. The grape's development has been a roller coaster ride. Zinfandel started off as an overblown tannic monster. It went through an awkward adolescence trying to find itself in terms of style, and it has now settled into a more self-assured wine. Today, the lucky consumer can find a wide diversity of Zinfandel styles. Zinfandel can also be made into a light blush style labeled White Zinfandel, which has a bright flavor and a taste of ripe berry fruit and peppery spice.

PINOT NOIR

Those who love Pinot Noir are fanatic about it. A finesse wine of deep flavor and supple structure, the best Pinot Noirs show many layers of complexity. A well-made Pinot Noir sings of cherries and raspberries, spice and hints of licorice and mocha. Like a white wine, it offers tremendous diversity. Pinot Noir matches food beautifully, as happy with a grilled piece of tuna as it is with a lamb chop. The grape, which is French in origin, has proven to be very fickle — with more misses than hits. But oh those hits...

CALIFORNIA ITALIAN VARIETALS

On the cutting edge of the wine world, California's Italian varietals show great promise. These grapes include Sangiovese from Tuscany, and Dolcetto and Nebbiolo from the Piedmont region. Although a handful of wineries are currently working with these varietals, more and more are planning to join in soon. True to their roots, California's Italian varietals offer the same cherry, truffle and roasted coffee notes you find in the old country.

RHONE-STYLE VARIETALS

California is close to the same latitude as France's Rhone Valley and Provence. Therefore, it makes sense that varietals from that region would do well in California — and they do. In fact, many of their grapes, including Mourvedre (Mataro), Syrah and Grenache, are among some of the oldest planted in the state. As you would expect, the wines are true to their roots: deep plummy and jammy fruit, cracked black pepper and smoky flavors, either melded together if in a blend or as stand-alone features when individual grapes are isolated.

WHITE WINE VARIETALS

CHARDONNAY

The queen of white wines well deserves her claim to the throne. Not only is Chardonnay the most popular of white wines, it is almost always one of the best — if not the best — white wine offered by a winery. The Chardonnay boom of the past decade means that there are a lot of examples from which to choose, from all parts of the state. You will find some diversity of style in the wines but almost all premium Chardonnays are produced using some form of oak barrel aging to enhance the flavors and textures of the wine.

In addition to their regular bottling, many wineries produce Chardonnays which are unique in one of two ways. The wine is either made from grapes coming from a single vineyard, like the cru wines of Burgundy's fabled Cote d'Or in France, to exhibit distinctive attributes, or the wine may be labeled a reserve, which by definition represents a select wine. A winery designates its Chardonnay a reserve when it feels the wine is a cut above, perhaps because of its grape selection or its vinification method. In either case, the consumer is sure to receive a wine that is quite special in the winery's esteem.

SAUVIGNON BLANC & FUME BLANC

Many avid diners feel that Sauvignon Blanc or Fume Blanc — they are one and the same — is the quintessential white wine for American food. Its angular character and bold flavor make it a natural when paired with contemporary cuisine. There are two distinctive styles: one, which has a lean, crisp taste, favors the more green herbaceous flavors, while the other is round, rich and elegant. This style flirts with Chardonnay and emphasizes tastes of green melon, fig, sweet cream and lime.

GEWURZTRAMINER

In German, Gewurz means spicy. A transplant from France's Alsace by way of Italy (the grape originated in northeastern Italy), this heavily perfumed wine is often overlooked in the spectrum of white wine varietals. Usually rich and full bodied, the flavor of Gewurz is unmistakably that of sweet spices. Cinammon, allspice and clove are classic flavors, alongside fragrant blossomy qualities frequently found in this wine.

JOHANNISBERG RIESLING

Truly a global favorite, Johannisberg Riesling "disputes with Chardonnay the title of the world's best white wine grape," according to noted English wine authority Hugh Johnson. Unfortunately, in America we have not yet caught that fervor. Riesling, or White Riesling, as it is also known, is a very delicate grape. It requires specific cool climates for the grape to show its often subtle nuances. Hints of nectarine, pear and apricot dominate the bouquet while mineral overtones can often be detected in the most classic Rieslings.

CHENIN BLANC

Chenin Blanc has its roots in France's Loire Valley, where the grape produces a wide variety of wines. In America, this grape shows the classic red apple, light melon and guava flavors in wines that range from bone dry to just short of dry.

SPARKLING WINES

In France, they call it Champagne. Here, we call it sparkling wine, although many estates in California have French affiliations. The winemaking process is the same, only the name is different. Champagne is technically a sparkling wine produced in France's Champagne district. One taste of our selected sparklers and you'll realize that those tiny bubbles don't need to be French to be sublime!

BRUT

Brut-style sparkling wine represents not only the driest wine made by a property but also the majority of its production. It is generally a blend of Pinot Noir and Chardonnay, but some houses also use a little Pinot Blanc or Pinot Meunier, which are additional white and red grapes, to create a house style.

BLANC DE NOIRS

Blanc de Noirs translates as "white of blacks," which in winespeak means a white wine from dark-skinned or red fruit. Here the grape of choice is Pinot Noir, and the resulting wine, often light pink or faintly orange in tone, is spicy, accented by flavors of strawberries and raspberries. It is slightly more ample than the Blanc de Blancs.

BLANC DE BLANCS

Translated from French, Blanc de Blancs means "white of whites." It's a sparkling white wine made from white grapes, almost exclusively Chardonnay. Blanc de Blancs are delicate and fragrant, laced with nuances of flowers and bright citrus fruit.

ROSE

A rose by any other name is a rose, but in the category of sparkling wines, it's quite special. Tinted a color that may range from Pacific Coast salmon to Mediterranean sunset, these wines get their color from the addition of Pinot Noir to the blend, either as an added component wine or bled from the grapes during the initial fermentation. Either way, the striking appearance sets the stage for a complex array of flavors.

CALIFORNIA PORT

The state's southern Mediterranean climate is ideal for generous Port-style dessert wines: late-harvested Zinfandel, Zinfandel blends or those made from indigenous Port grapes from Portugal's Douro Valley. All offer diverse, tremendously concentrated flavors of plummy fruit and sweet spice, making California Ports the perfect climax to a delicious meal.

CALIFORNIA DESSERT WINES

Dessert wines, like people, come in all types. While most are produced from white grapes, their variety is stunning. They range from apricot-scented late harvest Rieslings to honied dessert-style Sauvignon Blanc or Semillon. Muscat, a global favorite, does exceedingly well in California. Mix and match, play and experiment — California's dessert wines are among the most fun wines you can taste.

Winning Wines

CABERNET SAUVIGNON

1989 Arrowood Cabernet Sauvignon
Sonoma County

This wine melds firm, rich flavors of black plum, blackberry and spice with a great structure underlined by ample acidity and a solid backbone of tannin. It is quite tasty now but will benefit from additional aging. Needs rich food to show off its pedigree.

1989 B.R. Cohn "Olive Hill Vineyard" Cabernet Sauvignon
Sonoma County

Full-bodied, with plentiful flavors of vanilla, stone fruits and red licorice, this well-made wine is showing well right now. It has medium length with apparent oak in both a spicy toast flavor and a velvety texture. A nice mouthful of wine.

1988 Beaulieu Vineyards "Georges de Latour Private Reserve" Cabernet Sauvignon
Napa Valley

Rich, textured and of medium weight and intensity, this distinctive wine has flavors of black pepper, chocolate and fresh black currants, with just a nuance of dusty earth and soft yet firm tannins. Spicy overtones provide an engaging accent.

1989 Beringer Cabernet Sauvignon
Knights Valley, Proprietor Grown

Enticing aromas of plum, black raspberry and exotic small dark fruits, with round, approachable tannins.

This wine is medium in body and has a shade of oak aging that adds intricacy to its flavor. A lightly herbal taste is also present. Good quality, with supple texture.

1987 Beringer "Private Reserve" Cabernet Sauvignon
Napa Valley

Deep and rich, with a pleasant earthiness, this wine has great breed. Complex and balanced, it is very concentrated with flavors of mint, dark cherry, currants and leather. A slight cedar component enhances the plum and berry core.

1989 Cakebread Cabernet Sauvignon
Napa Valley

Cassis, dried plums and rich berry fruit underline this full-bodied yet supple wine. Good intensity and balance, with a touch of vanilla and sweet toasty oak. Drinks well now although it could benefit from a few years of bottle-aging.

1986 Cakebread "Rutherford Reserve" Cabernet Sauvignon
Napa Valley

Massive and powerful, this full-bodied wine has a pronounced classic Cabernet aroma, accented by flavors of green tea and strawberry. Extremely long on the finish, with a nice balance between fruit and charred oak. Ample in tannin, it would benefit from some aging.

1988 Caymus "Special Selection" Cabernet Sauvignon
Napa Valley

Deep ruby in appearance and extremely well made. Aromas of dark cherry, dark chocolate, cinnamon and spice dominate. Toasty oak and supple texture marry with the fruit on the palate. This wine has layers of complexity and a wonderful fruit finish marked by a sweet blueberry note.

1989 Caymus Vineyards Cabernet Sauvignon
Napa Valley

Medium in intensity with cassis and blackberry flavors and a lasting finish. Sweet oak nuances are attractive in both taste and texture. Rich in the mouth, this wine is quite pleasing now but will develop gracefully.

1988 Chateau Montelena Estate Cabernet Sauvignon
Napa Valley

Dense and opaque-looking, with a concentrated nose of small black fruits, eucalyptus and earth. Full bodied in the mouth, this wine echoes rich fruit on the palate while picking up herbal overtones in its long finish. Needs at least five years in the cellar for maximum appreciation.

1988 Clos du Bois "Briarcrest" Cabernet Sauvignon
Alexander Valley, Sonoma County

A warm dusty scent underlines sweet vanilla, dill and light blackberry flavors. Medium in both intensity and body, this wine has ripe fruit, bell pepper and herbal flavors that mirror the aroma. A hint of toffee in the finish offers complexity, and a frame of tannin and acidity provides good structure. Elegant and balanced, this wine offers immediate charm but should age for several years.

1988 Clos du Val Cabernet Sauvignon
Stag's Leap District, Napa Valley

Plum, spice and a trace of vanilla mark this deep ruby-colored wine. A solid core of balanced berry flavor and a balanced supple finish. Adequate tannins and earth are present on the palate.

1989 Far Niente Cabernet Sauvignon
Napa Valley

A beautifully balanced wine with attractive flavors of cassis, cocoa and thyme. A prominent flavor of smoky oak comes through on both the nose and palate, lending a note of complexity. Medium-full in body, it has good structure and sufficient tannin for the long haul.

1986 Grgich Hills Cabernet Sauvignon
Napa Valley

With mint, black pepper and a nuance of blackberry in the aroma, this medium-bodied wine has excellent intensity of flavor and good persistence in the finish. The mint comes through on the palate along with eucalyptus and a trace of black plum. Well-balanced in the mouth, it drinks beautifully.

1989 Groth Cabernet Sauvignon
Napa Valley

The scent of herbs and soft prunes marks this full-bodied wine. Opulent in the mouth, it has good intensity and a restrained finish. Works well with vegetable dishes and entrees stressing olive flavors.

1987 Heitz Cellar Cabernet Sauvignon
Napa Valley

Hints of cocoa and fresh mint surround a core of ripe, rich cassis. Forward but with a long finish, the flavors complement the appealing bouquet, and a moderate amount of oak rounds out the flavor profile. This well-made wine has all of its elements in the right place.

1987 Heitz Cellar "Martha's Vineyard" Cabernet Sauvignon
Napa Valley

Deep and concentrated with mint and eucalyptus aromas, generous ripe fruit and a piercing quality of currant and black raspberry. Ripe and youthful, this blockbuster of a full-bodied wine merits its reputation but will require patience to see it to its zenith.

1989 Hess Collection Cabernet Sauvignon
Napa Valley

Long, full and quite concentrated, with pronounced flavors of plum and currant and a hint of vanilla. Ample and generous, this wine displays complexity and unabashedly powerful fruit. Rounded out with balanced oak and adequate tannins, it is a fine effort and will age gracefully.

1988 Jordan Cabernet Sauvignon
Alexander Valley, Sonoma County

Medium in body, balanced with rosemary, jammy blackberry and light peppery flavors, this Cabernet has a nice finish. Although no earth is present in the aroma, there is a trace of fertile earth in the mouth. With good balance and supple tannins, it is forward and approachable.

1989 Joseph Phelps Napa Cabernet Sauvignon
Napa Valley

Medium-full-bodied and powerful, this Cabernet has mint, bitter chocolate and slight blackberry aromas, with exotic spicy flavors in the mouth. Ample tannins and sufficient acidity provide a solid finish and promise a good future.

1989 Kenwood "Artists Series" Cabernet Sauvignon
Sonoma Valley

Leather, black cherry, a kiss of clove and a strong shot of oak give this formidable wine a terrific intensity. A pretty flavor of black licorice is evident in the middle palate. Tremendous synergy of flavor with a complex, lingering finish make it very seductive.

1989 Ridge Cabernet Sauvignon "Monte Bello"
Santa Cruz

Layered with intense blackberry, dark plum and a kiss of oak, this wine is medium-full-bodied, with a long, lingering finish. Expansive flavors, with an attractive light hint of pepper, and smooth yet defined tannins frame an elegant and promising future.

1988 Robert Mondavi Cabernet Sauvignon
Napa Valley

Stylish and substantial, with delicious soft red fruit and powerful flavor. A reserved but stated character of oak with a nuance of spice offers a very Bordeaux-like flavor profile reminiscent of a St. Julien. Good weight and body complete this age-worthy bottling.

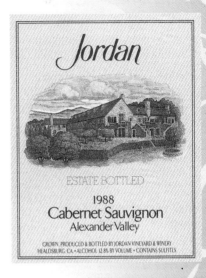

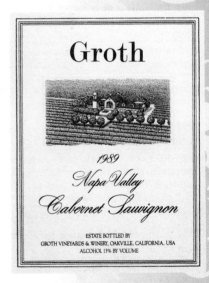

1988 Robert Mondavi "Reserve" Cabernet Sauvignon
Napa Valley

A perfumed wine with lovely scents of eucalyptus, mint and ripe currants. Full in body, with good intensity of flavor and balanced, up-front tannins, it is well integrated and packed with potential.

1989 Shafer Cabernet Sauvignon
Stag's Leap District, Napa Valley

Full bodied and long on the palate, with aromas of rich earth and black cherries. The palate echoes this concentration of flavor with a vivacious and silky mouthfeel. Blended-in Merlot and Cabernet Franc provide complexity, and plum and blackberry flavors explode in the finish. This well-balanced wine can be enjoyed now but is full of future.

1987 Shafer "Hillside Select" Cabernet Sauvignon
Stag's Leap District, Napa Valley

Red bell pepper, juicy blackberries and plum provide the flavor foundation for this concentrated and harmonious wine. The rich, well-focused flavors are offset by sufficient tannin and an appealing nuance of anise. Long on the palate, with ample acidity, this wine has a great future for those who wait.

1988 Simi "Alexander Valley Reserve" Cabernet Sauvignon
Sonoma County

Tight and youthful, with ample currant and cedar aromas, this rich wine bursts in the mouth with beautiful rich berry fruit. Substantial but balanced tannins provide a genuine balance of structure to support the formidable flavor. Will age gracefully.

1988 Simi Cabernet Sauvignon
Alexander Valley, Sonoma County

Understated, with a pleasant earthy aroma, this wine combines flavors of cedar, mint and mature dark cherry fruit. Moderate acidity and tannins provide sound structure, and an impression of sweet oak adds a note of complexity.

1989 Spottswoode Cabernet Sauvignon
Napa Valley

A concentrated nose of chocolate and spicy black cherry mirrors the dense layers of flavor in the mouth. The youthful intensity is in perfect balance and of tremendous length, accented with anise and hints of small berry fruit. This wine will age well into the next decade.

1989 Stags Leap Wine Cellars Cabernet Sauvignon
Napa Valley

Pronounced aromas of marjoram, green leaves and pepper overlay this relatively lean wine, with a dense middle palate of cassis and spearmint. The tannins and acid show the wine somewhat on the hard side, although it should round out with time.

RED MERITAGE WINES

1987 Cain Cellars "Cain 5"
Cabernet Sauvignon, Cabernet Franc, Merlot, Petit Verdot & Malbec; Napa Valley

Herbal notes of laurel and rosemary augment a rich core of blueberry and blue plum fruit. Intensely concentrated, with firm acid and tannins lending good structure. Pleasant nuances of oak and earth provide complexity. A well-knit, well-integrated wine that goes beautifully with food.

1987 Carmenet Red Table Wine
80% Cabernet Sauvignon, 9% Cabernet Franc, 11% Merlot; Sonoma County

Green olives and rich earth are the focus of this firm, full-bodied wine. Ample tannins and super persistence provide great structure, with black cherry, dried herbs and leather in the middle palate. Great with lamb.

1989 Clos du Bois "Marlstone"
61% Cabernet Sauvignon, 13% Malbec, 26% Merlot; Sonoma County

Deep, firm but not overpowering, with integrated notes of cinnamon, dry earth and a kiss of vanilla. Black licorice, black raspberry and a hint of green olive form the foundation of this medium-full-bodied wine. A pronounced flavor of black cherry marks the palate, with ample acidity and finish. A well-made wine with several years ahead of it.

1988 Flora Springs "Trilogy"
Cabernet Franc, Cabernet Sauvignon & Merlot; Napa Valley

Medium in body, with well-integrated tannins and excellent length and complexity in the finish, this wine is underscored with aromas of cassis, black olive and green bell pepper. A dustiness is apparent in the mouth, and a kiss of toasty oak adds complexity.

1988 Joseph Phelps "Insignia"
50% Cabernet Sauvignon, 20% Cabernet Franc, 30% Merlot; Napa Valley

Full-bodied with a supple mouthfeel, this wine is marked by ripe cassis, black cherry and traces of fresh herbs. Spice and toasty oak are present on the palate, with good acidity and a flurry of cranberry flavor in the finish. A well-balanced wine of medium intensity.

1987 Merryvale Meritage
Cabernet Sauvignon & Cabernet Franc;
Napa Valley

Sour cherries and sweet spices are the focus of this medium-bodied Bordeaux blend, with soft but adequate tannins and a light dusty quality in the mouth. Pleasing texture and balanced oak; good persistence and finish.

1988 Mondavi-Rothschild Opus One
85% Cabernet Sauvignon, 13% Cabernet Franc,
2% Merlot; Napa Valley

Cassis, dark plums and blackberries are evident in this polished, medium-bodied, well-integrated wine. Bitter-sweet cocoa, sage and earth highlight the rich fruit flavors, and attractive qualities of vanilla and cedar add depth. Needs more time in the bottle to show its true colors. Serve with full-flavored dishes.

1988 Pahlmeyer Red Table Wine
Cabernet Sauvignon, Cabernet Franc, Merlot,
Malbec, Petit Verdot; Napa Valley

Strong earth and gravel notes punctuate a nucleus of juicy blueberry and dark cherry fruit. This wine has incredible length and complexity, with firm tannins and a lovely marriage of fruit and oak. A weighty, complex wine, it will show even more flavor layers after several years of bottle-aging.

MERLOT

1989 Clos du Val Merlot
Stag's Leap District, Napa Valley,
Estate Bottled

Plums, tobacco and a pleasing component of sandalwood combine with supple tannins and a light-medium body. With a trace of earth and cherry in the mouth, this wine has good harmony and subtlety and an enticing herbal perfume in the finish. Shows better with food.

1989 Cuvaison Merlot
Napa Valley

A beautiful quality of defined dark cherries and a whisper of chocolate form the base of this formidable wine. Gravelly earth tones and a delicate touch of oak provide additional complexity. Soft yet firm tannins make it approachable, and the long, expansive finish bodes well for its aging potential.

1990 Duckhorn Vineyards Merlot
Napa Valley

Excellent balance and a fine, well-defined structure showcase concentrated fruit flavors of blackberry, damson plum and bing cherries. Spice and a hint of herbs and oak provide further depth. Medium- to full-bodied, with immense length and a toasty aftertaste, this wine is delicious.

MERRYVALE

PROFILE

A NAPA VALLEY RESERVE RED WINE
PRODUCED AND BOTTLED BY MERRYVALE VINEYARDS.
ST. HELENA, CALIFORNIA, USA, ALCOHOL 13% BY VOLUME

RAVENS

WOOD

MERLOT
SONOMA COUNTY
1 9 9 0
MADE AND BOTTLED BY
RAVENSWOOD
SONOMA, CALIFORNIA
CONTAINS SULFITES.
ALCOHOL 13.8% BY VOL.

1989 Ferrari Carano Merlot
Sonoma County

Blackberry, rhubarb and jammy strawberry aromas dominate this delicious Merlot. Ample tannin and acidity provide the necessary structure, with an inviting center of sweet brambly-plummy fruit. Inviting and forward, with light floral scents.

1989 Franciscan Merlot
Oakville Estate, Napa Valley

Well-defined and medium in body, with anise, sweet black cherries and a hint of marjoram, this wine is well integrated and balanced. A pleasant dusty quality is evident in the fragrance. Light flavors of herbs and mild vanilla stand out in the finish. While soft enough for immediate consumption, it has sufficient structure to age for a few years.

1989 Matanzas Creek Winery Merlot
Sonoma County

Full and soft, with delicate flavors of red plums, cherries and a whisper of new oak, this wine has tremendous intensity throughout and long, lingering flavors. Well made and stylish, it is one of the best of the vintage.

1990 Ravenswood Merlot
Sonoma County

A rich, dense wine with coffee, plum and a faint nuance of mint in the aroma. Medium in body and very round, this moderately intense wine is balanced with a broad spectrum of fruit flavors in the mouth, most notably red currant and blue plums. Crisp acidity and fairly dense tannins indicate a solid future.

1990 Shafer Merlot
Napa Valley

Sweet berries and violets distinguish the aroma of this elegant, harmonious wine. Developed with a core of mature juicy fruit, it has the same ripe power in the palate. Long and lingering, it is a classic of the varietal.

1989 Sterling Vineyards Merlot
Napa Valley, Estate Bottled

Soft and appealing, with supple yet stated tannins and an expansive finish, this Merlot is medium to full in body. Attractive flavors of cassis, thyme and green bell pepper dominate, with some spicy oak and a light charry oak taste.

ZINFANDEL

1989 Burgess Cellars Zinfandel
Napa Valley

Rich, full and mouth-filling, this wine has good length and enough tannin to balance the charming fruit. With a stylish nose of raspberry, currant and cracked black pepper, it is textbook Zinfandel, with all the attributes that make this grape so lovely.

1990 Caymus Zinfandel
Napa Valley

Opaque in appearance and overtly dusty in the nose, this wine is dense and powerful, with a mouthful of dark cherries, sweet oak and exotic spice. Soft tannins and a good backbone of acidity provide the necessary structure. A youthful wine, it is an example of Zinfandel that drinks well now.

1990 Chateau Montelena Zinfandel
Napa Valley

Berries and cherries dominate the flavor of this warm, lightly spicy wine. Earthy components in both the aroma and mouth, with soft spice and a touch of vanilla. Pleasant tannins offer good structure without being astringent, and the more formal, lighter style is enticing. Drinks well now but should age with elegance.

1990 Frogs Leap Zinfandel
Napa Valley

Floral and plummy, with a dense core of spicy, brambly berry fruit. Warm flavors of mission fig and sasparilla are attractive. Good intensity, medium tannins and a nice finish round out this straightforward and exemplary Zinfandel. Its light-medium body is a nice change from the cumbersome styles often encountered.

1988 Grgich Hills Zinfandel
Sonoma County

This is a rich, dense wine with a big, opulent style, replete with tarry black raspberry flavors and fat luscious fruit. It has good balance and striking tannins. Light oak seems apparent on the nose, enhancing its sexy allure.

1990 Lytton Springs Zinfandel
Sonoma County

Faint aromas of cedar and boysenberry underscore the solid foundation of sweet-tart blackberry and sour cherry. Medium in body, with a medium finish and adequate acidity, this wine is rather closed, implying a good future. Warmer in alcohol, it is extremely food friendly and pairs well with both lamb and dry sharp cheeses.

1990 Nalle Zinfandel
Dry Creek Valley, Sonoma County

Well-balanced and elegant, this Zinfandel has medium body and long jammy flavors. Blackberry, raspberry and sweet vanilla embellish its concentration. Not a huge wine, but one that nonetheless packs a punch.

1990 Quivira Zinfandel
Dry Creek Valley, Sonoma County

Long and fruity, with aromatic, earthy forest floor aromas, this fuschia-colored Zinfandel is laden with plum, black pepper, jammy black raspberry and a touch of coffee bean. Intense in concentration, it is packed with ripe jammy fruit flavor. Delicious now, it will taste even better in a few years.

1990 Ravenswood Zinfandel
Sonoma County

Hints of cherry, tar and smoke dominate the flavor of this Zinfandel. Medium in body, it has generous flavors of black cherry and black plum. The ripe stone fruit is captivating and makes for a tasty wine.

1990 Storybook Mountain Zinfandel
Napa Valley

This powerful wine bursts with deep cherry flavor and a slight lacing of oak. It has great depth and balance, with firm tannins and long persistence. Its bright fruit flavors and fragrant aroma of fresh herbs are appealing.

PINOT NOIR

1990 Acacia "Carneros" Pinot Noir
Napa Valley

Bright and vibrant, with a soft attack and a silky texture, this wine sings of tart small red fruits, including raspberry and sour cherry. Hints of cinnamon and coriander lend an exotic note, and a taste of mint can be found in the finish. Good length and soft, supple tannins are just enough. A stylish, well-made wine with clean, classic Pinot Noir flavors.

1990 Byron Vineyard & Winery Pinot Noir
Santa Barbara County

An assertive wine with light-medium body and a refreshing, lively finish. Explosive flavors of cherry and black raspberry and a delicate nuance of cinnamon form the primary flavor profile, enhanced by mocha tones of sweet new oak. Supple and versatile, this wine is very compatible with food.

1990 Calera "Jensen Vineyard" Pinot Noir
Mt. Harlan, Hollister

A full-bodied Pinot Noir, with perfumed earth and opulent fruit. Ripe strawberries, red cherries and a light sweet toast are the standout flavors. Pleasantly intense and full in style, it has a Burgundian charm that makes up in power what it lacks in finesse. Great length and acidity.

1990 Chalone Vineyards Pinot Noir
Monterey County, Estate Bottled

Bright and lively, with aromas of cranberry, mature cherries and faint cedar, this is a Pinot of moderate intensity.

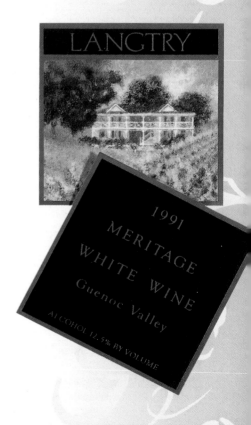

Toast and a flavor of bay leaf are unmistakable in the mouth, with great balance and depth and a clean, focused finish. Restrained in style despite its power.

1988 Etude Pinot Noir
Napa Valley

Rich and spicy, with a seductive perfume of violets, berries and Burgundian-like earth, this wine is medium in body, with soft tannins and long-lasting flavor. A well-made Pinot Noir, it starts out a bit closed, like a rose, then shows petal after beautiful petal.

1990 Gary Farrell "Allen Vineyard" Pinot Noir
Russian River Valley, Sonoma County

Wonderful and explosive, with a delightful intensity of raspberries, strawberries and red cherries and a slight presence of oak. Black cherry in color, this wine has good body and great persistence of flavor. Well-made, well-integrated and very refined.

1990 Robert Mondavi Pinot Noir
Napa Valley

A lively and refreshing Pinot Noir, with good plum and cherry flavors and a long clean finish. Cherry tomatoes and a kiss of mint are noticeable in the palate, and an earthy, dusty note offers additional complexity. Some oak peeks through the vibrant fruit. Almost transparent tannins give just enough structure to this tempting wine.

1990 Rochiolo Pinot Noir
Sonoma County, Estate Bottled

Powerful yet elegant, with an outstanding blend of earth and sweet oak tones and a delicately stated finish, this wine abounds with a proverbial fruit basket of flavors, with noticeable cherries, strawberries and a hint of anise. Round in style and medium in body, it is an outstanding example of Pinot Noir and reflects the attention to the fruit that this varietal demands.

1990 Saintsbury Carneros Pinot Noir
Napa Valley

Hints of earth, clove and cinnamon are layered over cherries, plums and crushed red berries. Concentrated, with a touch of spice and vanilla from the oak, this is a finely balanced Pinot Noir, lush and supple in texture, with a velvety mouthfeel and a long finish. Excellent with less oily styles of fish, such as tuna and salmon.

1990 Williams Selyem "Allen Vineyard" Pinot Noir
Russian River Valley, Sonoma County

Rich, layered and fascinating, this wine bursts with red plums and spicy cherry fruit. Defined spice notes of cumin and cinnamon and a noteworthy but subtle earth tone provide layers of flavor. As Beaune-like a Pinot Noir as you will find in California.

ITALIAN VARIETALS

1990 Atlas Peak Sangiovese
Napa Valley, Estate Bottled

Clean and vibrant, with explosive flavors of cranberry and pomegranate. A little like a Pinot Noir in style, this wine possesses enticing spicy qualities of coriander, cumin and dried flowers. Appropriate amounts of tannin and acidity give it a slightly lighter weight.

1990 Robert Pepi "Colline di Sassi" Sangiovese Grosso
Napa Valley

Strawberry and red cherry aromas enhance a center of dry earth. Medium in body and intensity, with soft tannins and a moderate finish. Reminiscent of Pinot Noir with its soft velvety fruit and immediate charm. This wine epitomizes elegance.

RHONE-STYLE VARIETALS

1989 Bonny Doon Vineyard "Le Cigare Volant"
44.6% Grenache, 12.2% Syrah, 43.2% Mourvedre

Firm and assertive aromas of violets, raspberries and anise, with a core of similar tastes in the mouth augmented by qualities of charred earth, pepper and boysenberry. Slightly meaty and earthy, this wine shows minimal evidence of wood aging. A big wine, it is beginning to show the gamey profile of the Rhone varieties.

1990 Joseph Phelps "Vin du Mistral" Le Mistral
52% Mourvedre, 26% Grenache, 9% Syrah, 7% Cinsault, 6% Carignan

Balanced and drinkable, with aromas of red plum and mature raspberry. Light oak and a hint of black pepper add interesting flavor notes to the nice definition of fruit. On the palate, some bing cherry comes out. Good acid balance and medium weight add to this truly tasty wine, which proves the merit of these varietals in California.

1991 Joseph Phelps "Vin du Mistral" Viognier
Napa Valley

Perfumed and intensely scented, with tropical aromas of pineapple, lychee and a hint of guava and mint. Rich and concentrated, this wine has sufficient length and body and a delayed fragrance of rose petals. It will develop even more complexity with moderate bottle aging.

1991 Qupe Syrah
Central Coast

Black pepper and crushed raspberries are apparent in the aroma of this medium-full-bodied wine. Soft but pleasant tannins provide the frame for the jammy crushed fresh fruit in the mouth. Interesting notes of molasses, brown sugar and lavender add complexity.

CHARDONNAY

1990 Arrowood Chardonnay
Sonoma County

Clean and rich, with almost muscular aromas of yellow apples and ripe green pears. An interesting taste of mandarin orange adds complexity on the palate, and extraordinary persistence prevails. This splendid wine has great distinctness and a bright future.

1990 Chalone Chardonnay
Monterey County

Full bodied and mouth-filling, with aromas of toast, pear and clove. An apparent but not overwhelming use of oak and very good intensity and concentration mark this wine. One of the few California Chardonnays with a true sense of "terroir," it has excellent balance and breed, with pleasantly youthful fruit and a sufficiently long finish.

1990 Chalone "Reserve" Chardonnay
Monterey County

Pear, apple and fresh flowers dominate the aromas of this full-bodied wine. It is sumptuous and round, with a rich center, a weighty intense palate, and a beautiful balance of fruit and sweet oak. This fine Chardonnay has the depth and power of a red wine and bursts forth with generous developed fruit.

1990 Chateau Montelena Chardonnay
Napa Valley

Elegant in a generous style, this wine is medium in body, with nice length and concentration, and good breed. Apple, spice, coconut and a lime quality of citrus dominate the nose. More lemon and vanilla are on the palate, with mouthfilling texture.

1990 Cuvaison "Carneros Reserve" Chardonnay
Napa Valley

Intense and brilliant, with crisp acidity, defined citrus flavors and excellent length. A trace of earth and spice overlay a nice element of toasty oak and pippin apples. Elegant and concentrated, this is one of the finest examples of Carneros Chardonnay. Should age gracefully.

1990 Far Niente Chardonnay
Napa Valley

Firm and tight, with superior definition and a snappy young finish, this wine is medium to full in body.

CALERA
JENSEN
Mt. Harlan Pinot Noir

1990

GROWN, PRODUCED & BOTTLED
BY CALERA WINE COMPANY
HOLLISTER, CALIFORNIA
Table Wine

RIDGE   1989
SANTA CRUZ
MOUNTAINS
MONTE BELLO

86% CABERNET SAUVIGNON, 12% MERLOT, 2% PETITE VERDOT
SANTA CRUZ MOUNTAINS   ALCOHOL 13.4% BY VOLUME
GROWN, PRODUCED AND BOTTLED BY RIDGE VINEYARDS
BW 4488, 17100 MONTE BELLO ROAD, CUPERTINO, CALIFORNIA

Honey, citrus and green pear flavors predominate, with an expansive lemon-lime finish. Spicy vanilla-flavored oak lends an appealing note to the fruit. An attractive, well-made wine that will develop with bottle age.

1990 Ferrari Carano Chardonnay
Alexander Valley, Sonoma County

Lush and supple, with balanced aromas of allspice, pear and wild flowers, this wine has distinctive flavors of green apple, sweet cream and tropical fruit. Stylish and spicy, it has incredible persistence and zippy acidity. Simply delicious, this Chardonnay is hard not to like.

1989 Ferrari Carano Reserve Chardonnay
Alexander Valley, Sonoma County

Round and honeyed, with bright acidity, a long, buttery finish and a sensational mouthfeel. Ripe peach and pear, mature tropical fruit and caramel form the nucleus of flavor, with nutmeg and other sweet spices providing grace notes. A sophisticated wine that shows deft wine-making skills yet remains true to the fruit.

1990 Flora Springs Chardonnay
Napa Valley, Barrel Fermented

Rich and ripe, with pronounced flavors of honey, mango and nectarine. Very smooth in the mouth, this wine is full in body and concentration, long and lingering with attractive yeasty notes. A fine effort in winemaking that respects the quality of the fruit.

1989 Grgich Hills Chardonnay
Napa Valley

Lemon, anise and butter form the base of this medium-full-bodied wine. Vanilla-tinged oak and tropical fruit add depth of flavor. This is a classic example of the best California Chardonnay: long-lasting, well-structured and full of complexity.

1989 Jordan Chardonnay
Alexander Valley, Sonoma County, Estate Bottled

An enormous wine with lasting flavors and dynamic full body. Lemon and loquat aromas are sandwiched nicely between the suggestion of oak aging and careful wine-making. Bold and full, this wine will please lovers of big-style Chardonnay.

1990 Matanzas Creek Chardonnay
Sonoma Valley

Pear, red apple and some pineapple, with complex notes of oak, toast and peach. Full in the mouth and suffi-ciently long, this is another fine effort from a top-notch producer. Classic and typical of Sonoma's opulent style, this Chardonnay has a striking bright gold appearance.

1991 Morgan Chardonnay
Monterey County

Pineapple, mango and ripe pear aromas, with plenty of toasty oak adding complexity. Silky in texture, with medium body, a soft, buttery finish, and toast and a lit-tle coconut in the aftertaste. A well-crafted wine, it should improve with bottle age.

1990 Mount Eden Chardonnay
Santa Cruz, Estate Bottled

Deep and full bodied, with layers of apple, pear and but-tered popcorn in the nose and lemon and light banana on the palate. Spicy new oak and an intense earthiness lend genuine pedigree to this wine. Complex in the fin-ish, it has good acidity and overall structure. A real keeper.

1990 Robert Mondavi "Reserve" Chardonnay
Napa Valley

Bold in nature, with pronounced aromas of butter, toast and rich oily fruit, this wine has tremendous concen-tration and full body, with a creamy-textured mouth-feel, a nice extraction of flavor, and a soft but stated fin-ish. Opulent in style, it should age well.

1990 Saintsbury Carneros Chardonnay
Napa Valley

Clove and butterscotch aromas add complexity to a basic fruit core of apple, pear and cantaloupe. Full and ripe in the mouth, with similar flavors and a rich waxy texture. Attractive in a full-bodied style, this is a real mouthful of wine, with satisfying concentration and a good finish.

1990 Saintsbury "Reserve" Chardonnay
Carneros, Napa Valley

Green apple, grapefruit and faint toast are the aromas of this wine, with sweet oak, citrus fruit and banana on the palate. Medium full in body, with good acidity and tremendous persistence. This is a very opulent style of Chardonnay, epitomizing balance of mature fruit and judicious use of oak.

1990 Simi Chardonnay
Sonoma County

Clean and compact, with an extreme nose of yellow apples and Crenshaw melon and a trace of oak. Rich vari-etal fruit with similar apple flavors on the palate and a long-staying finish. Defined and flavorful, this well-focused Chardonnay is as good with food as it is by itself.

1988 Sonoma Cutrer "Les Pierres" Chardonnay
Sonoma Coast

Candied pineapple and ripe green apple, with steely lean acidity. Integrated and balanced, this Chardonnay has a trace of mint and mineral overtones. Medium in body, with an endless finish and lively lemony-oak grace notes, it is well crafted and moderately complex. Zippy acidity should allow it to age well.

1990 Sonoma Cutrer
"Russian River Ranches Chardonnay"
Sonoma County

Green apple and cherimoya with a kiss of oak, good depth of flavor and some intensity. This wine explodes on the palate initially, then expands as it crosses the tongue. Balanced and adequately long, this wine has appealing flavors and deserves its reputation.

1990 Trefethen Vineyards Chardonnay
Napa Valley, Estate Bottled

A trace of vanilla on relatively steely acidity and a lemon/green apple quality of fruit. Medium full in body, with fine persistence and continuity of complexity as the wine crosses the palate. Traditionally one of the state's finest Chardonnays, this well-made wine lives up to its reputation. Most certainly a keeper.

1990 ZD Chardonnay
California

Ripe banana, custard and spicy oak aromas underline a surprisingly austere structure. Medium in body, with pineapple and other tropical notes in the finish. Good acidity and a warming persistence. More old fashioned in style than many, it is nonetheless quite tasty.

SAUVIGNON
& FUME BLANC

1991 Caymus Vineyards Sauvignon Blanc
Napa Valley, Barrel Fermented

Golden delicious apples and juicy green melon, with very crisp acidity and some smoky oak in the finish. Quite rich, with medium body and assertive apple and grapefruit flavors, this Sauvignon has an interesting nuance of honey. Distinctive in style, it is devoid of the grassiness that some dislike in Sauvignon Blanc.

1991 Duckhorn Sauvignon Blanc
Napa Valley

Light grass and fig aromas, with medium richness and bright acidity. Light herbal flavors and minimal oak, with seductive flavors of ripe melon in the middle palate. Fairly rich in style for a Sauvignon Blanc, this wine is one of the best examples of the varietal.

1991 Ferrari Carano Fume Blanc
Sonoma County

A wide spectrum of aromas is marked by fresh-cut herbs and a pleasing flinty mineral note. This wine has a ripe, lush impression in the mouth, with fig and Crenshaw melon flavors. It is a clean, bright wine with nice citrusy overtones, crisp acidity and moderate length.

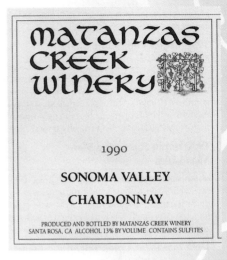

MATANZAS CREEK WINERY

1990

SONOMA VALLEY

CHARDONNAY

PRODUCED AND BOTTLED BY MATANZAS CREEK WINERY
SANTA ROSA, CA ALCOHOL 13% BY VOLUME CONTAINS SULFITES

ESTATE BOTTLED CHARDONNAY

1988

SONOMA-CUTRER

LES PIERRES

SONOMA COAST CHARDONNAY BOTTLED BY SONOMA-CUTRER, WINDSOR, CA. TABLE WINE

1991 Frog's Leap Sauvignon Blanc
Napa Valley

Light and angular, with lemon, green olive and lightly floral aromas, this wine is medium in body and quite concentrated. Lovely flavors of Meyer lemon and pink grapefruit dominate the palate. Quite long, with ample acidity, it is perfect with seafood.

1990 Grgich Hills Fume Blanc
Napa Valley

Classic grassy aromas, with traces of asparagus and green bell peppers. A hint of dill and sweet peaches in the mouth. Well made, with excellent body and balance. Interesting flavors of green olive and light smoke add a note of complexity to this varietally typical wine.

1990 Honig Sauvignon Blanc
Napa Valley

Melon, apple and honeyed pears, with a slight evidence of new oak in the aroma. Apricot and light herbs augment the melon in the mouth with an almost sweet impression from the exceedingly ripe fruit. Medium in both intensity and body, this wine has a pleasing silky texture.

1990 Matanzas Creek Sauvignon Blanc
Sonoma County

Ripe and rich, with delicate flavors of anise, straw and green grass, a firm core of fruit and a long, warm finish. A touch of grapefruit lends complexity. This Sauvignon Blanc has excellent varietal definition without being aggressive.

1991 Murphy Goode Fume Blanc
Alexander Valley, Sonoma County

Clean and refreshing, with a dominant anise and light pepper earthiness in the aroma. A soft attack gives way to pleasing flavors of Meyer lemon, Crenshaw melon and a trace of grassiness, which here is quite delightful. Light-medium in body, this dry Sauvignon has excellent structure and an enjoyable finish of gooseberries.

1990 Robert Mondavi Fume Blanc
Napa Valley

Assertive flavors of herbs, mineral and oak dominate the aroma of this wine. It has fairly good concentration and a medium to full body, with pleasant earthy nuances and a little melon. Well-balanced, it will be a favorite of those who prefer an oakier style of Sauvignon.

1991 Spottswoode Sauvignon Blanc
Napa Valley

Melon, fig and sun-warmed summer grass dominate the aroma of this fine wine. Light citrus and slightly under-ripe cantaloupe flavors, with creamy mild acidity and rich, assertive concentration. Great balance exists between the herbal/grassy and melon/fig notes. A little honey marks the finish of this tasty northern Napa Valley style.

WHITE MERITAGE WINES

1990 Benziger "A Tribute"
60% Sauvignon Blanc, 40% Semillon;
Sonoma Mountain

Flavorful aromas of pink grapefruit, cream and a little citrus mark this Meritage wine. A fairly rich mouthfeel, with ample acidity and a warm, satisfying finish. Curiously complex and beautifully assembled, it offers much enjoyment now but will certainly improve in the near future.

1990 Langtry Meritage
70% Sauvignon Blanc, 30% Semillon;
Guenoc Valley

An exemplary white wine, with good structure and a combination of lime, kumquat and dried fig aromas. Medium in body, it has adequate acidity and a mouthful of flavor. Pairs well with a variety of foods, including poultry, veal and pork.

1991 Merryvale Meritage
72% Sauvignon Blanc, 28% Semillon;
Napa Valley

Slightly grassy, with notes of green melon, fresh herbs and a kiss of smoky oak. Nice intensity of fruity flavors in the mouth, with ample body, good balance and a long finish. The oak comes through on the palate as slightly more charry than smoky. This wine works well with food.

GEWURZTRAMINER

1991 Chateau St. Jean Gewurtzraminer
Sonoma County

Apricot, a touch of honey and wild flowers are pronounced, along with spicy notes of clove and cinnamon. An attractive hint of sweetness adds a thought-provoking foil. The wine has nice weight in the mouth and a pleasing finish.

1991 DeLoach Gewurztraminer
Russian River Valley, Sonoma County

Refreshing and crisp, with aromas of honeydew melon, rose petal and sweet juicy citrus fruits, and a very healthy acidity. A sweet vanilla quality is present on the palate in addition to melon, banana, rosewater and apricot notes. Medium in body and quite flavorful.

1991 Joseph Phelps Gewurztraminer
55% Napa, 25% Sonoma, 20% Mendocino

Perfumed with floral and grapefruit aromas and flavored with allspice, cinnamon and some anise. Light earth tones and saturation of taste make for a full-bodied and mouth-filling wine. Dense and compact, it has a lovely light acidity that lends an appealing finish.

1990 Navarro Gewurztraminer
Anderson Valley, Mendocino

Pear, subtle citrus blossom and a trace of resin distinguish the bouquet. Delicate flavors of honeysuckle and pear predominate, with a restrained smoky characteristic. Adequate acidity and medium-full-bodied, this wine is extremely well balanced and provocative.

JOHANNISBERG RIESLING

1991 Chateau St. Jean Johannisberg Riesling
Sonoma County

This wine is marked with distinctive floral notes and a sweet fruity perfume. Light medium body in the mouth and sufficient length. The classic nectarine and delicate peach notes are here.

1991 Jekel Vineyards Johannisberg Riesling
Arroyo Seco, Estate Bottled

Sweet apples, honey and apricot aromas, with moderate power and a soft, lingering finish. Medium in body, with a kiss of sweetness, this wine has flavors of spiced apples and some attractive minerals and earth. Sufficient acidity and a pleasant finish.

1990 Joseph Phelps Johannisberg Riesling
Napa Valley

Soft and medium bodied, with an intricate aroma of apricot, nectarine and a trace of green apple, this wine has a dry, sharp finish. Perfumed and concentrated, with delicate fruit flavors in the mouth and a very clean, refreshing acidity. Light, elegant and enjoyable, it has enticing floral characteristics.

1991 Navarro White Riesling
Anderson Valley, Mendocino

Lemon, citrus sorbet and flower blossoms mark this wine's distinctive aroma. An earthy flavor of slate and lush lemon and lime in the mouth, with complex tropical notes in the long finish. Crisp, racy acidity balances a slight sweetness. Delicious.

1991 Trefethen White Riesling
Napa Valley

Always one of the state's finest offerings in White Riesling, this wine possesses refreshing lemon and nectarine aromas and a light-medium body, with a nice finish. Rose petals and citrus flavors dominate the palate, and good acidity indicates a healthy future. This wine consistently ages well.

JORDAN SPARKLING WINE COMPANY

CHENIN BLANC

1990 Chappellet Chenin Blanc
Napa Valley

A slightly spicy note of peppermint lends exquisite complexity to the tropical fruit flavors that dominate the bouquet. Always a standout among California Chenin Blancs, this wine is light-medium in body, with exceptional acidity and a long, racy finish. Should continue to develop nicely in the bottle.

1991 Dry Creek Vineyards Chenin Blanc
Sonoma County

Ripe melon, guava and hints of peach in the bouquet, with moderate concentration, youthful acidity and a fine structure. Medium in body, this wine is packed in the mouth with red apple and lemon, a little flower blossom and fresh, fresh fruit. Clean and flavorful.

1991 Hacienda Dry Chenin Blanc
Clarksburg, Sonoma County

Bright and fresh, with a basket of fruit in the aroma, including notes of pineapple, peach and mature Rome Beauty apples. This wine has medium power and intensity, with a slight sweetness and ample acidity. Well made and tasty, it calls for a warm day and good friends.

1991 Pine Ridge Chenin Blanc
Yountville Cuvee, Napa Valley

Refreshing and soft, with friendly aromas of honeydew melon, menthol and tart lemons, and a light but adequate body. This wine has a pleasant intensity and appealing melon and light grassy flavors in the mouth. Beautiful balance of fruit, sugar and acidity.

1990 Robert Mondavi Chenin Blanc
Napa Valley

Red apples and a trace of orange zest distinguish this forward wine. The flavors seem centered in the front of the mouth and echo the perfume with the addition of delightful floral qualities. Soft and lush in body with good acidity, it is an excellent wine for day-to-day drinking.

1990 Simi Chenin Blanc
Sonoma County

Youthful white fruit including melon and pear, with a hint of mineral and spicy earth and a faint scent of vanilla and sweet cream. The palate shows pear and citrus fruits with a dash of the same earthiness. Medium in concentration and body, with good length and crisp acidity, it is excellent with poultry and light fish dishes.

BRUT SPARKLING WINES

Domaine Carneros Non Vintage Cuvee
Carneros, Napa Valley

Vibrant apple and kumquat aromas, with substantial intensity and beautiful fruit flavors. Medium in body and silky in texture, this sparkling wine has excellent persistence and just the right amount of light earth. It is distinguished by terrific balance and lively acidity.

Domaine Chandon Brut Cuvee Non Vintage
Napa Valley

Light to medium body, with good balance and adequate length. Melon, hay and notes of ripe fruit dominate the bouquet, with similar flavors on the palate. A slight nuttiness adds an appealing accent, and sound acidity provides good length. Nice flavor and broad appeal.

1989 Iron Horse Vineyards Brut Cuvee
Green Valley, Sonoma County

Hints of green apple, pear and a trace of licorice, with soft yeasty notes in the aroma and a brilliant, bracing acidity. Forward fruit in the mouth with a slightly steely, austere texture. Refreshing and intriguing, this wine has a clearly defined personality, very fine bead and excellent bubble formation.

Maison Deutz Brut Cuvee Non Vintage
78% San Luis Obispo, 22% Santa Barbara

Nuances of rich earth and apple blossoms are dominant in the nose, with flavors of bread dough, toast and yeast in the palate. Medium intensity of perfume, clean citrusy apple fruit and crisp acidity. This wine's delicate symmetry makes it a sumptuous aperitif.

Mumm Cuvee Napa Brut Prestige Non Vintage
Napa Valley

Small, well-defined streams of bubbles, with a light bread crust aroma and a formidable foundation of lemon and green apple fruit. Medium in body, with lively acidity and a refreshing long finish. Somewhat creamy in texture, this wine has great style.

Roederer Estate Brut Cuvee Non Vintage
Anderson Valley, Mendocino

Green pear, wild flowers and an unusual perfume of light soy, cocoa and biscuits, with delicate layers of flavor and a velvety, silky texture. A kiss of vanilla lends complexity, and a nutty finish adds appeal. A sophisticated wine, it has a long, lingering finish.

1985 Schramsberg Brut Reserve
Napa Valley

Medium straw in color, with a faint trace of copper and a steady fine mousse, this wine is marked by aromas of tart green and ripe yellow apples, toasted bread and honey — a most agreeable perfume. Medium in body and richness, it has tart apple flavors and a kiss of strawberry in the finish, which is quite long and expansive. Complex and well constructed.

BLANC DE NOIRS

1989 Iron Horse Vineyards Wedding Cuvee
Napa Valley

Bright and intense, with apple, quince and a dash of honey as the standout aromas. A superb balance of fruit to acid to sweetness, with a soft lively finish of red apple and ripe pear. A pleasing quality of hay and mineral adds appealing earth elements to this bone-dry wine.

Mumm Cuvee Napa Blanc de Noirs Non Vintage
Napa Valley

An attractive appearance, with a pale salmon color and very fine beading. Forward cherry blossom and red apple fruit with a hint of dry earth in the nose. Medium in body with brisk acidity, this well-made wine has crisp cherry flavors in the palate and a very velvety mouthfeel.

1988 Schramsberg Blancs de Noirs
Napa Valley

Elegance and refinement distinguish this wine, with red cherry and faint wild strawberries in the aroma and a velvety mouthfeel. Medium in body, it has a spicy berry flavor and a hint of blood orange in the finish. Nice acidity and balance.

BLANC DE BLANCS

1987 Iron Horse Vineyards Blanc de Blancs
Green Valley, Sonoma County

Toasted nuts, green pippin apples and fragrant flowers in a medium-full-bodied style, with balanced acidity and suitable length. Roasted hazelnuts, toasted bread crust and bright apple flavors are in the mouth, with a faint scent of coffee bean. A well-made Blanc de Blancs, exemplary of the style.

1988 Scharffenberger Blanc de Blancs
Mendocino County

Bursting with lemon, butter and pear aromas, this wine has bold, rich flavors on the palate. Honeyed pear, soft lemon and a hint of underripe pineapple underscore a complex, harmonious package. Long and slightly tart, this wine has racy acidity and a mild floral finish.

1987 Schramsberg Blanc de Blancs
Napa Valley

Light gold in color, with defined, consistent streams of small bubbles and a light-medium body. Aromas of

California Orange Muscat
sweet Dessert wine
Vintage 1990
Produced & Bottled by
Andrew Quady, Madera, California
alcohol 15% by volume
750 ml.

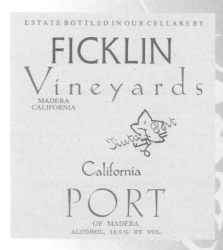

ESTATE BOTTLED IN OUR CELLARS BY

FICKLIN
Vineyards
MADERA
CALIFORNIA

California

PORT
OF MADERA
ALCOHOL, 18.5% BY VOL.

peach and earth dominate, with an underlying note of Meyer lemon. An adequate persistence of flavor echoes the nose, and exquisite Chardonnay flavors stamp the palate. Good balance and admirable intensity.

ROSE SPARKLING WINES

1989 Iron Horse Vineyards Brut Rose
Green Valley, Sonoma County

Almost orange-red in hue, with tremendous intensity and beautiful streams of fine bubbles. Hints of raspberry and strawberry give the bouquet great richness, while flavors on the palate follow the nose. Very long and lingering, with great breeding.

Scharffenberger Brut Rose Non Vintage
Mendocino County

Clean and subdued, with a pale coppery pink hue, moderate length and the muted strawberry, dry toast and earthy notes of Pinot Noir. Strawberry appears again on the palate. Not as overtly fruity as many examples, this is a serious, well-made wine with excellent balance and restraint.

1988 Schramsberg Cuvee de Pinot Brut Rose
Napa Valley

Gorgeous salmon pink in hue, with a sweet Pinot Noir nose and tremendous texture. This elegant wine has sound intensity and firm fruit, with faint raspberry and red berry qualities and attractive yeasty elements. A well-made showcase for Pinot Noir, it has a complex, dry finish.

PORTS & DESSERT WINES

1990 Bonny Doon Vineyard "Vin de Glaciere" Muscat Canelli
California

Playful and luscious, with fresh flavors of lychee, apricot and tangy tangerine. A trace of toffee and almond comes through in the mouth, and an engaging finish sings of golden raisins and lemon. Truly hedonistic.

Ficklin California Port Non Vintage
Madera, Estate Bottled

Prunes, tobacco, orange and a trace of menthol in the aroma, with a full, warm mouthfeel and nice intensity of flavor. Buttery nuts, menthol and jam on the palate add complexity. Ripe and somewhat coarse, this wine has pleasing attributes of wood-aging melded with dense, attractive fruit flavors.

1989 Frog's Leap "Late Leap-Le Baiser Magique" Late Harvest Sauvignon Blanc
Napa Valley

A delicious wine packed with flavors of peach, honey, buttered nuts and a generous note of spice and vanilla. A strong floral honey flavor in the mouth, with just a hint of lemondrop and peach. Full and rich on the palate, it has a slightly nutty flavor that comes through in the finish.

1990 Joseph Phelps Scheurebe Late Harvest
Napa Valley

A light gold hue, with stunning aromas of ripe fig, peaches and sweet spice and a balanced acidity. Concentrated and full, with cinnamon and mace in the finish. This clean, well-made wine is delicate for such substance, with a splendid balance of sweetness to acidity and abundant flowery attributes.

1989 Joseph Phelps Vineyards "Delice du Semillon" Late Harvest
Napa Valley

Orange, honey, melon and faint citrus in the bouquet, with a delicate amount of sweet oak. Orange peel, cantaloupe and peach are standout flavors on the palate. This wine has power, richness and tremendous persistence. Lovely with rich fruit desserts.

1989 Navarro "Cluster Select" Late Harvest White Riesling
Anderson Valley

Dark gold in color, with seductive aromas of sweet cream, vanilla and ripe, deep apricot. Peach and honeyed nuances come out in the mouth, and a lovely flavor of candied pineapple characterizes the finish. Full and rich in body, it has ample acidity for a wine of such weight, balancing out the sweetness. Luscious.

Quady Non Vintage Port "Starboard-Batch 88" Rich Ruby
Amador County

Rich and mature, with sweet floral and spicy notes and a jammy quality of ripeness. Medium in both weight and body, this wine demonstrates elements of development without sacrificing any of its captivating fruit flavors. Chilled, it could easily be enjoyed as an aperitif.

1986 Quady Vintage Port "Frank's Vineyard"
Amador County

Plums and black fruit, with plowed earth in the nose and a weighty palate of huckleberry, blue plums and rich earth. An intense wine, it has great concentration and massive power, with a prolonged finish that shows its youth. Very classic in style, this wine has tremendous potential.

THE NAPA VALLEY WINE AUCTION

The Napa Valley Wine Auction is *the* social event of the year in Napa Valley. Since its debut in 1981, the auction has become recognized as a major wine function, attracting bidders from around the world. The event has raised millions of dollars to benefit local health-care facilities.

Vintners and private collectors throughout Napa Valley donate old, rare and collectible wines for the auction, which takes place on the grounds of the Meadowood Resort Hotel in St. Helena.

The auction caps three day of events sponsored by the Napa Valley Vintners Association. Wineries throughout the county hold special food and wine events, including brunches prepared by gourmet chefs. Lunch and dinner parties, barrel tastings, wine seminars and food pavilions showcase the nation's premier winegrowing region.

On the eve of the auction, Meadowood hosts a four-course Vintner Dinner, created by chef Henri Delcros of Meadowood and other guest chefs. The dinner, which is open to the public, is held under Meadowood's giant outdoor tent. Tickets to the event are available separately from the auction.

Some 1,500 guests are expected annually for the auction, with more than 500 bidders raising their paddles in the bidding.

In 1994, the Napa Valley Wine Auction will be held June 9-12. For an invitation, contact the auction director at 707-963-5246.

WITH NEARLY 60 YEARS OF WINEMAKING EXPERIENCE IN THE NAPA VALLEY, the Robert Mondavi family is proud to have been part of Northern California's food and wine revolution. Thanks to the innovative cooking and great wines that began to emerge here in the mid-sixties, America's tables have changed forever.

When I started my winegrowing career in 1937, wine critics, experts and consumers agreed that the only internationally recognized fine wines came from Europe. After I had been in the business for 25 years, I challenged that assumption. By then I knew that California's North Coast regions had the climate, soil and grape varieties to produce wines in the same league as Europe's best. Today, the world's most respected critics give our wines rave reviews, and collectors everywhere prize them.

Introduced by Robert Mondavi

Robert Mondavi is founder and chairman of the Robert Mondavi Winery in Oakville, Napa Valley, and an internationally respected authority on wine.

Success is also measured by growth. When my family founded the Robert Mondavi Winery in Oakville in 1966, it was one of only 26 wineries in the Napa Valley. Today, there are more than 165 wineries in the Napa Valley, and more than 725 in California — a tribute not only to the fine wines we produce, but also to the public's appreciation of their quality.

At the Robert Mondavi Winery, we view wine as part of our culture and heritage, integral to gracious living. Wine has been with us since the beginning of civilization. It feeds both the body and the spirit, adding pleasure, creativity and happiness to life.

The Wine Country

Whether you are a wine aficionado or a novice eager to learn more, *AM/PM's* guide to Wines & Wine Country is invaluable. You'll find many of the best wines described by Northern California's Master Sommeliers, along with wineries to visit, places to stay, restaurants to enjoy and attractions to discover in both Sonoma and the Napa Valley. Before you start your journey, however, share a glass of wine and a toast with us: to good friends, good food and good wine, the things that make life worth living. Cheers!

Thank you: Dwayne March, Jennifer Wolf, EPIC Models

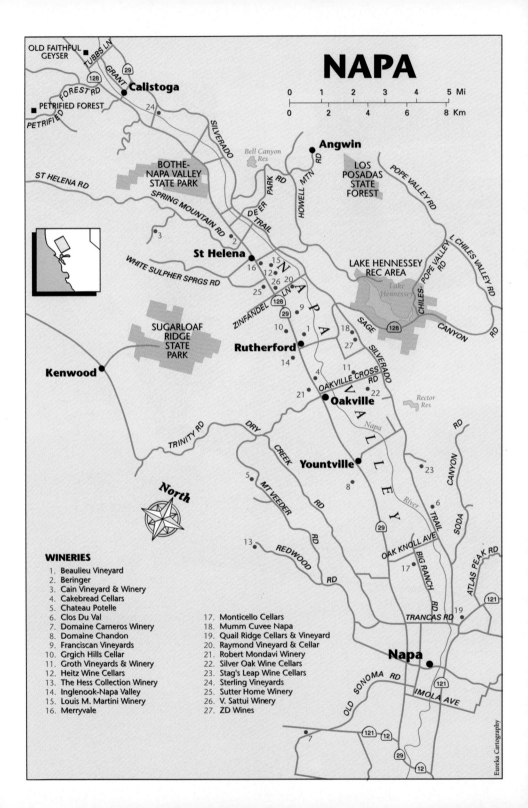

NAPA INFORMATION

BED & BREAKFAST INNS

Ambrose Bierce House, St. Helena 707-963-3003
Bordeaux House, Yountville 707-944-2855
Brannan Cottage Inn, Calistoga 707-942-4200
Burgundy House, Yountville 707-944-0889
Churchill Manor, Napa......................707-253-7733
La Residence, Napa 707-253-0337
Old World Inn, Napa 707-257-0112
Pine Street Inn, Calistoga 707-942-6829
Pink Mansion, Calistoga....................707-942-0558
Silver Rose Inn, Calistoga 707-942-9581
Wine Way Inn, Calistoga 707-942-0680

BIKE RENTALS

Napa Valley Cyclery, Napa 707-255-3377
St. Helena Cyclery............................707-963-7736

GLIDER RIDES

Calistoga Gliders 707-942-5000

GOLF

Chimney Rock Golf Course, Napa 707-255-3363
Napa Community Golf Course 707-255-4333
Silverado Country Club......................707-257-0200

HORSEBACK RIDING

Wild Horse Valley Ranch, Napa 707-224-0727

LODGING

Accommodations Referral..................707-963-8466
Napa Valley's Finest Lodgings 707-257-1051
Napa Valley Reservations 707-253-2929
Wine Country Reservations................707-257-7757

MUSEUMS & WINE HISTORY

Napa Valley Wine Library, St. Helena
.... 707-963-5145
Sharpsteen Museum and Sam Brannan Cottage
Calistoga..707-942-5911
Silverado Museum, St. Helena 707-963-3757

PICNIC SUPPLIES

Oakville Grocery, Oakville 707-944-8802

TOURS

Wine Adventures 707-944-8468
Napa Valley Excursions.....................707-252-6333
Napa Valley Wine Train 707-253-2111

VISITOR INFORMATION

Calistoga Chamber of Commerce 707-942-6333
Napa Chamber of Commerce 707-226-7455
St. Helena Chamber of Commerce 707-963-4456
Yountville Chamber of Commerce 800-959-3604

NAPA VALLEY DIRECTORY

POINTS OF INTEREST

BALE GRIST MILL
St. Helena / 707-963-2236

English physician Edward T. Bale married into Sonoma's Vallejo family in the 1840s and was given a land grant near St. Helena. An early entrepreneur, Bale noted an increase in the region's corn and wheat crops and in 1846 built a flour mill on a creek three miles north of town. The mill saw continuous use until 1905. Now a state historic park, the mill's 36-foot waterwheel has been restored and is back in operation. Grinding demonstrations are given every Saturday and Sunday at 1PM and 4PM.
Open daily 10AM to 5PM

BOTHE-NAPA VALLEY STATE PARK
St. Helena / 707-942-4575

Coastal redwoods, Douglas fir, oak and madrone are interlaced with hiking trails, campgrounds, picnic areas and a swimming pool on 2,000 acres, open mid-June through Labor Day. It's a cool respite from the hot valley floor in the summertime. Reservations are advisable for camping, especially in summer: 800-444-PARK.
Open daily 8AM to sunset

OLD FAITHFUL GEYSER OF CALIFORNIA
Calistoga / 707-942-6463

Calistoga's Old Faithful shoots its beautiful plume of steam and water skyward at intervals of approximately 40 minutes day and night. The boiling water and vapor roar out of the ground at 350 degrees and rise to 60 feet or more. Barometric pressure, the moon, the tides and tectonic stresses along the California coast determine the exact height and time of the eruption.
Open daily 9AM to 6PM in summer; 9AM to 5PM in winter

WINES & WINE COUNTRY

Where the Wine Country Experience Begins...

Yountville

Shops, Dining & Accommodations

Napa Valley's Finest

**One Hour North of San Francisco
Visitors Information (800) 959-3604**

PETRIFIED FOREST
Calistoga / 707-942-6667

The slow petrification of redwoods, covered by ash when nearby Mt. St. Helena was an active volcano millions of years ago, is dramatically displayed here. A 20-minute walking trail will lead you to the "Queen of the Forest," an 80-foot-long and 12-foot-diameter petrified redwood, or "The Monarch," 126 feet long and four feet in diameter.

Open daily 10AM to 6PM in summer; 10AM to 5PM in winter

ROBERT LOUIS STEVENSON STATE PARK
Mt. St. Helena, Calistoga / 707-942-4575

Not many know that the famous Scottish author of *Treasure Island* and *Dr. Jekyll and Mr. Hyde* once called the Napa Valley home. Robert Louis Stevenson and his bride moved into a vacant miners' bunkhouse near an abandoned mine in Mt. St. Helena's Silverado City following the town's fruitless "Silver Rush." Stevenson later wrote a series of sketches called *The Silverado Squatters* based on their idyllic 1880 summer there. A marble tablet in the beautiful park (day use only) marks the spot of Stevenson's cabin. Fans of the author's work should also visit the Silverado Museum in St. Helena.

Open daily 8AM to sunset

EXCURSIONS

ADVENTURES ALOFT
P.O. Box 2500, Yountville / 707-255-8688

Adventures Aloft offers champagne balloon flights that let you experience the Napa Valley from a bird's eye view. Float above the vineyards and hills, completely relaxed and confident, while an experienced pilot guides the way. The entire excursion lasts between three and four hours, and lives on in your memories forever. All flights depart in the early morning ($165 per person, half-price for children 8-12). Hotel and massage packages are also available.

Daily; reconfirm reservations 24-hours prior to flight date

BALLOON AVIATION OF NAPA VALLEY
P.O. Box 2500, Yountville / 707-944-4400

Called the "ultimate California experience" by *The New York Times*, a champagne balloon flight with Balloon Aviation is not to be missed. Now celebrating its 19th year in business, Balloon Aviation provides an unforgettable adventure above the Napa Valley.

Daily; reconfirm reservations 24-hours prior to flight date

CALISTOGA GLIDERS
1546 Lincoln Ave., Calistoga / 707-942-5000

Want to experience total freedom and breathtaking views while soaring in a glider over miles and miles of vineyards? Calistoga Gliders will provide just the vehicle for your sense of adventure and will guarantee a unique and exhilarating morning or afternoon. Gliders hold one or two passengers.

Flights begin daily at 9AM all year

SPAS

CALISTOGA VILLAGE INN & SPA
1880 Lincoln Ave. at the Silverado Trail
Calistoga / 707-942-0991

Nestled in the tranquil Napa Valley vineyards and close to the Mayacamas Mountains, Village Inn & Spa is dedicated to relaxation. Mud baths, massages, salt scrubs, seaweed wraps, herbal wraps and natural facials are available in various combination spa packages, and accommodations are comfortable with an array of modern amenities. Mineral water swimming pool, sauna and jacuzzi are also available. Some rooms feature Roman tubs or private whirlpools.

Doubles & suites $50 - $150

DR. WILKINSON'S HOT SPRINGS
1507 Lincoln Ave., Calistoga / 707-942-4102

Dr. Wilkinson's renowned full spa services are available to the public as well as to guests staying in its comfortable lodgings. You'll enjoy three mineral pools, mud baths, massage, whirlpool baths, steam rooms and a state-of-the-art salon offering facials, acupressure facelifts, hand and foot massage and makeup application. Reservations are advised.

Singles $44- $84; doubles $49- $94

GOLDEN HAVEN HOT SPRINGS
1713 Lake St., Calistoga / 707-942-6793

Let your tensions dissolve at the Golden Haven Spa and Resort, located in a quiet neighborhood just five minutes from the center of Calistoga. Pamper yourself with a complete range of relaxing treatments, including massage, herbal facials, hot mineral pools and private mud baths, for both couples and individuals. Walk-in spa reservations are welcome. For an overnight stay, you'll find a variety of comfortable accommodations, some with kitchenettes, private sauna and jacuzzi.

Singles & doubles $49- $105

LINCOLN AVENUE SPA
1339 Lincoln Ave., Calistoga / 707-942-5296

Lincoln Avenue Spa has taken Calistoga mud to a new level of luxury. A mud treatment here features rejuvenating and health-giving herbs combined with a fine warm clay mixed to order for each client. You'll find many Spa packages that allow you to combine a body mud treatment with a facial or massage, including the popular Ultimate Pamper Package, a 4½-hour extravaganza of relaxing self-indulgence. The Spa is open every day from 9AM to 9PM, and both reservations and walk-in appointments are welcome.

YOUNTVILLE

Yountville's beautiful Beard Plaza

Yountville is a walking town full of small encounters with history, where an old door or odd fence suddenly strikes the viewer with its beauty, and mental photographs are forever engraved in the memory. Surrounded by hills and vineyards, Yountville's "Old Town," with its trees leaning over irregular streets, is like a poem to the past, blending seamlessly with the town's newer sections.

In the seventeenth century, the Wappo Indian tribe had a large encampment and trading center here. Even the Plains Indians would make the long journey to the Napa Valley to trade for the Wappo tribe's renowned obsidian arrowheads.

George Yount visited the Napa Valley in 1831 while on a hunting expedition. Four years later, Mexican General Mariano Guadalupe Vallejo gave him a land grant to most of the region. Yount planted the Napa Valley's first vineyard in the 1840s and founded Yountville in 1855.

Today, Yountville evokes a world many long to return to, if only for a day or two. Peaceful yet dynamic, it beckons visitors with its yellow fields of mustard in the spring and its lush grapevines laden with fruit in summer and fall. In the heart of Yountville, Beard Plaza abounds with seasonal flowers, a focal point for both residents and visitors who appreciate this unique town: a place to shop, eat, sip a glass of wine and savor life at a relaxed pace.

SHOPPING

ANTIQUE FAIR
6512 Washington St. at Mulberry, Yountville / 707-944-8440

French walnut, mahogany, oak and cherry furniture is displayed in a pristine, uncluttered 3,000-square-foot environment. Proprietors George and Alice Rothwell import a most inspiring collection of antique French goods as well as accessories for home and attire. Since merchandise sells quickly, new stock is brought in every week. Antique Fair's reputation as purveyors of fine antiques has been impeccably upheld for 21 years of business and promises to continue for many years to come.
Open daily

BEARD PLAZA
Washington Street, Central Yountville

Located in the heart of historic Yountville, beautiful Beard Plaza is within walking distance of outstanding restaurants, accommodations and shops. Constructed in 1985 by the Beard family, one of the oldest families in Yountville, the plaza abounds with colorful flowers that change seasonally. Many interesting specialty shops, including two not-to-be-missed galleries, **RASberry's** and **Images Fine Art**, are located in the plaza, making this a popular place to meet and relax for visitors to this charming town.
Open daily

CALISTOGA DEPOT
1458 Lincoln Ave., Calistoga

The second oldest train station in California and a historic landmark, the Calistoga Depot has been turned into a charming bazaar of boutiques and restaurants, including some housed in restored railcars.

MAIN STREET
St. Helena

In St. Helena, Highway 29 becomes Main Street, lined with 19th century false-front buildings housing shops, craft and antique stores and eateries.

OVERLAND SHEEPSKIN CO.
6505 Washington St., Yountville / 707-944-0778

Located at the original site of the Southern Pacific train station in the Whistle Stop center, Overland Sheepskin Co. offers handmade, natural and unique merchandise. You'll find fabulous sheepskin and leather coats, handmade rugs and, of course, seat covers, as well as leather luggage, boots, purses and accessories. Also not to be missed: fashionable cotton and denim clothing for men and women, including a great selection of canvas jackets. Overland Sheepskin Co. is open every day from 10AM until 6PM and until 8PM on Fridays and Saturdays. Another Overland Sheepskin Co. is located in San Francisco at 21 Grant Street.
Open daily

VINTAGE 1870
6525 Washington St., Yountville / 707-944-2451

You can spend an entire day exploring Vintage 1870, a restored, 122-year-old winery complex housing 40 exquisite specialty stores. Shop for antiques, art, crafts, imported goods, gourmet cookware, gifts, clothing, jewelry, handmade chocolates and more; have lunch or a snack at **Red Rock Vintage Cafe, Yountville Pastry Shop, Cafe Kinyon** or **Compadres Mexican Bar & Grill**, or enjoy the lovely picnic garden; and taste the fine wines of the Napa Valley at **Winewrights Wine Shop** tasting bar, and take a bit of Napa Valley home with you. Vintage 1870 is open every day from 10AM until 5:30PM.
Open daily

WASHINGTON SQUARE
Washington & Madison Sts., Yountville

Just off Highway 29, Washington Square is a small, open-air village of cottage-like shops with shingled roofs and bricked walkways. Start with an early morning balloon flight from **Napa Valley Balloons** or a cup of coffee from **Java Express**. Then, enjoy a day of shopping at gift and fashion stores such as **Pentacle, Trish's** and **Threads**. Dine on imaginative American cuisine at **California Cafe's** outdoor tables or superb Italian specialties at **Ristorante Parma**. Complete your visit with wine tasting at **Audubon Cellars**, a beauty treatment from **Details** or a relaxing massage at **Massage Werkes**.
Open daily

GALLERIES

DONLEE GALLERY OF FINE ART
1316 Lincoln Ave., Calistoga / 707-942-0585

Wander through Donlee Gallery's four rooms of fine Southwestern painting and sculpture and the informative staff will put both the connoisseur and neophyte collector at ease. Pastoral Calistoga is the perfect setting to enjoy Howard Carr's bold, colorful still lifes and Santa Fe scenes.
Open daily

IMAGES FINE ART
6540 Washington St., Beard Plaza
Yountville / 707-944-0404

This showplace gallery features limited edition graphics, sculpture and original art. The friendly, knowledgeable staff will assist you with all your art needs. Nationally and internationally known artists represented by Images of Fine Art include Alvar, Behrens, Delacroix, Earle, Erte, Fairchild, Gorman, Hatfield, Markes, McKnight, Neiman, Orlando and more than 40 others. Worldwide shipping and financing available.
Open daily

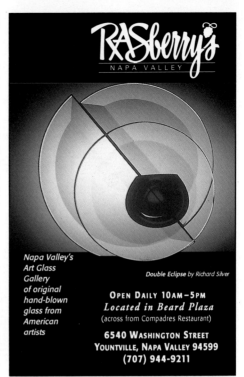

WINES & WINE COUNTRY

WITH STERLING VINEYARDS, YOU'LL GET MORE THAN A TASTE OF THE WINE COUNTRY

At Sterling Vineyards, we believe that the more you know about wine, the more you enjoy it. That's why we offer a variety of half-day and full-day "courses" on wine that can be made to order, so to speak.

Our refreshingly fun and informative courses give you or your group a one-of-a-kind opportunity to learn all about how wine is made and how to enjoy it.

And if your group can't come to the wine country, we'll bring the wine country to you. The pleasure is ours.

For more information, call the School toll-free at 1-800-955-5003. Or write us at the Sterling Vineyards School of Service and Hospitality, P.O. Box 365, Calistoga, California 94515.

I. WOLK GALLERY
1235 Main St., St. Helena / 707-963-8800

The I. Wolk Gallery features a unique, sophisticated and comprehensive collection of contemporary paintings, works on paper and sculpture by established and emerging artists from the San Francisco Bay Area, Santa Fe, Los Angeles, Chicago and New York City. The emphasis is on new realism, and exhibitions change regularly. Call for information on current shows. The gallery is open from 10AM until 5:30PM.
Closed Tuesday

RASBERRY'S ART GLASS
6540 Washington St., Beard Plaza
Yountville / 707-944-9211

The works of nearly 100 contemporary American glass artists combine to make RASberry's the only museum-quality art glass gallery in the Napa Valley. The collection includes scent bottles, wine goblets, paperweights, vases, plates and sculptural forms. All pieces are signed by the artist, and most are numbered limited editions.
Closed Tuesday

WINERIES

BEAULIEU VINEYARD
1960 St. Helena Hwy. 29, Rutherford / 707-963-2411
TOURS, TASTING & RETAIL SALES

The Beaulieu Vineyard Visitors Center is located in the Rutherford Square complex. Beaulieu is best known for their varietals, particularly the acclaimed Cabernet Sauvignon.
Monday through Sunday: 10AM to 5PM

BERINGER
2000 Main St., St. Helena / 707-963-7115
TOURS, TASTING, RETAIL SALES & GIFTS

The winery's most unique features are the spectacular Rhine House, a copy of the Beringers' ancestral home in Germany, and the hand-hewn aging tunnels carved out of the mountainside. Beringer is the oldest continuously operating winery in the Napa Valley and a current leader in vineyard-designated wines. Both current and Private Reserve wines are available for tasting.
Daily: 9:30AM to 6PM summer; 9:30AM to 5PM winter

CAIN VINEYARD AND WINERY
3800 Langtry Rd., St. Helena / 707-963-1616

The mountaintop Cain Vineyard and Winery is dedicated to the creation of its proprietary Cabernet blend, the Cain Five. Some 100 acres of the five Bordeaux varieties (Cabernet Sauvignon, Merlot, Cabernet Franc, Malbec and Petit Verdot) have been planted here on steep terraces dramatically cut into hillsides facing north, east, south and west. These parcels form a stunningly diverse collection from which to draw the Cain Five. Cain does not welcome walk-in visitors. If you wish to visit, please call ahead to make arrangements.
Tours & tasting by appointment

CAKEBREAD CELLARS
8300 St. Helena Hwy., Rutherford / 707-963-5221
TASTING & RETAIL SALES

Cakebread Cellars is located in the heart of the Napa Valley, on Highway 29 between Oakville and Rutherford. Founded in 1973, Cakebread specializes in three varietals: Sauvignon Blanc, Chardonnay and Cabernet Sauvignon. Cakebread Cellars' style emphasizes finesse and balance. The winery also produces two reserve wines, a Chardonnay Reserve and a Rutherford Reserve Cabernet Sauvignon.
Retail sales daily: 10AM to 4PM. Tours & tasting by appointment

CHATEAU POTELLE
3875 Mt. Veeder Rd., Napa / 707-255-9440
TASTING & RETAIL SALES

Located high on Mt. Veeder at the end of a twisting road, Chateau Potelle creates elegant wines that respect the unique personality of the winery's grapes. The secret is a separate harvesting, fermenting and aging of each vineyard according to soil type. The smashing results: their 1986 Chardonnay graced the tables of the Inaugural Dinner for President Bush, and their 1990 Chardonnay sold for the highest bid in the history of the Napa Valley Wine Auction.
Open Friday through Monday noon to 5PM. Closed December to March

CLOS DU VAL
5330 Silverado Trail, Napa / 707-252-6711
TOURS, TASTING, PICNIC, RETAIL SALES & GIFTS

Founded in 1972 by French winemaker Bernard Portet, Clos Du Val has successfully established its label among the world's finest. Clos Du Val produces award-winning Cabernet Sauvignon, Merlot, Zinfandel, Pinot Noir, Chardonnay and Semillon from estate vineyards in Napa Valley's Stags Leap and Carneros districts. Located on the scenic Silverado Trail in Napa, the winery is surrounded by its Merlot vineyard, with a traditional French rosebush planted at the end of each row.
Daily: 10AM to 5PM. Tours by appointment

DOMAINE CARNEROS WINERY
1240 Duhig Rd., Napa / 707-257-0101
TOURS, TASTING, & RETAIL SALES

Owned by Champagne Taittinger, Domaine Carneros Winery produces super-premium sparkling wines exclusively from Carneros appellation grapes. This beautiful region, with its cool climate, is known for superb Pinot Noir and Chardonnay grapes, which together give Domaine Carneros sparkling wines their characteristic delicacy and creaminess. Enjoy a glass with complimentary hors d'oeuvres in the elegant salon or on the sunny

WINES & WINE COUNTRY

terrace overlooking the rolling Carneros vineyards. Designed in the tradition of the Taittinger Chateau de la Marquetterie, the dramatic Domaine Carneros winery is only 50 minutes from San Francisco on Highway 121/12 between the towns of Sonoma and Napa.
Daily: 10:30AM to 5:30PM May to October; 10:30AM to 4:30PM Friday through Tuesday November to April

DOMAINE CHANDON
1 California Dr., Yountville / 707-944-2280
TOURS, TASTING, RESTAURANT & RETAIL SALES

The winery, owned by Moet-Hennessy Louis Vuitton, harvests acreage in the Carneros area and the Napa Valley. Domaine Chandon produces six million bottles annually of *méthode champenoise* sparkling wines, and offers a tour that illuminates the age-old art of champagne making. Plan to visit Le Salon, where wine may be purchased by the glass or bottle and is served with complimentary hors d'oeuvres, or stay for a delightful meal at the winery's four-star restaurant.
Daily: 11AM to 6PM May to October; 11AM to 5PM Wednesday through Sunday November to April

FRANCISCAN VINEYARDS
1178 Galleron Rd., north of Rutherford / 707-963-7111
TASTING, WEEKEND TOURS & RETAIL SALES

This winery offers the visitor an array of gold-medal-winning wines for tasting. The hospitality center sells current and rare inventory wines at special prices and displays antique viticultural equipment and corkscrews.
Daily: 10AM to 5PM

GRGICH HILLS CELLAR
1829 St. Helena Hwy., Rutherford / 707-963-2784
TOURS, TASTING & RETAIL SALES

Grgich Hills Cellar was established in 1977 through the efforts of Miljenko "Mike" Grgich and Austin Hills of the Hills Brothers Coffee family. The stellar attraction is the rich and complex Chardonnay with flowery aromas and intense fruitiness. Other wines include a crisp Fume Blanc, a berrylike Zinfandel and a Cabernet Sauvignon worthy of aging. Visitors to the winery are offered the opportunity to purchase carefully selected and matured older vintages from the winery's collection.
Daily: 9:30AM to 4:30PM. Tours by appointment

GROTH VINEYARDS & WINERY
750 Oakville Crossroad, Oakville / 707-944-0290
TOURS, TASTING & RETAIL SALES

Located in the center of the Napa Valley, Groth Vineyards & Winery produces estate-grown Sauvignon Blanc, Chardonnay and Cabernet Sauvignon. Oakcross Vineyard, Dennis and Judy Groth's first purchase of 121 acres along Oakville Crossroad, produces all the Cabernet and Chardonnay fruit for Groth wines. In 1982, they added the 43-acre Hillview Vineyard just south of Yountville for Sauvignon Blanc and Merlot grapes. The

winery at Oakcross Vineyard was completed in 1990, with Nils Venge, part-owner and winemaker, responsible for producing 40,000 cases of wine annually.
Monday through Saturday: 10AM to 4PM for retail sales. Tours & tasting by appointment

HEITZ WINE CELLARS
436 S. St. Helena Hwy., St. Helena / 707-963-3542
TASTING & RETAIL SALES

Heitz winery was established in 1961 by Joe and Alice Heitz. Today, they are joined by their children, David, Kathleen and Rollie, making Heitz Cellars truly a family operation. The Heitz family is dedicated to producing outstanding wines, exemplifying an ongoing tradition of the art of fine winemaking in the Napa Valley. Among the renowned Cabernets are the Martha's Vineyard and Bella Oaks. Heitz is the only Napa Valley winery that produces Grignolino, Grignolino Rose and Grignolino Port.
Daily: 11AM to 4:30PM

THE HESS COLLECTION WINERY
4411 Redwood Rd., Napa / 707-255-1144
TOURS, TASTING & RETAIL SALES

Located 6½ miles up Redwood Road West from the Highway 29/Trancas intersection, this historic turn-of-the-century stone winery is home to Donald Hess's two passions: wine and art. Visitors enjoy a self-guided tour that includes an overview of the winemaking operation, an audio-visual presentation highlighting the four seasons of the mountain vineyards, and a permanent exhibition of Joanna and Donald Hess's contemporary art collection acquired over the past 25 years. The richly textured Hess Collection wines display the unique character of the grapes from estate vineyards on Mt. Veeder. Tastings are $2.50 per person.
Daily: 10AM to 4PM; groups by appointment only

INGLENOOK-NAPA VALLEY
1991 St. Helena Hwy., Rutherford / 707-967-3362
TOURS, TASTING & RETAIL SALES

The confluence of soil and climate has consistently produced the award-winning Cabernet Sauvignon for which Inglenook is famous. They have been producing wines since 1879 when Gustav Niebaum founded the winery. In recent years their Chardonnay, Pinot Noir, Sauvignon Blanc and Zinfandel have achieved acclaim as outstanding wines.
Daily: 10AM to 5PM. Tours 10:30AM to 4PM

LOUIS M. MARTINI WINERY
254 S. St. Helena Hwy, St. Helena / 707-963-2736 or 800-321-9463
TOURS, TASTING, RETAIL SALES, GIFTS & PICNIC

One of the oldest winemaking families in the Napa Valley, the Martinis built their winery in St. Helena in 1933. Today, third-generation winemaker Michael Martini specializes in Cabernet Sauvignon, Merlot, Barbera and Chardonnay. The tasting room frequently offers decade-old Cabernets and limited-release Vineyard Selection bottlings for tasting. Visitors are welcome to picnic in the winery's beautiful garden courtyard.

Daily: 10AM to 4:30PM

MERRYVALE
1000 Main St., St. Helena / 707-963-2225
TASTING, RETAIL SALES & GIFTS

Since 1983 when William Harlan, John Montgomery, the late Peter Stocker and Robin Lail established Merryvale Vineyards, the winery's reputation has grown nationally, and with the establishment of Merryvale's European office headed by Swiss partner Jack W. Schlatter, Merryvale's prominence has grown overseas as well. The secret is wine-maker Robert Levy's selection of grapes from premier vine-yards in the Napa Valley. His wines dictate their own style, reflecting the inherent qualities of both the grapes and their growing regions.

Daily: 10AM to 5:30PM. Group tours by appointment

MONTICELLO CELLARS
4242 Big Ranch Rd., Napa / 707-253-2802
TOURS, TASTING, PICNIC & RETAIL SALES

Founded in 1970 by Jay Corley, Monticello Cellars adopted its name and winemaking philosophy from Thomas Jefferson, one of America's first oenophiles. The winery's Jefferson House is a scaled-down replica of Jefferson's home in Charlottesville, Virginia. Adopting a "hands-off" approach, the winemaking team keeps cellar handling to a minimum, allowing the natural components of the grapes to craft the finished product: Pinot Noir, Merlot and two styles of both Chardonnay and Cabernet Sauvignon. To celebrate Jefferson's 250th birthday, Monticello Cellars will host special dinners and wine-tasting seminars throughout 1993. Visitors are welcome to enjoy the tasting room, the beautiful grounds and the picnic grove.

Daily: 10AM to 4:30PM. Tours at 10:30AM, 12:30PM & 2:30PM

MUMM CUVEE NAPA
8445 Silverado Trail, Rutherford / 707-942-3434
TOURS, TASTING, RETAIL SALES & GIFTS

On an oak-dotted hill with a wonderful view of the May-acamas Mountains, Mumm Cuvee Napa is home to some of the region's top *méthode champenoise* sparkling wines. Four sparkling wines are available by the glass or bottle, as well as a "tasting sampler" of three wines. A complimentary snack accompanies the wine.

Daily: 10AM to 5PM. Tours on the half hour from10:30AM to 3:30PM

WINES & WINE COUNTRY

QUAIL RIDGE CELLARS AND VINEYARDS
1055 Atlas Peak Rd., Napa / 707-257-1712

Quail Ridge makes its home in the historic Hedgeside Caves, handhewn more than a century ago. Founder and winemaker Elaine Wellesley established her reputation with her first vintage, a 1978 barrel-fermented Chardonnay. Other vintages include Sauvignon Blanc, Cabernet Sauvignon and Merlot.
Tours by appointment

RAYMOND VINEYARD & CELLAR
849 Zinfandel Lane, St. Helena / 707-963-3141
TASTING & RETAIL SALES

As fourth-generation Napa Valley vintners, Walter and Roy Raymond, Jr. have been bottling award-winning wines under their own label since 1971. Today, Raymond Vineyard & Cellar exemplifies the finest in Napa Valley wineries. With its beautiful grounds, friendly and knowledgeable staff, comfortable Visitor Center and first-class wines, Raymond is an enjoyable destination for visitors and residents alike. Wines featured in the tasting room include Chardonnay, Cabernet Sauvignon, Sauvignon Blanc and Private Reserve.
Daily: 10AM to 4PM. Tours by appointment

ROBERT MONDAVI WINERY
7801 St. Helena Hwy., Oakville / 707-963-9611
TOURS, TASTING & RETAIL SALES

Robert Mondavi is credited with leading the wineries of California to their current level of success. Since founding the winery in 1966, he has continued to produce world-class wines and to educate the public about wine and its proper role as a mealtime beverage of moderation. Complimentary tastings at the winery are part of the tours, and the wines change every day. Tastings of Reserve and older vintage wines are available for a nominal charge. Call for information on wine and food seminars and special tours.
Daily: 10AM to 4:30PM November to April; 9AM to 5PM May to October. Reservations recommended (extension 4312)

SILVER OAK WINE CELLARS
915 Oakville Cross Rd., Oakville / 707-944-8808
TASTING & RETAIL SALES

Winemaker and owner Justin Meyer vinifies only Cabernet Sauvignon — and he does it very well. With grapes from the Alexander Valley, Napa Valley and Bonny's Vineyard in Napa, Meyer produces Cabernets of unique complexity.
Tours by appointment Monday through Friday at 1:30PM

STAG'S LEAP WINE CELLARS
5766 Silverado Trail, Napa / 707-944-2020
TOURS, TASTING & RETAIL SALES

Warren and Barbara Winiarski founded the winery in 1972. The second vintage, a 1973 Cabernet Sauvignon, took top honors in the U.S.A. bicentennial Paris tasting.

It rocked the wine world that an obscure, new-world winery could surpass century-old wineries like Chateau Haut-Brion and Chateau Mouton-Rothschild. Although the winery is known for its Cabernet Sauvignons, the Stag's Leap Wine Cellar Chardonnays, Sauvignon Blancs and White Rieslings are consistently excellent, and the Merlots are outstanding.
Daily: 10AM through 4PM. Tours by appointment

STERLING VINEYARDS
1111 Dunaweal Ln., Calistoga / 707-942-5151
TOURS, TASTING, GIFT SHOP & RETAIL SALES

Sterling focuses on vintage-dated, estate-bottled Napa Valley varietals — Cabernet Sauvignon, Cabernet Blanc, Merlot, Sauvignon Blanc, Pinot Noir and Chardonnay. Visitors travel up the hill to the winery by aerial tramway, leaving their worldly cares behind. The design of the winery brings to mind an eastern Mediterranean monastery. The $6 visitor's fee includes the tram ride, a discount on wine purchases, and three tastings plus a "guest's choice."
Daily: 10:30AM through 4:30PM. Self-guided tours

SUTTER HOME WINERY
277 S. St. Helena Hwy., St. Helena / 707-963-3104
TASTING, GIFTS & RETAIL SALES

Originally built in 1874, Sutter Home was sold to the Sutter family in 1906. Mario and John Trinchero purchased the long-dormant winery in 1947. Sutter Home now leads the industry in producing several varietals, and the Trinchero family continues to welcome visitors to its popular tasting room and charming Victorian grounds. Garden tours are offered daily, and the tasting room features live music most Saturdays and holidays. Sutter Home has also introduced two new brands of non-alcoholic White Zinfandel and Chardonnay wines.
Daily: 9AM to 5PM; garden tours on the hour

V. SATTUI WINERY
White Ln. at Hwy. 29, St. Helena / 707-963-7774
TASTING, DELI, PICNIC, RETAIL SALES & GIFTS

Established in 1885 in North Beach, V. Sattui Winery was revived in 1975 by the founder's great-grandson, Daryl Sattui. Nestled amid towering oaks, his stone winery boasts award-winning vintages that garnered 41 gold medals in 1992 alone. The only winery in the Napa Valley to sell its entire production of wines directly from the winery, V. Sattui also houses a gift shop, gourmet deli, acclaimed cheese shop and two acres of tree-shaded picnic grounds.
Daily: 9AM to 6PM summer; 9AM to 5PM winter

ZD WINES
8383 Silverado Trail, Napa / 707-963-5188
TASTING & RETAIL SALES

Family owned and operated, ZD is a small winery located mid-valley on the Silverado Trail. Founded in 1969,

it is staffed by five members of the de Leuze family, including CEO Norman de Leuze and his winemaker son, Robert de Leuze. ZD produces Pinot Noir, Cabernet Sauvignon and a Chardonnay that has gained the winery international prominence. Tastings are $3 a glass, good toward purchase of wine.
Daily: 10AM to 4:30PM. Tours by appointment

RESTAURANTS

AUBERGE DU SOLEIL
180 Rutherford Hill Rd., Rutherford / 707-963-1211
Breakfast, lunch & dinner daily
WINE COUNTRY

Set on a hillside amid spreading oaks and grassy knolls, this unique wine country restaurant and inn has an unsurpassed view of the valley's vineyards. Auberge du Soleil, which means "inn of the sun," serves Wine Country cuisine hailed as brilliant by delighted gourmets. The restaurant has a 48-room inn for overnight accommodations.
Specialties: Roasted Sterling Salmon with Wild Rice, Root Vegetables, Wild Mushroom Broth; Braised California Pheasant with Savoy Cabbage, Portobello Mushrooms, Oregon Huckleberries; Roasted Mint Valley Rack of Lamb with Spinach & Goat Cheese Souffle

BRAVA TERRACE
3010 St. Helena Hwy. N., St. Helena / 707-963-9300
Lunch & dinner daily; closed Wednesdays November-April
AMERICAN

At the time of day when shadows grow long, Brava's tranquil terrace and surrounding greenery create the illusion of late afternoon in the South of France. Chef/owner Fred Halpert, who has studied with some of France's finest chefs, makes the restaurant a personal obsession. His seasonal menu ranges from basic to inspired, and unpretentious presentation and prices earn him a loyal following.
Specialties: Spicy Peppered Fried Oysters with a Romesco Sauce; Grilled Filet of Beef with Garlic Mashed Potatoes & Crispy Fried Onions; Grilled Veal Chop with Ragout of Local Mushrooms & a Tarragon-flavored Jus

CAFFE NAPA
1075 California Blvd., Napa / 707-253-9540
Lunch & dinner daily; Sunday brunch
AMERICAN

Located in the Inn at Napa Valley's atrium court, Caffe Napa offers a superb setting for dining. Enjoy a sunny ambiance by day, and lively entertainment by night in Joe's lounge. Specializing in pasta, seafood and mesquite grilling, Caffe Napa also offers award-winning

"Relax on the terrace deck while soaking up the warmth & beauty of California's wine country. After dining explore the adjoining gardens where Chef Halpert grows his fantastically fresh ingredients."

WINES & WINE COUNTRY

Meadowood
Napa Valley

A World Apart in the Napa Valley

Fireplace Suites, The Restaurant,
The Grill, Tennis, Golf, Croquet,
Pools, Hiking Trails, Wine School
and a new,
State-of-the-Art Health Spa

Meadowood Resort • 900 Meadowood Lane • St. Helena, CA 94574
TEL (707) 963-3646 FAX (707) 963-3532

Napa Valley wines.

Specialties: Oregano Pesto with Grilled Chicken Breast; Seafood Grill; Pork Tenderloin with Polenta; Warm Goat Cheese Salad

CALIFORNIA CAFE
6795 Washington St., Yountville / 707-944-2330
Lunch & dinner daily
CALIFORNIA/AMERICAN

Located in a picturesque vineyard setting, the California Cafe in Yountville is a favorite dining destination.

CHANTERELLE
804 First St., Napa / 707-253-7300
Lunch & dinner daily; Sunday brunch
MEDITERRANEAN

A charming restaurant adjacent to the Wine Train depot, Chanterelle gives a Mediterranean flavor to fresh Wine Country ingredients. The wine list is extensive, featuring reasonably priced Napa Valley wines. A light, airy decor of large windows and comfortable chairs and a relaxing, informal ambiance add to the dining enjoyment — as does the ample free parking.
Specialties: Medallions of Veal Sauteed with Fresh Artichoke Hearts, Sundried Tomatoes & Capers; Poached Salmon with Champagne Sauce & Fresh Basil; Rack of Lamb with a Hazelnut Crust, Cognac & Fresh Herbs

COMPADRES MEXICAN BAR & GRILL
6539 Washington St., Yountville / 707-944-2406
Lunch & dinner daily; breakfast Saturday & Sunday
MEXICAN

Housed in a historic building that was once a private home, Compadres has beautifully landscaped grounds and a brick patio ideal for warm-weather dining. The cuisine has a healthy dose of California style, and the festive ambiance lends itself to parties and celebrations. Compadres also offers a sensational breakfast on Saturdays and Sundays, and the best margarita in the Napa Valley.
Specialties: Carnitas: Lean Pork Roasted Slowly Served with Fresh Tortillas, Fresh Salsa, Frijoles Catrines, Fiesta Rice, Mexican Salad & Marinated Vegetables; Fajitas: Grilled Marinated Steak or Chicken Served Thinly Sliced with Grilled Onions & Peppers, Soft Tortillas, Salsa Fresca, Sour Cream & Guacamole

DOMAINE CHANDON
1 California Dr., Yountville / 707-944-2892
Lunch & dinner daily May-October, Wed-Sun off season
FRENCH

The architecturally dramatic restaurant is perched on an oak knoll at the Domaine Chandon winery. Chef Philippe Jeanty creates delicate, fresh lunch and dinner dishes that complement the Chandon sparkling wines. Reservations are recommended.
Specialties: Tuna Pepper Steak with Potato Puree, Leek

Coulis & Leek Tumbleweed; Sonoma Muscovy Duck Breast with Foie Gras & Brown Rice Stuffing & a Fig Merlot Sauce; Grilled Ribeye Steak with Garlic Potato Puree & a Cabernet Black Pepper Sauce

THE FRENCH LAUNDRY
6640 Washington St., Yountville / 707-944-2380
Dinner Wed-Sun
COUNTRY FRENCH

Relaxed and idyllic, The French Laundry has a reputation for friendliness and excellent cuisine in a beautiful garden setting.

THE GARDEN GRILL
Rancho Caymus Inn, 1140 Rutherford Rd.
Rutherford / 707-963-1777
Lunch daily; weekend brunch
COSTA RICAN/CENTRAL AMERICAN

The Garden Grill offers relaxed dining in a rustic early California dining room or the flower-filled courtyard of the Rancho Caymus Inn. Instead of sticking to the usual California cuisine, Chef Michael Weiler creates tantalizing dishes of Southwestern and Costa Rican inspiration. The Garden Grill makes a lovely private setting for weddings and parties as well as business retreats and conferences. But be warned: it's not open for dinner.
Specialties: Rock Shrimp & Hearts of Palm on Masa Griddle Cakes; Garlic-braised Lamb Shanks with Ancho Chili Polenta

MUSTARDS GRILL
7399 St. Helena Hwy., Yountville / 707-944-2424
Lunch & dinner daily
AMERICAN

Mustards is a favorite haunt of local vintners, winemakers, growers and cognoscenti. The mood is light and the conversation level high. Specialties include hardwood-grilled steaks, fish, fowl and rabbit. Interesting appetizers, salads and desserts are other fortes. The extensive wine list features small local wineries. You can also order from the bar's impressive collection of liqueurs, ports, madeiras and sherries, or try the sensational rum punch. Mustards Grill also prepares picnic food to go.
Specialties: Grilled Sonoma Rabbit with Mushrooms, Mustard & Bacon; Yucatan-style Chicken Breast on Black Beans with Mango Salsa

NAPA VALLEY WINE TRAIN
1275 McKinstry St., Napa / 707-253-2111
Operates daily
CALIFORNIA

Enjoy a movable feast on the Napa Valley Wine Train, a treat for the eyes as well as the palate. While the train chugs through the scenic wine country, passengers dine in a meticulously restored dining car appointed with etched glass, brass and mahogany. A second, more casual dining car serves a la carte sandwiches and light fare.

WINES & WINE COUNTRY

THE PENGUINS FISH GROTTO
1533 Trancas St., Napa / 707-252-4343
Lunch Mon-Fri; dinner daily
SEAFOOD

Born in Greece, chef/owner Denny Drossos adds dishes from his Mediterranean heritage to the house specialty, the freshest seafood available. Try the restaurant's delicious moussaka and lamb shish kabob combination. Penguins Fish Grotto also serves live Maine lobster, grilled fish, seafood salads and shellfish plates. Pasta, charbroiled steaks, veal dishes and housemade desserts are also on the menu. All are generously portioned and reasonably priced. The comfortable dining room and the friendly service have made Penguins Fish Grotto a favorite with locals for more than a decade.
Specialties: Bouillabaisse; Petrale Sole Dore; Abalone Steak; Prawns Scampi Provencale; Pacific Lobster Thermidor; Filet Mignon in Bearnaise Sauce Wrapped in Lean Bacon, Topped with Mushroom Caps; Veal Saltimbocca; Spaghetti Carbonara; Housemade Kahlua Cheesecake

PIATTI
6480 Washington St., Yountville / 707-944-2070
Lunch & dinner daily
ITALIAN

Chef Renzo Beronese took over the kitchen of Piatti and has maintained the Northern Italian style this warm, lively restaurant is famous for. With its large open kitchen and rustic decor of wood and terracotta tiles, Piatti feels just right for a relaxed meal in the wine country. The menu changes regularly, and the pizza and calzone are out of this world.
Specialties: Pappardelle Fantasia: Wide Saffron Fettuccine with Shrimp, Arugula & Fresh Tomato; Cannelloni Mamma Concetta: Homemade Cannelloni Filled with Ground Beef, Spinach, Ricotta, Mozzarella & Wild Mushrooms; Pollo Arrosto: Oak Wood Roasted Chicken with Rosemary Potatoes & Seasonal Vegetables

THE RESTAURANT AT MEADOWOOD
900 Meadowood Ln., St. Helena / 800-458-8080
Dinner daily; brunch Sun
WINE COUNTRY

Overlooking the beautiful golf course at the Meadowood Resort, the restaurant is a secluded oasis nestled in a small valley just off the Silverado Trail. High ceilings, large windows and spacious decks make the most of an idyllic setting, and the award-winning cuisine, combining Catalan, French and Italian influences, celebrates Napa Valley's fresh ingredients. The Restaurant at Meadowood now serves a Sunday brunch and afternoon tea. You can also enjoy breakfast and lunch in the

WINES & WINE COUNTRY

more casual Grill.

Specialties: Paella with Duck Sausage, Chicken, Mussels, Clams, Monkfish, Lobster, Calamari, Chorizo & Saffron; Pan-seared Scallops with Ratatouille Puree, Fennel & Saffron Oil; Roasted Loin of Venison with Apples, Mushrooms, Shallot Confit & Game Sauce

RISTORANTE PARMA
6795 Washington St., Yountville / 707-944-9509
Dinner Wed-Sun
ITALIAN

Chef/owner Pietro Elia invites you to enjoy authentic regional cuisine from his beloved Parma, Italy. This cozy European-style restaurant features white tablecloths, a warm mauve decor and contemporary original artwork from top San Francisco galleries. The music of renowned European artists relaxes diners as they enjoy homemade pasta, veal, chicken and fish entrees. The Parma also offers an extensive selection of fine Italian and Napa Valley wines.

Specialties: Agnolotti della Casa: Half-moon Pasta Filled with Roasted Peppers, Onions & Eggplant, with a Light Cream Tomato Sauce; Tortellini della Nonna: Veal Tortellini with Prosciutto in a Light Cream Sauce; Filetto di Agnello: Grilled Lamb Filet Served with Balsamic Vinegar Sauce & Mushrooms

RIVER CITY RESTAURANT
505 Lincoln Ave., Napa / 707-253-1111
Lunch & dinner daily
AMERICAN/CONTINENTAL

There's no trouble in this River City. With large windows overlooking the Napa River, the inviting restaurant features fresh seafood, steak, chicken and wonderful desserts served in a restful blue-and-gray dining room, or on an intimate patio shaded by lush oak trees. Two banquet rooms are available.

Specialties: Baked Halibut with Spinach, White Wine, Olives & Artichokes; Double Breast of Chicken with Sundried Tomatoes & Capers; Half Rack of Lamb with Mustard Sauce

RUFFINO'S RESTAURANT
645 First St. at McKinstry, Napa / 707-255-4455
Dinner Thurs-Tues; lunch Mon & Tues, Thurs & Fri
ITALIAN

A striking stucco building set behind an herb garden dotted with olive trees, Ruffino's Restaurant takes the garden indoors with plenty of greenery and privets that line the inviting entranceway. A lounge with a circular, mahogany bar, a dining room that overlooks the streets of Napa and terracotta floors complement the contemporary Northern Italian dishes prepared by proprietor/chef Joseph Ruffino.

Specialties: Spiedini alla Romano: Skewered Grill of Mozzarella & Bread with Warm Garlic Anchovy Butter; Baby Spinach Salad with Prosciutto, Pistachios, Asiago & Balsamic Vinaigrette; Osso Bucco

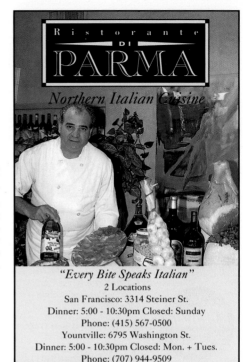

WINES & WINE COUNTRY

TERRA
1345 Railroad Ave., St. Helena / 707-963-8931
Dinner Wed-Mon
FRENCH/ITALIAN

In a stone structure dating back to 1884, two former Spago chefs opened Terra, featuring the simple, robust foods of Southern France and Northern Italy.

TRA VIGNE
1050 Charter Oak Ave., St. Helena / 707-963-4444
Lunch & dinner daily
ITALIAN

Tra Vigne serves innovative, mouth-watering cuisine in a striking setting, with a casual Northern Italian elegance. The Italian-inspired menu changes often, but there is always a sizable choice of appetizers, grilled meats and fish, homemade pasta, gourmet pizzas and California and Italian wines. Sunny days make for pleasant al fresco dining on Tra Vigne's vine-bedecked brick patio. A retail store on the premises, Cantinetta, offers food to go, as well as local and Italian wines.
Specialties: Pappardelle with Asparagus, Artichokes & Spinach in a Garlic Chicken Broth; Bruschetta with Just-made Mozzarella on a Warm White Bean Salad with Basil Oil & Arugula; Grilled Sonoma Rabbit with Teleme-layered Potatoes, Ovendried Tomatoes & Mustard Pan Sauce

ACCOMMODATIONS

AUBERGE DU SOLEIL
180 Rutherford Hill Rd., Rutherford / 707-963-1211

A Mediterranean-style inn on 33 acres of flowers and trees, Auberge du Soleil offers privacy, luxury and unsurpassed beauty. The 48 rooms are actually villas scattered among the trees, each with a private veranda and rustic decor of tiles and terracotta. The main building houses the renowned restaurant with its beautiful valley views and inviting bar. A swimming pool, tennis courts and small spa round out the amenities.
Doubles $215- $315

CALISTOGA VILLAGE INN & SPA
1880 Lincoln Ave. at the Silverado Trail
Calistoga / 707-942-0991

Nestled in the tranquil Napa Valley vineyards and close to the Mayacamas Mountains, Village Inn & Spa is dedicated to relaxation. Mud baths, massages, salt scrubs, seaweed wraps, herbal wraps and natural facials are available in various combination spa packages, and accommodations are comfortable with an array of modern amenities. Mineral water swimming pool, sauna and jacuzzi are also available. Some rooms feature Roman tubs or private whirlpools.
Doubles & suites $55-$150

THE CHATEAU HOTEL
4195 Solano Ave., Napa / 707-253-9300

This 115-room hotel has the atmosphere of a country inn combined with the conveniences of a city hotel.

CHURCHILL MANOR
485 Brown St., Napa / 707-253-7733

In an 1889 mansion — now a national historic landmark — Churchill Manor has ten delightful rooms, all with private baths. Each is unique and charming, furnished with antiques and filled with light. A hearty breakfast buffet is included in the price, and complimentary Napa Valley wines are served in the gracious parlor or on the veranda every evening.
Doubles $75- $145

COMFORT INN
1865 Lincoln Ave., Calistoga / 707-942-9400

The Comfort Inn provides many of the amenities of a resort at reasonable prices. A mineral-water swimming pool and whirlpool, sauna, steamroom, meeting room, remote-control television with premium cable channels, and complimentary Continental breakfast make your stay in the Napa Valley a pleasant one.
Doubles $55- $105

DR. WILKINSON'S HOT SPRINGS
1507 Lincoln Ave., Calistoga / 707-942-4102

In addition to having some of the best spa facilities in Calistoga, Dr. Wilkinson's is a great place to stay. Choose from 43 rooms in five separate buildings, including bungalows, a Victorian-style house, kitchen units and a honeymoon cottage, all opening onto a patio area and three mineral pools. Massage, mud baths, whirlpool baths, steam rooms and an all-new salon offering facials, acupressure face-lifts, hand and foot massage and make-up application make this a full-service spa.
Singles $44- $84; doubles $49- $94

HARVEST INN
One Main St., St. Helena / 800-950-VINO

Nestled in a 14-acre vineyard, the 54-room Harvest Inn, located 1½ hours north of San Francisco, is handsomely furnished with antiques and stained glass. Most of the English Tudor-style rooms have used-brick fireplaces, wet bars, refrigerators and dressing vanities. Firewood is free of charge and every room has color TV, air-conditioning, king or queen size beds and telephones. Public areas include two swimming pools, two spas and a wine bar. Two conference rooms can accommodate up to 80 people. Bike rentals are also available.
Singles & doubles $110- $325

INDIAN SPRINGS
1712 Lincoln Ave., Calistoga / 707-942-4913

Within walking distance of Calistoga's shopping and restaurants, Indian Springs offers suite accommodations with spa amenities. An Olympic-size mineral pool is on the premises, and mud baths and massage are offered.

INN AT NAPA VALLEY
1075 California Blvd., Napa / 707-253-9540

The Inn at Napa Valley is nestled in the heart of California's wine country, just 45 miles northeast of San Franciso. Relax in the comfort and elegance of two-room suites, each featuring two color televisions, a sofa sleeper and a wet bar with microwave, coffeemaker and refrigerator. Complimentary extras include a cooked-to-order breakfast and a beverage reception nightly from 5:30PM to 7:30PM. Other amenities: a heated indoor pool, spa and sauna, an outdoor pool and plenty of free parking. Golf, wineries, the Wine Train and much more are nearby. *Suites $129-$179*

MAGNOLIA HOTEL
6529 Yount St., Yountville / 800-788-0369

A lovely antique-filled hostelry in the quiet town of Yountville, the Magnolia Hotel is a romantic place to stay. The century-old main building features quaintly intimate rooms, while the newer Garden Court has large rooms with fireplaces and bay windows overlooking the pool and jacuzzi. All accommodations have private baths and include a full breakfast served family-style. *Singles & doubles $99-$189; suite $300*

MEADOWOOD RESORT HOTEL
900 Meadowood Ln., St. Helena / 800-458-8080

Located in its own miniature valley, Meadowood is a full-service resort, featuring golf, tennis, croquet and a new fitness spa. Meadowood also has an executive conference center. You'll find total privacy here, in charming one-bedroom suites nestled in the hillside, with views of the golf course, pool area or a mountain panorama. The Croquet Lodge, overlooking the perfectly manicured croquet lawns, houses an additional 13 guestrooms. The **Restaurant at Meadowood** and the casual **Grill** both overlook the golf and croquet lawns. *Singles & doubles $235-$500; suites $325-$500*

MOUNT VIEW HOTEL
1457 Lincoln Ave., Calistoga / 707-942-6877

Built in 1918 and enlarged in 1938, this historic landmark is a showplace of Art Deco and Victorian motifs. A cozy, fire-warmed lobby leads to two outstanding restaurants: **Valeriano's**, offering Northern Italian cuisine for dinner only, and **Johnny's**, a casual cafe for breakfast and lunch that becomes a lively lounge by night, with live music Thursday through Sunday. A recent addition to the hotel is the **Mount View Spa**, a

European spa with everything from Shiatsu massage to seaweed wraps. The large heated pool and hot tub are surrounded by palm trees and fountains. With 22 rooms, 8 suites, 3 renovated cottages and meeting facilities for 75 people, the Mount View Hotel is a year-round resort. *Singles & doubles $90-$105; suites $130-$165*

RANCHO CAYMUS INN
1140 Rutherford Rd., Rutherford / 707-963-1777

Rancho Caymus offers early California elegance in a unique hacienda setting. Built on land given to George Yount in the first land grant of the 1830s, the two-story inn offers small and large suites that surround a beautiful central courtyard. Each room has a separate sitting area, with wetbar and refrigerator, and a balcony or patio, and the four master suites also have kitchenettes and jacuzzi tubs. Handmade beds, handhewn beams and Mexican wallhangings reflect the handcrafted warmth of a bygone era. Relax in front of an adobe-style beehive fireplace with a bottle of special Rancho Caymus wine and enjoy the Southwestern cuisine of the **Garden Grill** for lunch or weekend brunch. Weddings and small meetings are a specialty. *Basic suites $115-$150; master suites $175-$275*

SILVERADO COUNTRY CLUB AND RESORT
1600 Atlas Peak Rd., Napa / 707-257-0200

A 1,200-acre resort and country club, Silverado features private cottage suites clustered around hidden courtyards and secluded swimming pools, two 18-hole championship golf courses and a 20-court tennis complex.

VILLA ST. HELENA
2727 Sulphur Springs Ave., St. Helena / 707-963-2514

A grand Mediterranean-style villa hidden in the Mayacamas Mountains above St. Helena, Villa St. Helena combines quiet country comfort with panoramic views of the Napa Valley vineyards. Romantic antique-filled rooms have private entrances and baths, and some have fireplaces. Walking trails crisscross the wooded 20-acre estate, and guests can also enjoy the tranquility of Villa St. Helena's spacious courtyard. *Singles & doubles $145-$225*

VINTAGE INN
6541 Washington St., Yountville / 707-944-1112

This 80-room contemporary country inn is located on a historic winery estate in the walking town of Yountville. Centered amidst some of Napa Valley's finest vineyards, the luxury resort offers pool, spa, tennis, cycling, hot air ballooning and meeting facilities. A complimentary California champagne breakfast is included. The Vintage Inn offers superb accommodations for year-round comfort, each with a wood-burning fireplace, whirlpool bath and many extras. *Singles & doubles $129-$189; suites $179-$199*

CALENDAR OF EVENTS

For specific dates, contact the Napa Chamber of Commerce at 707-226-7455.

JANUARY

GREAT CABARET OF THE NORTH BAY
Cabaret and concerts at the Domaine Chandon Winery in Yountville. The winery presents Monday evening concerts throughout the year, including the Great Performers Series from February through April.

FEBRUARY

VALENTINE WEEKEND EXCURSION
Romantic excursion aboard the Napa Valley Wine Train.

MARCH

NAPA VALLEY FOOD & WINE EXTRAVAGANZA
Wine and food paired by Napa chefs and winemakers, Christian Brothers Greystone Cellars in St. Helena.

APRIL

GREAT CHEFS AT ROBERT MONDAVI WINERY
Menu demonstrations by leading chefs from the United States and abroad at the Robert Mondavi Winery in Oakville. The chef program is offered four times a year: April, May, October and November.

MAY

NAPA VALLEY SENSATIONAL
Restaurants and wineries participate in a festival with food, wine and entertainment in downtown Napa.

JUNE

NAPA VALLEY WINE AUCTION
Auction of rare Napa wines culminates three days of events including a gala dinner, tastings and wine seminars throughout the valley. For information on this year's auction, see the special feature on the Napa Valley Wine Auction.

WINE COUNTRY POPS
Summer pops concerts at the Robert Mondavi Winery in Oakville.

NAPA COUNTY FAIR
Art, livestock shows and carnival attractions at the Napa County Fairgrounds in Calistoga.

JULY

FOURTH OF JULY CELEBRATIONS
Domaine Chandon Winery in Yountville has special festivities. The Napa Valley Wine Train features an excursion with a fireworks show. Events are also planned at the Napa County Fair, including fireworks and a parade down Lincoln Avenue in downtown Calistoga.

ROBERT MONDAVI SUMMER FESTIVAL
World-renowned jazz artists at the Oakville winery.

BASTILLE DAY CELEBRATION
Music, food and entertainment at Domaine Chandon Winery in Yountville.

JAZZ & ART FESTIVAL
Music, food and art at Veterans Memorial Park, Napa.

AUGUST

PICCOLA FESTA ITALIANA
Food, dancing and bocce ball contests on the grounds of the Charles Krug Winery in St. Helena.

NAPA TOWN & COUNTRY FAIR
Wine tasting, contests, rodeo and live entertainment at the Napa Valley Expo, Napa.

THE GREAT NAPA VALLEY DUCK RACE
Plastic ducks race down the Napa River. This popular event in downtown Napa includes food, wine and crafts.

SEPTEMBER

NAPA WINE FESTIVAL & CRAFTS FAIRE
Entertainment, food, wine and crafts in Napa.

HARVEST FESTIVAL
Harvest festival, featuring family games, music, dancing and a tasting at the Charles Krug Winery in St. Helena.

OCTOBER

YOUNTVILLE DAYS PARADE & FESTIVAL
Saluting Napa's agriculture. Parade, food, music and entertainment in downtown Yountville.

HOMETOWN HARVEST FESTIVAL
Wine and food, arts and crafts, music, dancing and a parade on Oak Street in St. Helena.

NOVEMBER

NAPA VALLEY WINE FESTIVAL
Wine tasting, dinner and silent auction of wines at the Napa Valley Expo, Napa.

FESTIVAL OF LIGHTS & HOLIDAY FAIRE
Holiday celebrations at Vintage 1870 and throughout downtown Yountville.

DECEMBER

CHRISTMAS BAZAAR
Holiday gifts at the Napa County Fairgrounds, Calistoga.

CHRISTMAS IN CALISTOGA
Appearance by Santa Claus, caroling and other events along Lincoln Avenue in Calistoga.

WINES & WINE COUNTRY

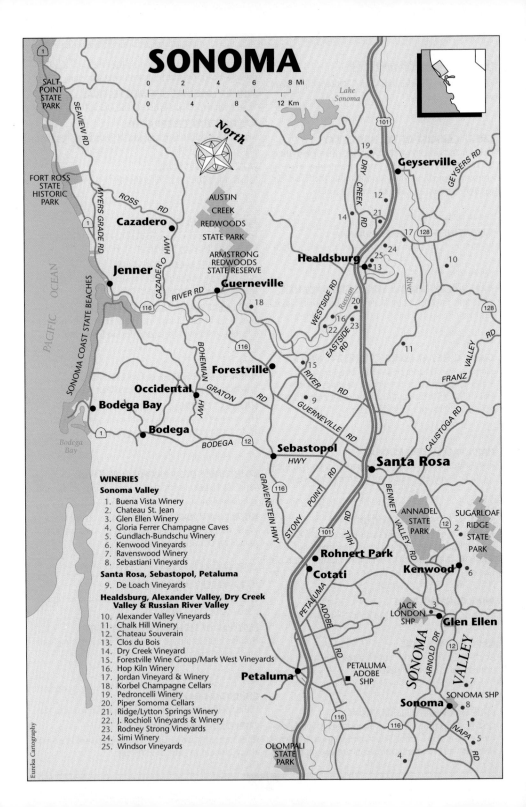

SONOMA

0 2 4 6 8 Mi
0 4 8 12 Km

North

SALT POINT STATE PARK

FORT ROSS STATE HISTORIC PARK

SEAVIEW RD

ROSS RD

CAZADERO HWY

Cazadero

AUSTIN CREEK REDWOODS STATE PARK

ARMSTRONG REDWOODS STATE RESERVE

Jenner

RIVER RD

Guerneville

18

MYERS GRADE RD

PACIFIC OCEAN

SONOMA COAST STATE BEACHES

116

BOHEMIAN HWY

GRATON RD

Forestville

15

Occidental

Bodega Bay

Bodega

1

BODEGA

12

Sebastopol

HWY

Bodega Bay

GRAVENSTEIN HWY

116

RIVER RD

GUERNEVILLE RD

9

STONY POINT RD

101

Lake Sonoma

101

19

Geyserville

GEYSERS RD

DRY CREEK RD

12

14

21

17 128

24

25 13

Healdsburg

Russian River

WESTSIDE RD

20

16
22 23

EASTSIDE RD

11

128

FRANZ

VALLEY RD

CALISTOGA RD

Santa Rosa

BENNET VALLEY

ANNADEL STATE PARK

SUGARLOAF RIDGE STATE PARK

12

2

Kenwood

6

WINERIES

Sonoma Valley

1. Buena Vista Winery
2. Chateau St. Jean
3. Glen Ellen Winery
4. Gloria Ferrer Champagne Caves
5. Gundlach-Bundschu Winery
6. Kenwood Vineyards
7. Ravenswood Winery
8. Sebastiani Vineyards

Santa Rosa, Sebastopol, Petaluma

9. De Loach Vineyards

Healdsburg, Alexander Valley, Dry Creek Valley & Russian River Valley

10. Alexander Valley Vineyards
11. Chalk Hill Winery
12. Chateau Souverain
13. Clos du Bois
14. Dry Creek Vineyard
15. Forestville Wine Group/Mark West Vineyards
16. Hop Kiln Winery
17. Jordan Vineyard & Winery
18. Korbel Champagne Cellars
19. Pedroncelli Winery
20. Piper Somoma Cellars
21. Ridge/Lytton Springs Winery
22. J. Rochioli Vineyards & Winery
23. Rodney Strong Vineyards
24. Simi Winery
25. Windsor Vineyards

Rohnert Park

Cotati

PETALUMA

ADOBE RD

Petaluma

PETALUMA ADOBE SHP

OLOMPALI STATE PARK

116

116

JACK LONDON SHP

3

Glen Ellen

ARNOLD DR

SONOMA VALLEY

12

7

Sonoma

SONOMA SHP

8

1

5

NAPA RD

4

Eureka Cartography

SONOMA INFORMATION

ART
Sonoma County ARTrails....................707-579-ARTS

BED & BREAKFAST INNS
Belle de Jour Inn, Healdsburg.............707-433-7892
Camellia Inn, Healdsburg 707-433-8182
The Estate, Guerneville 707-869-9093
Gaige House, Glen Ellen.....................707-935-0237
Haydon House, Healdsburg 707-433-5228
Hope-Merrill House, Geyserville 707-857-3356
Inn on the Plaza, Healdsburg 707-433-6991
Melitta Station Inn, Santa Rosa.........707-538-7712
Murphy's Jenner Inn, Jenner...............707-865-2377
Victorian Garden Inn, Sonoma 707-996-5339
Wine Country Inns..............................707-433-INNS

BIKE RENTALS
Spoke Folk Cyclery, Healdsburg..........707-433-7171

GOLF
Bodega Harbour Golf Links................707-875-3538
Fountaingrove Golf Course 707-579-4653
Healdsburg Golf Course.....................707-433-4275
Mountain Shadows Golf Course, Rohnert Park
....707-584-7766
Oakmont Golf Club, Santa Rosa........707-538-2454
Sonoma Golf Club 707-996-0300

HORSEBACK RIDING
Armstrong Woods Pack Station Trail Rides
....707-579-1520
Horseback Adventures........................707-887-2939

HOT AIR BALLOONING
Air Flambuoyant.................................707-575-1989
Once in a Lifetime..............................707-578-0580
Sonoma Thunder Balloon Safaris 707-LETSFLY

PICNIC SUPPLIES & CHEESEMAKING
The Creamery Store, Petaluma 707-778-1234
Healdsburg Charcuterie......................707-431-7213
Marin French Cheese Company 707-762-6001
Sonoma Cheese Factory, Sonoma 707-996-1931
Vella Cheese Company, Sonoma 707-938-3232

TOURS
Viviani Touring Company 707-938-2100
Wine Country Wagons.......................707-833-2724

VISITOR INFORMATION
Healdsburg Chamber of Commerce ...707-433-6935
Petaluma Chamber of Commerce 707-762-2785
Russian River Chamber of Commerce..707-869-9009
Sonoma County Visitors Bureau.........707-575-1191
Sonoma Valley Visitors Bureau...........707-996-1090

SONOMA & SONOMA VALLEY

POINTS OF INTEREST

JACK LONDON STATE HISTORIC PARK
Glen Ellen / 707-938-5216

The Wolf House ruins, The House of Happy Walls Museum and Beauty Ranch are the main attractions of this spectacular former estate of Jack London. An adventurous world traveler and writer (53 books in 16 years), London was buried overlooking the ruins of Wolf House, his dream house that mysteriously burned to the ground immediately after its completion in 1913. Restoration of the ranch buildings, including London's cottage, is now partially complete.

MISSION SAN FRANCISCO SOLANO DE SONOMA
1st St. East & Spain St., Sonoma / 707-938-1519

The northernmost in the chain of Spanish California missions, Mission San Francisco Solano is the oldest building in Sonoma, consecrated on July 4, 1823, and completed in 1841. In 1881, the church sold the adobe chapel and its adjoining residence, which were then used as a hay barn, winery and blacksmith shop. Now a state historic landmark, the mission and its museum are open to the public for tours.

WINES & WINE COUNTRY

SONOMA PLAZA
Sonoma / 707-996-1090

The largest town square in California, Sonoma Plaza was commissioned by General Vallejo in 1835 as a site for his troop maneuvers. Since then, the plaza has seen an aborted Indian uprising, several duels and the California Bear Flag Revolt. The plaza's grassy park is perfect for picnicking. There's a duck pond to enchant children, and plenty of room for sunning, strolling and soaking up the Sonoma ambiance.

VALLEJO'S HOME (LACHRYMA MONTIS)
Spain St. & 3rd St. West / 707-938-9559

Completed in 1852, General Mariano Guadalupe Vallejo's estate home is located half a mile from Sonoma Plaza, near a spring the Indians called *Chiucuyem* (crying mountain), latinized by Vallejo to Lachryma Montis. Built in the Victorian style, the house is surrounded by orchards, vineyards and decorative plants. The beautiful house, furnished with many of Vallejo's personal effects, is open to visitors and is part of the Sonoma State Historic Park.

SPAS

SONOMA SPA
457 First St. West, Sonoma / 707-939-8770

Located on the historic Sonoma Plaza, just one hour from the Golden Gate Bridge, Sonoma Spa is perfect for a day of relaxation. You'll enjoy all-natural health and beauty treatments, including massage, herbal facials, herbal wraps, foot reflexology and body mud treatments. Whether you're exploring the wine country or escaping city stress, you'll leave refreshed, rejuvenated and looking radiant.

WINERIES

BUENA VISTA WINERY
18000 Old Winery Rd., Sonoma / 707-938-1266
TOURS, TASTING, PICNIC, ART GALLERY, RETAIL SALES

After years of searching for the perfect grape-growing area in America, Hungarian Count Agoston Haraszthy planted his grapes in the romantic Sonoma Valley in 1857. The 2PM daily guided historical presentation celebrates the founding of the Sonoma wine country and Buena Vista's history as California's oldest premium winery. A wooded country path leads to the ivy-covered stone Press House, where you can sample award-winning wines, make purchases at the gourmet shop or visit the art gallery. The winery's picnic areas are perfect for a relaxed afternoon.
Daily: 10:30AM to 5PM summer; 10:30AM to 4:30PM winter

CHATEAU ST. JEAN
8555 Sonoma Hwy., Kenwood / 707-833-4134
SELF-GUIDED TOURS, TASTING, PICNIC, RETAIL SALES

Chateau St. Jean produces Chardonnay, Cabernet,

Sauvignon Blanc, Johannisberg Riesling, Gewurztraminer and *méthode champenoise* sparkling wines.
Daily: 10AM to 4:30PM

GLEN ELLEN WINERY
1883 London Ranch Rd., Glen Ellen / 707-935-3000
TASTING, RETAIL SALES

In 1980 the Benziger Family purchased the 100-acre Julius Wegener Estate, granted to Wegener by General Vallejo in 1868, and have continued the winery's history of grape growing and winemaking.
Daily: 10AM to 4:30PM

GLORIA FERRER CHAMPAGNE CAVES
23555 Hwy. 121, Sonoma / 707-996-7256
TOURS, TASTING, RETAIL SALES

Gloria Ferrer Champagne Caves, the first sparkling wine house to open in the famous Carneros region of Sonoma, invites visitors to its tasting room to sample its award-winning sparkling wines. Enjoy the spectacular view from the Vista Terrace or, in winter, warm yourself in front of a crackling fire. Guided tours are offered daily and include a walk through the subterranean caves. With its warm ambiance and decor, Gloria Ferrer provides visitors with a taste of Spain right in Sonoma.
Daily: 10:30AM to 5:30PM. Tours on the hour from 11AM to 4PM; group tours by appointment

GUNDLACH-BUNDSCHU WINERY
2000 Denmark St., Sonoma / 707-938-5277
TASTING, PICNIC, NATURE HIKES, RETAIL SALES

While small in size, this enterprise is large in stature and renowned for wines of the highest quality.
Daily: 11AM to 4:30PM

KENWOOD VINEYARDS
9592 Sonoma Hwy., Kenwood / 707-833-5891
TASTING, RETAIL SALES

Producer of premium varietal wines, Kenwood is housed in a historic Sonoma County barn.
Daily: 10AM to 4:30PM

RAVENSWOOD WINERY
18701 Gehricke Rd., Sonoma / 707-938-1960
TOURS, TASTING, PICNIC, RETAIL SALES

Built of stone and nestled in a quiet valley close to Sonoma's historic plaza, Ravenswood is an award-winning producer of Zinfandel, Cabernet Sauvignon and Merlot. The small winery also holds weekend barbecues in the summer, from May 15th to Labor Day.
Daily: 10AM to 5PM

SEBASTIANI VINEYARDS
389 4th St. East, Sonoma
707-938-5532 or 800-888-5532
TOURS, TASTING, RETAIL SALES

This 89-year-old winery produces complex, elegant wines. The winery hosts a large collection of hand-

Jordan®

Elegance in a Bottle

JORDAN VINEYARDS
PO BOX 878
HEALDSBURG, CALIFORNIA
95448

707 431 5250

carved wine casks. Professionally trained guides conduct tours at regular intervals throughout the day. Follow the signs throughout Sonoma to reach this distinctive winery. *Daily: 10AM to 5PM. Bus groups by reservation only*

RESTAURANTS

BLUM'S JAVA CAFE
452 First St. East, Sonoma / 707-939-8081
Breakfast, lunch & dinner daily
BISTRO

An informal cafe right on Sonoma's historic plaza, Blum's Java offers fresh, reasonably priced bistro fare. You can get anything from pastas and vegetable and fruit salads to creative daily specials such as chicken satay and risotto with ratatouille. Morning starters might be a cracked wheat bran Belgian waffle topped with whipped cream and berries or a croissant with chicken-apple-sausage-scrambled egg, jack cheese and housemade hot mustard. Don't forget to start your morning with one of several brewed coffees or a fabulous espresso drink, perhaps the chocolate raspberry truffle. The cafe opens early for bagels, scones, muffins and other light fare. Blum's Java Cafe also has Italian gelati, great on a hot summer day, and live music on Friday and Saturday.
Specialties: Caesar Salad; Mediterranean Pita Pocket; Spinach Quiche; P.L.T (Pancetta, Lettuce & Tomato Sandwich); Grilled Eggplant Sandwich; Hot Reuben

THE CAFE
Sonoma Mission Inn & Spa
18140 Sonoma Hwy. 12, Boyes Hot Springs / 707-938-9000
Breakfast, lunch & dinner daily
ITALIAN

At the north end of the Sonoma Mission Inn & Spa, The Cafe offers Italian cuisine with an innovative twist. Casual and lively, the cafe has a daily lunch and dinner special, in addition to its regional Italian dishes. The cafe has a full bar, with cocktails and wine tastings offered at the Wine Bar.
Specialties: California Pizza with Eggplant, Goat Cheese & Sundried Tomatoes; Grilled Pacific Swordfish, Artichoke Salsa & Wilted Spinach; Herb-roasted Garlic Chicken with Natural Juices & Grilled Polenta

DEPOT 1870 RESTAURANT
241 First St. West, Sonoma / 707-938-2980
Lunch Wed-Fri, dinner Wed-Sun
ITALIAN

A historic stone building just off Sonoma's Plaza is home to Depot 1870. The country-style dining rooms overlook a garden and poolside terrace, creating a romantic, relaxed atmosphere for award-winning Chef Michael Ghilarducci's innovative Northern Italian cuisine. Subtle, elegant sauces, lavish portions, an extensive Sonoma Valley wine list and moderate prices make Depot 1870

a favorite of locals and visitors alike.
Specialties: Housemade Ravioli Di Pomodori Al Bosco; Green Peppercorn Steak; Fresh Local Seafood; Tiramisu; Housemade Ice Creams & Sorbets

EASTSIDE OYSTER BAR & GRILL
133 East Napa St., Sonoma / 707-939-1266
Lunch Mon-Sat, dinner daily, brunch Sun
CALIFORNIA

Opened last September, Eastside Oyster Bar & Grill has won raves from Bay Area food writers.

THE GRILLE
Sonoma Mission Inn & Spa
18140 Sonoma Hwy. 12, Boyes Hot Springs / 707-938-9000
Lunch Mon-Sat, dinner daily, brunch Sun
SONOMA CUISINE

In the luxurious Sonoma Mission Inn & Spa, The Grille is located off the lobby. The elegant dining room features a seasonal menu, prepared with fresh local products. With a full bar, excellent service and an outstanding wine list with European, California and more than 200 premium Sonoma County wines, the restaurant offers sumptuous dining in the wine country. An innovative, low-calorie menu is also available for lunch and dinner.
Specialties: Roast Pork Tenderloin; Grilled Swordfish with Penne Pasta; Sonoma Leg of Lamb; Grilled Black Angus New York Steak

KENWOOD
9900 Sonoma Hwy. at Warm Springs Rd.
Kenwood / 707-833-6326
Lunch & dinner Tues-Sun
FRENCH

Enjoy the bucolic view from Kenwood's sunny deck as you feast on imaginative, colorful, light French country fare.

L'ESPERANCE
464 1st St. East, Sonoma / 707-996-2757
Lunch & dinner Wed-Mon
FRENCH

Located just off Sonoma Plaza, the restaurant serves classic French dishes such as coarse duck pate and rack of lamb.

ORESTE'S GOLDEN BEAR
1717 Adobe Canyon Rd., Kenwood / 707-833-2327
Lunch & dinner Wed-Sun
ITALIAN

The Golden Bear serves authentic Italian cuisine created by Chef Adriano Orsi, who renamed the restaurant in honor of his father, Oreste.

PIATTI
405 First St. West, Sonoma / 707-996-2351
Lunch & dinner daily
ITALIAN

A lively restaurant in the landmark El Dorado Hotel, Ristorante Piatti serves rotisserie items, pizzas from a wood-burning oven and regional Italian cuisine.

WINES & WINE COUNTRY

REGINA'S SONOMA
110 West Spain St., Sonoma / 707-938-0254
Lunch & dinner daily
CREOLE

No visit to Sonoma is complete without a meal at Regina's. Fans of Regina Charboneau's San Francisco restaurant, who despaired when it closed after the Regis Hotel changed hands, rejoiced to find her in business again in the charming Sonoma Hotel on the Plaza. Here, you'll find buttery biscuits, bouillabaisse, grilled catfish, chocolate bread pudding — and all the other Southern specialties that reflect Regina's Mississippi roots and New Orleans culinary training.

Specialties: Mississippi Bouillabaisse; Southern Pot Roast; Smoky Grilled Catfish Sandwich; Spinach-stuffed Gulf Shrimp with Pecan Crust & Apple-Wild Rice Dressing; Chocolate Bread Pudding with White Chocolate Sauce

ACCOMMODATIONS

BEST WESTERN SONOMA VALLEY INN
550 2nd St. West, Sonoma / 707-938-9200

Just a short walk from historic Sonoma Plaza, the Sonoma Valley Inn is built around an inviting courtyard with gazebo, spa and heated pool.

KENWOOD INN
10400 Sonoma Hwy., Kenwood / 707-833-1293

The Kenwood Inn has four exquisite suites, richly appointed with imported tapestries and velvets, working fireplaces, down mattresses and comforters, huge European pillows and private baths. A complimentary breakfast is served at 9AM, featuring such gourmet delights as Mediterranean-style egg dishes served with polenta, Sicilian sausage with olives and tiny new potatoes, freshly baked breads or croissants and other tantalizing fare. The staff at Kenwood Inn is dedicated to accommodating every wish to ensure an unforgettable stay.
Suites $175-$225

SONOMA HOTEL
110 West Spain St., Sonoma / 707-996-2996

"Close to the city but a hundred years away" is how the owners of the Sonoma Hotel describe their romantic inn on Sonoma Plaza. Enjoy a drink in the magnificent saloon, or Creole specialties in **Regina's**.

SONOMA MISSION INN & SPA
18140 Sonoma Hwy. 12, Boyes Hot Springs / 707-938-9000

Sonoma Mission Inn & Spa is a Mobil four-star luxury resort situated on eight beautifully landscaped acres. Pink

WINES & WINE COUNTRY

and palatial, the California mission-style inn offers 170 luxury guest rooms, many with fireplaces, a world-class spa, two acclaimed restaurants, **The Grille** and **The Cafe**, a market and a deli, two swimming pools, tennis courts, seminar and conference facilities, and award-winning service and amenities. This spring, the Sonoma Mission Inn has brought to the surface the legendary hot springs that made the resort famous in the 1920s. Hot mineral water fills both pools and whirlpools, and is used as the hot water source in the spa and historic inn buildings. *Singles & doubles $135-$340; suites $375-$780*

SANTA ROSA SEBASTOPOL & PETALUMA

POINTS OF INTEREST

CHEESE PLANT/CREAMERY STORE
Western Ave. & Baker St., Petaluma / 707-778-1234

Shop for award-winning California Gold butter and cheeses, dairy products and unique items at the creamery store adjacent to this 80-year-old cheese plant. The ultra-modern plant is an engaging facility to tour.

LUTHER BURBANK HOME & MEMORIAL GARDENS
Sonoma & Santa Rosa Ave., Santa Rosa / 707-524-5445

Famous horticulturist Luther Burbank called Santa Rosa home for more than 50 years. Docent-led tours of Burbank's home and self-guided tours of his fascinating experimental gardens are available.

PETALUMA
Petaluma Area Chamber of Commerce
215 Howard St. at Washington / 707-762-2785

Just 32 miles north of the Golden Gate Bridge, Victorian Petaluma welcomes you to step back in time. Pick up a free brochure from the Chamber of Commerce and take a walking tour of the city's famous Ironfront buildings and Victorian homes, survivors of the 1906 earthquake. You can tour the town's two cheese factories and winery, visit local farms for fresh produce, or explore California's largest adobe at the Petaluma Adobe State Historic Park. Downtown, you'll find more than 100 antique stores and, at last count, 142 restaurants. Enjoy a river cruise on the Petaluma Queen paddlewheeler, and don't forget to visit the museum and the Cinnabar Theatre. For more ideas, stop by the Visitor Center at the Penngrove exit off Highway 101 or the Chamber's downtown office, open weekdays 9AM to 5PM and weekends during the season. The Chamber can also provide information on dining, shopping, lodging and camping.

PETALUMA ADOBE STATE HISTORIC PARK
3325 Adobe Rd., four miles southeast of Petaluma
707-762-4871

On a low knoll overlooking the Petaluma Valley, the Petaluma Adobe was the main residence and center of activity for General Vallejo's 100-square-mile Rancho Petaluma. Although only half of the original four-sided structure remains, the Mexican flag still flies and historical representations of the adobe's industry are on display.

WINERIES

DE LOACH VINEYARDS
1791 Olivet Rd., Santa Rosa / 707-526-9111
TOURS, TASTING, RETAIL SALES

The vineyards surrounding the tasting room date back to a 1905 planting of Zinfandel vines, which now produce De Loach's fine estate-bottled Zinfandel.
Daily: 10AM to 4:30PM; tours twice daily

RESTAURANTS

ALFRED'S
17 Keller St., Petaluma / 707-778-7787
Lunch Tues-Fri, dinner Tues-Sun, brunch Sun
STEAKHOUSE

A converted turn-of-the-century Gothic Lutheran church is home to Alfred's, an elegant steakhouse for people with big appetites.

CAFFE PORTOFINO
535 4th St., Santa Rosa / 707-523-1171
Lunch & dinner Mon-Sat
ITALIAN

Enjoy fresh Italian cuisine at Santa Rosa's downtown Caffe Portofino, owned and operated by the Belmontes, who have been in the restaurant business for more than 25 years. A lively, well-dressed crowd can usually be found gathered around the bar or in the stylish dining room, enjoying the European ambiance, or sipping espresso at the sidewalk cafe, "just like in Roma." Dedicated to today's *cucina moderna* Italian cooking, Chef Maria Belmonte has made Caffe Portofino one of the most popular restaurants in the wine country.
Specialties: *Homemade Seafood & Chicken Ravioli; Saltimbocca; Veal Scalloppine Bolognese*

ITALIAN AFFAIR
1612 Terrace Way, Santa Rosa / 707-528-3336
Lunch & dinner Tues-Sat
NORTHERN ITALIAN

Enjoy an aperitif at the wine bar while you wait for a table at this small yet popular restaurant.

JOHN ASH & CO.
4330 Barnes Rd., Santa Rosa / 707-527-7687
Lunch Tues-Fri, dinner Tues-Sun, brunch Sun
CALIFORNIA

John Ash & Co., adjacent to the elegant Vintners Inn, offers distinctive regional cuisine, an award-winning wine list, outdoor seating and a full bar.

LA GARE
208 Wilson St., Santa Rosa / 707-528-4355
Dinner Tues-Sun
FRENCH

Chef Marc Praplan serves fresh seafood daily; his specialty is baked salmon. Other specialties are sweetbreads, beef Wellington and duck a l'orange.

LISA HEMENWAY'S
714 Village Court Mall, Santa Rosa / 707-526-5111
Lunch Mon-Sat, dinner daily, brunch Sun
SONOMA CUISINE

Located in Montgomery Village, Lisa Hemenway's is an award-winning restaurant. Lisa Hemenway, who has appeared as a guest chef in restaurants from the United States to Thailand, serves regional cuisine prepared with local ingredients. The menu changes daily, featuring innovative dishes, a choice of heart-healthy items and fantastic desserts. Enjoy outdoor dining on the patio or purchase box lunches and picnic gourmet selections from the restaurant's Tote Cuisine, offered next door from 8:30AM to 7PM daily.
Specialties: Lamb Tenderloin with Hazelnuts & Sweet Mustard Glaze; Halibut in Potato Corn Crust with Southwest Salsa; Filet Mignon with Two-color Peppercorns in a Brandy Shallot Sauce; Hungarian Nut Torte

PROSPECT PARK
515 4th St., Santa Rosa / 707-526-2662
Dinner daily
AMERICAN

A California-style bistro with an impressive beer list, this eatery offers such specialties as grilled peppered lamb tenderloins and Korean-style duck.

TRUFFLES
234 South Main St., Sebastopol / 707-823-8448
Dinner Fri-Sun
INTERNATIONAL

The menu here offers an intriguing mix of Asian, Latin and Sonoma County cuisines.

ACCOMMODATIONS

DOUBLETREE INN
3555 Round Barn Rd., Santa Rosa / 707-523-7555

Recognizable by its historic round winery, the Fountain Grove Ranch is the site of this luxurious hotel. Its 247 rooms are complemented by a meeting facility, swimming pool, spa complex and a restaurant, **The Sonoma Harvest**, overlooking the Santa Rosa basin.
Singles & doubles $85-$129; suites $129-$350

FLAMINGO RESORT HOTEL
4th St. & Farmers Lane, Santa Rosa / 800-848-8300

The Flamingo Resort Hotel offers luxurious accommodations in the midst of tranquil vineyards. A heated

Olympic-size pool, jacuzzi, five tennis courts, shuffleboard and table tennis are available for active guests. The **Picasso's Palm Room**, serving fine local cuisine, is a great place to end your day.

VINTNERS INN
4350 Barnes Rd., Santa Rosa / 707-575-7350

Home to the acclaimed **John Ash & Co.** restaurant, the Vintners Inn resembles a small European country inn.

HEALDSBURG
ALEXANDER, DRY CREEK & RUSSIAN RIVER VALLEYS

POINTS OF INTEREST

ARMSTRONG REDWOODS STATE RESERVE
Guerneville / 707-869-2015

This 700-acre redwood forest was set aside as a natural park and botanic garden in the 1870s. You'll see some of the tallest trees remaining in this part of California, among them the 310-foot Parson Jones Tree, more than 1,400 years old.

LAKE SONOMA
Geyserville / 707-433-9483

Eight thousand acres of wildlife preserve, some of the best bass fishing in the state, and secluded campsites make Lake Sonoma a distinctive place for recreation. Bring a picnic lunch or water skis, and be sure to see the exhibits and fish hatchery at the visitors center.

WINERIES

ALEXANDER VALLEY VINEYARDS
8644 Hwy. 128, Healdsburg / 707-433-7209
TASTING, RETAIL SALES

In 1842 Cyrus Alexander settled in the southeast area of the valley that bears his name. The Wetzel family purchased the property in 1963 and built a reputation for producing classic, well-balanced wines.
Daily: 10AM to 5PM. Tours by appointment

CHALK HILL WINERY
10300 Chalk Hill Rd., Healdsburg / 707-838-4306
TASTING, RETAIL SALES

Chalk Hill Winery is the only estate winery located in Sonoma's Chalk Hill appellation. When Frederick Furth purchased the property, he recognized its great potential for producing world-class wines. The estate covers 1,100 acres, with 250 acres producing Cabernet Sauvignon, Chardonnay and Sauvignon Blanc.
Monday through Friday: 10AM to 5PM. Tours, tasting and retail sales by appointment

CHATEAU SOUVERAIN
Independence Lane & Hwy. 101, Geyserville / 707-433-8281
TASTING, RETAIL SALES

Situated on a knoll commanding views of the Alexander Valley, the twin-towered Chateau Souverain is a striking winery with old-world architectural overtones and new-world winemaking techniques. Winemaker Tom Peterson oversees the vinification of five varietals, including Chardonnay, Sauvignon Blanc, Merlot and Cabernet Sauvignon.
Daily: 10AM to 5PM in summer; Thursday through Monday 10AM to 5PM in winter

CLOS DU BOIS
5 Fitch St., Healdsburg / 707-433-5576
TASTING, RETAIL SALES

Just a few blocks from Healdsburg Plaza is the prestigious Clos du Bois winery, producing Sauvignon Blanc, Chardonnay, Gewurztraminer, Pinot Noir, Merlot and Cabernet Sauvignon.
Daily: 10AM to 5PM. Tours by appointment

DRY CREEK VINEYARD
3770 Lambert Bridge Rd., Healdsburg / 707-433-1000
TASTING, PICNIC, RETAIL SALES

After owner David Stare replanted a prune orchard with grapevines in 1972, he was on his way to producing gold medal winners in Fume Blanc, Chardonnay, Chenin Blanc, Zinfandel and Cabernet Sauvignon.
Daily: 10:30AM to 4:30PM

FORESTVILLE WINE GROUP/ MARK WEST VINEYARDS
7010 Trenton-Healdsburg Rd., Forestville / 707-544-4813
TOURS, TASTING, PICNIC, RETAIL SALES

The estate-bottled Chardonnay, Gewurztraminer, Pinot Noir and Blanc de Noir sparkling wines are gaining national esteem for their flavor and balance.
Daily: 10AM to 5PM

HOP KILN WINERY
6050 Westside Rd., Healdsburg / 707-433-6491
TASTING, PICNIC, RETAIL SALES

Hop Kiln Winery is in a majestic, three-tiered hops barn — a national trust and a perfect spot for photographs and picnics.
Daily: 10AM to 5PM

JORDAN VINEYARD & WINERY
1474 Alexander Valley Rd., Healdsburg / 707-431-5250
RETAIL SALES

Founded by Tom Jordan and Sally Jordan in 1972, Jordan Vineyard & Winery is a family estate organized in the traditional style of a French chateau. Situated on an oak-covered knoll overlooking 1,300 acres of vineyards and wildlife reserve in the Alexander Valley, the winery exemplifies the Jordan family's care for detail and commitment to excellence. Jordan produces award-winning Cabernet Sauvignon and Chardonnay and markets J, a newly released *méthode champenoise* sparkling wine, produced by Jordan Sparkling Wine Company, also in

Healdsburg. There is no tasting room, but retail sales are permitted.
Monday-Friday: 9AM-5PM. Tours by appointment

KORBEL CHAMPAGNE CELLARS
13250 River Rd., Guerneville / 707-887-2294
TOURS, TASTING, PICNIC, RETAIL SALES

Korbel is the largest and oldest *méthode champenoise* facility in the United States. Tours include the brandy tower and the Korbel train station, family home and gardens.
Daily: 9AM to 5PM in summer; last tour 3:45PM.
In winter: 9AM to 4:30PM; last tour 3PM

PEDRONCELLI WINERY
1220 Canyon Rd., Geyserville / 707-857-3531
TASTING, RETAIL SALES

Pedroncelli Winery, the first winery to produce Zinfandel Rose, has always placed an emphasis on Zinfandel.
Daily: 10AM to 5PM

PIPER SONOMA CELLARS
11447 Old Redwood Hwy., Healdsburg / 707-433-8843
TASTING, RETAIL SALES, BANQUET FACILITIES

Classic French elegance is reflected in the ambiance of Piper Sonoma's Visitor Center and in their outstanding sparkling wines, made in the traditional *méthode champenoise.*
Daily: 10AM to 5PM

RIDGE/LYTTON SPRINGS WINERY
650 Lytton Springs Rd., Healdsburg / 707-433-7721
TASTING, RETAIL SALES

Ridge/Lytton Springs Winery is famous for its award-winning Zinfandels. Vintage-dated Zinfandels and Cabernets are also offered here.
Daily: 10AM to 4PM

J. ROCHIOLI VINEYARDS & WINERY
6192 Westside Rd., Healdsburg / 707-433-2305
TASTING, PICNIC, RETAIL SALES

Premium grape growers since the 1930s, the Rochioli family produces award-winning Chardonnay, Sauvignon Blanc, Gewurztraminer, Pinot Noir and Cabernet Sauvignon.
Daily: 10AM to 5PM

RODNEY STRONG VINEYARDS
11455 Old Redwood Hwy., Healdsburg / 707-431-1533
TOURS, TASTING, PICNIC, RETAIL SALES

Known for excellent Cabernet Sauvignon, Rodney Strong Vineyards also produces Chardonnay, Sauvignon Blanc, Pinot Noir and Zinfandel. Visitors are welcome to stroll on the esplanade, view working sections of the winery, and enjoy a casual, yet informative tasting with the staff. After perusing the art and gifts in the spacious tasting room, guests can relax and picnic under the trees.
Daily: 10AM to 5PM. Tours at 11AM, 1PM & 3PM

WINES & WINE COUNTRY

SIMI WINERY

16275 Healdsburg Ave., Healdsburg / 707-433-6981
TASTING, PICNIC, RETAIL SALES

Winemaker Nick Goldschmidt has led Simi, now owned by Moet-Hennessy and Louis Vuitton, from the wine shadows into the spotlight as one of California's top premium producers. Chardonnay and Cabernet Sauvignon are the major concentration of the 150,000 cases produced every year.
Daily: 10AM to 4:30PM

WINDSOR VINEYARDS

239A Center St., Healdsburg / 707-433-2822
TASTING, RETAIL SALES

Windsor Vineyards has quietly won the most awards of any winery in America for five years in a row. A half block from Healdsburg Plaza and an easy walk to restaurants and shops, Windsor Vineyards has 35 wines available for complimentary tasting. Windsor also has a tasting room in Tiburon, just across San Francisco Bay in Marin County. Both offer unique personalized labels for Windsor Vineyards gift sets.
Monday through Friday 10AM to 5PM; Saturday & Sunday 10AM to 6PM

RESTAURANTS

BISTRO RALPH

109 Plaza St., Healdsburg / 707-433-1380
Lunch & dinner Wed-Mon, brunch Sat & Sun
CALIFORNIA

Ralph Tingle, who was the chef at Sundial Grill and Fetzer Vineyard, runs this elegant bistro.

TRE SCALINI

241 Healdsburg Ave., Healdsburg / 707-433-1772
Lunch Mon-Fri, dinner Mon-Sat
ITALIAN

Tre Scalini's innovative Italian cuisine has won praise from *Gourmet Magazine* and *The Wine Spectator*.

ACCOMMODATIONS

MADRONA MANOR & RESTAURANT

1001 Westside Rd., Healdsburg / 707-433-4231

This Victorian mansion sits on eight acres of landscaped grounds in the heart of the wine country. Chef Todd Muir has earned national recognition for his superb California cuisine.

CALENDAR OF EVENTS

For events in Sonoma Valley, contact the Sonoma Valley Visitors Bureau at 707-996-1090. For events throughout the county, call the Sonoma County Convention & Visitors Bureau at 707-575-1191.

JANUARY

THREE KINGS DAY
Celebration in honor of the Magi. Champagne and complimentary Spanish treats, Gloria Ferrer Champagne Caves in Sonoma.

MARCH

HEART OF THE VALLEY BARREL TASTING
Open house, winemaker talks and tastings at various Sonoma County wineries.

SPRING BLOSSOM TOUR
Tour and events in the Alexander Valley.

RUSSIAN RIVER WINE FESTIVAL
Tastings at wineries throughout the Russian River area.

APRIL

EASTER SUNDAY AT SONOMA MISSION INN & SPA
Easter bunny and lavish Easter brunch at the Sonoma Mission Inn & Spa, Boyes Hot Springs.

SAINT JORDI DAY
Feast day celebrated at Gloria Ferrer Champagne Caves in Sonoma. The winery is among several participating in an open house of Carneros wineries.

JUNE

OX ROAST
Old-fashioned picnic with barbecue, live music and a wine tasting at the Plaza, Sonoma.

JULY

FOURTH OF JULY CELEBRATIONS
Kenwood sponsors the World Pillow Fighting Championships, Chili Cook-Off and Parade. At the Plaza in Sonoma, visitors can join in an old-fashioned celebration, with a parade, games, art show and tastings of Sonoma food and wines.

SONOMA VALLEY WINE FESTIVAL & LIBERTY RIDE
Wine tasting and 100-K noncompetitive bike ride through Sonoma County.

SONOMA COUNTY FAIR
Carnival attractions, fiddling and entertainment at the Sonoma County Fairgrounds, Santa Rosa.

REDWOODS SUMMER MUSIC FESTIVAL
Classical music program presented at various Sonoma County wineries.

AUGUST

SHAKESPEARE AT BUENA VISTA
Sunday evening performances at the Buena Vista Winery in Sonoma.

PETALUMA RIVER FESTIVAL & OLD ADOBE FIESTA
Raft races, street dancing, arts and crafts, and rides aboard a steamboat and a sternwheeler. The salute to Petaluma's past is also celebrated with the Old Adobe Fiesta, a recreation of California's rancho period. Weavers, blacksmiths, adobe bricklayers and others demonstrate their skills.

SONOMA COUNTY WINE AUCTION
Sonoma County's top event. Tastings, tours and luncheons are scheduled at wineries throughout the county, followed by a preview tasting and auction of barrel wines. The auction is held on the final day of the event.

SEPTEMBER

VALLEY OF THE MOON VINTAGE FESTIVAL
California's oldest wine festival. Grape stomp, parades, blessing of the grapes, tastings, entertainment and reenactments of Sonoma's history. Wineries from around the county participate in the event at the Plaza, Sonoma.

RUSSIAN RIVER JAZZ FESTIVAL
Jazz, food and wine in Guerneville.

OCTOBER

HARVEST FAIR
California's largest apple exhibit. Grape stomp and food and wine tasting in Santa Rosa.

NOVEMBER

HOLIDAY IN CARNEROS
Special events and tastings at Carneros wineries.

KENWOOD WINERIES OPEN HOUSE
Wineries in Kenwood open their doors to the public.

DECEMBER

CATALAN HOLIDAY LUNCHEON
Traditional Catalan holiday feast, Gloria Ferrer Champagne Caves in Sonoma.

CHRISTMAS AT THE MISSION
Candlelight procession, music and holiday food at the Plaza, Sonoma.

WINES & WINE COUNTRY

and beaches of Big Sur, the Monterey Peninsula is one of the most beautiful and distinctive places on earth. Everyone can find something to love here, whether it's nature, history, golf, treasure-hunting in local boutiques, or relaxing over fine food and wine.

John Steinbeck immortalized Monterey and its Cannery Row in his fiction. When the sardines mysteriously disappeared some years ago, the clanking of the canneries ceased. Yet the Row remains vibrant, blending the flavor of the old Cannery Row with an interesting mix of restaurants, hotels, shops and visitor attractions, including the Monterey Bay Aquarium and the value-filled American Tin Cannery outlet center.

Introduced by Ted Balestreri

Ted Balestreri is co-owner of The Sardine Factory Restaurant, internationally renowned for fresh seafood and pasta, fine wine and gracious service.

Adjacent to Monterey is Pebble Beach, the world's golf mecca. Farther south is the Carmel Mission and Carmel-by-the-Sea. There, in a European village-like setting, art galleries and restaurants share tree-lined streets with tiny shops of every description.

Whether your adventure leads you past the lush estates and panoramic vistas of 17-Mile Drive, down the rugged coast of Big Sur, or on an exploration of Monterey's bountiful food and wine, you'll find that everyone shares the same philosophy. It's one we've made famous at The Sardine Factory: "If we made you feel at home, we made a multi-

million-dollar mistake, because you might as well stay at home. Our job is to make you feel much better than at home."

Carmel·Monterey

Thank you: Dwayne March, Jennifer Wolf, EPIC Models

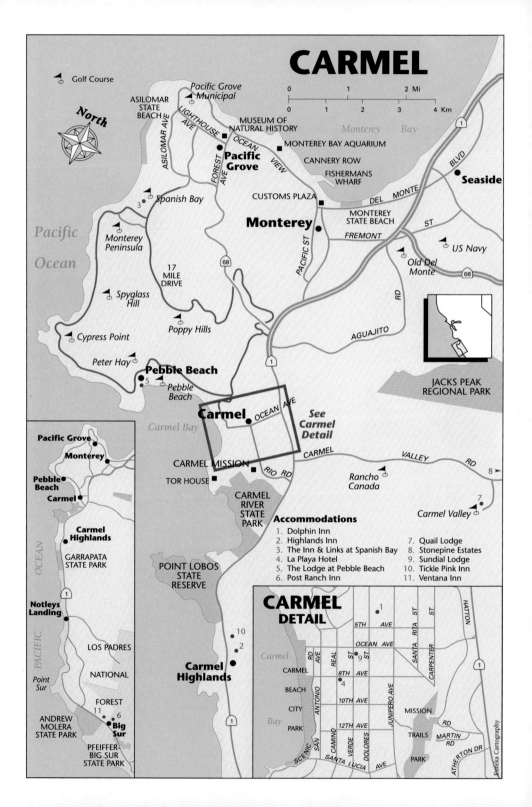

CARMEL

Golf Course

North

Pacific
Ocean

Monterey Bay

ASILOMAR
STATE
BEACH

Pacific Grove
Municipal

MUSEUM OF
NATURAL HISTORY

MONTEREY BAY AQUARIUM

CANNERY ROW

FISHERMANS
WHARF

**Pacific
Grove**

Spanish Bay

CUSTOMS PLAZA

Seaside

DEL MONTE

MONTEREY
STATE BEACH

Monterey

Monterey
Peninsula

17
MILE
DRIVE

FREMONT

US Navy

Old Del
Monte

Spyglass
Hill

Poppy Hills

AGUAJITO

JACKS PEAK
REGIONAL PARK

Cypress Point

Peter Hay

Pebble Beach

Pebble
Beach

Carmel

OCEAN AVE

*See
Carmel
Detail*

Carmel Bay

CARMEL

VALLEY   RD

CARMEL MISSION

RIO RD

Rancho
Canada

Carmel Valley

TOR HOUSE

CARMEL
RIVER
STATE
PARK

Accommodations

1. Dolphin Inn
2. Highlands Inn
3. The Inn & Links at Spanish Bay
4. La Playa Hotel
5. The Lodge at Pebble Beach
6. Post Ranch Inn
7. Quail Lodge
8. Stonepine Estates
9. Sundial Lodge
10. Tickle Pink Inn
11. Ventana Inn

Pacific Grove

Monterey

**Pebble
Beach**

Carmel

**Carmel
Highlands**

GARRAPATA
STATE PARK

OCEAN

POINT LOBOS
STATE
RESERVE

**Carmel
Highlands**

PACIFIC

Notleys
Landing

LOS PADRES

NATIONAL

*Point
Sur*

FOREST

ANDREW
MOLERA
STATE PARK

PFEIFFER-
BIG SUR
STATE PARK

**Big
Sur**

CARMEL
DETAIL

Carmel

CARMEL

BEACH

CITY

Bay

PARK

5TH   AVE

OCEAN AVE

8TH   AVE

10TH   AVE

12TH   AVE

SANTA LUCIA   AVE

SCENIC

SAN ANTONIO

CAMINO

VERDE

DOLORES

JUNIPERO AVE

SANTA RITA ST

CARPENTER

HATTON

MISSION

TRAILS

PARK

RD

MARTIN
RD

ATHERTON DR

Enrieka Cartography

CARMEL INFORMATION

AAA EMERGENCY ROAD SERVICE
Big Sur / Carmel 408-372-8131

AIRLINES
American Eagle / American Airlines ...800-433-7300
United / United Express 800-241-6522
USAir...800-428-4322

BUS
Monterey-Salinas Transit...................408-899-2555

GOLF
Carmel Valley Ranch Golf Club.. 408-626-2510
Golf Club at Quail Lodge..................408-624-1581
Pebble Beach Golf Links... 800-654-9300
Peter Hay Par 3 408-625-8518
Poppy Hills Golf Course... 408-625-2035
Rancho Canada Golf Course.............408-624-0111
Spanish Bay Golf Course...................800-654-9300
Spyglass Hill Golf Course... 800-654-9300

GUIDED TOURS
Steinbeck Country Tours....................408-625-5107

HORSEBACK RIDING
Molera Trail Rides 408-625-8664
Pebble Beach Equestrian Center........408-624-2756

LIMOUSINES
A-1 Chartered Limousine Service........408-649-1425
Bungays Limousine............................408-624-1407
Your Maitre d' Limousine...................408-624-1717

PUBLIC SWIMMING POOL
Carmel Valley Community Center 408-659-3983

TAXIS
Joe's Cabs...408-624-3885

TENNIS
Carmel Valley Inn & Tennis Resort 408-659-3131
Carmel Valley Racquet Club..............408-624-2737
Mission Tennis Ranch... 408-624-4335
Pebble Beach Tennis Club 408-624-0106

THEATRES
Cherry Hall.......................................408-624-7491
Forest Theatre (winter only)...............408-624-1531
(summer outdoor theatre) 408-626-1681
Hidden Valley Theatre 408-659-3115
Monterey County Theatre Alliance Box Office
....408-655-3200
Sunset Center 408-624-3996

VISITOR INFORMATION
Carmel Business Association 408-624-2522

POINTS OF INTEREST

CARMEL MISSION
West of Hwy. One on Rio Road / 408-624-1271

Mission San Carlos Borromeo del Rio Carmelo was the second mission outpost built by Father Junipero Serra, founder of the California missions. The complex consists of a museum and the residence and burial place of the Franciscan padre. The museum displays a collection of early Spanish and California Indian artifacts, relics and tools of mission days and a beautiful chapel.

PFEIFFER BIG SUR STATE PARK
Thirty miles south of Monterey on Hwy. One
408-667-2315

This state park is composed of 821 acres of coastal redwoods and chaparral bordering the Big Sur River. Group and individual picnic areas are open during the day. Campgrounds are available by reservation eight weeks in advance at 800-444-7275. Private accommodations are offered at the Big Sur Lodge, 408-667-2171. Hiking trails and nature walks enable visitors to surround themselves with acres of densely forested natural beauty. The park's Pfeiffer Falls should be on every hiker's list.

POINT LOBOS STATE RESERVE
Three miles south of Carmel on Hwy. One
408-624-4909

At Point Lobos all wildlife and plants are protected in order to preserve as nearly as possible the primeval state of the area. Certified divers can explore the underwater preserve known for its kelp forest and sea life, while the land-bound can observe colonies of sea otters, harbor seals, sea lions, deer, cormorants and birds. Park your car and explore the fascinating park on foot, then pause for a picnic in one of three scenic picnic sites.

17-MILE DRIVE
408-649-8500

One of the most famous roadways in the world, the 17-Mile Drive is a picturesque drive along the sea from Pacific Grove to Carmel and through the Del Monte Forest. Exclusive homes vie with the unspoiled scenery

CARMEL • MONTEREY

for the attention of passersby. Start from the Highway One gate into Del Monte Forest, bear to your right as you begin the drive and follow the 17-Mile Drive signs. This is private property and there is a $6 fee per car to enter.

TOR HOUSE
At Carmel Point on Ocean View, Carmel / 408-624-1813

Named for the craggy knoll or "tor" on which it was built, Tor House was the home of the famous poet and writer Robinson Jeffers. Guided tours of the house and gardens are given Fridays and Saturdays by appointment. Included are Hawk Tower and some of the writer's memorabilia. Children under 12 are not admitted.

SHOPPING CENTERS

THE BARNYARD
Hwy. One & Carmel Valley Rd., Carmel

Wooden barns joined by outdoor walkways and gardens with flowers year-round make up The Barnyard, an inviting shopping center with rural charm and dozens of delightful shops. Knowledgeable shopkeepers and exceptional wares make shopping here a pleasure.

CARMEL PLAZA
Ocean btwn. Junipero & Mission, Carmel

To experience Carmel, visit the Carmel Plaza with 50 shops and restaurants on Ocean Avenue across from the park. Carmel Plaza boasts a collection of fine fashion stores. Among them, **Saks Fifth Avenue**, **Mondi International** and **I. Magnin**, together with a variety of unique shops set amidst flower-decked hallways. From fashion, to books, to fine wines, to high-tech gadgetry at the **Sharper Image**, you'll find all the best at the Plaza. To please your palate visit one of Carmel Plaza's fine restaurants, featuring outdoor dining. Select from French, Greek, Japanese and California cuisine. For walkaway treats visit **Simply Nuts**, **Carmel Candy** & **Confection Co.** or **Yogurt of Carmel**. Validated parking is available in the Plaza parking facility on Mission.

THE CROSSROADS
Hwy. One & Rio Rd., Carmel

Nestled into rolling hills and surrounded by country farmlands and the beaches of Carmel, the Crossroads resembles a quaint English village more than a shopping center. Spend a day browsing through a multitude of shops and businesses, including fashion boutiques, purveyors of rare and imported goods, gift and specialty stores and wonderful restaurants, such as **Rio Grill** and **Chevys Mexican Restaurant**, to tempt every palate.

SHOPPING

BUFF LA GRANGE
Lincoln btwn. Ocean & 7th / 408-625-6506

Buff La Grange appeals to the woman with distinctive

taste for the cutting edge in fine European apparel, including collections by Moschino, Anvers and others.

DICK BRUHN
Ocean & San Carlos, Carmel / 408-624-8235

With a 42-year track record, Dick Bruhn has the largest selection of quality menswear in the area, including a complete Big and Tall department.

THE ELEGANT SET
San Carlos & 7th, Carmel / 408-625-6080
800-497-4994

The Elegant Set has the most extensive collection of hand-embroidered tablecloths, placemats and runners in the United States. All made from natural fabrics such as linen, cotton and silk, these beautiful table coverings come in all sizes, including banquet, for rectangular, square and hard-to-fit oval tables. The Elegant Set buys directly, so there are no added import or wholesale fees, which makes for outstanding values. The store also features California's largest selection of Saint Louis and Lalique crystal. Heirloom linens and exquisite French crystal make a dazzling combination for your table.
Open daily

LAUREL BURCH GALLERIE
Ocean & Monte Verde, Carmel / 408-626-2822

Artist-designer Laurel Burch applies brilliant colors and distinctive gold accents to her handcrafted collection of jewelry, apparel, totes, mugs and paper products. A former Haight-Ashbury street artist, Burch has developed a nationwide clientele for her vibrant, multicultural designs. Her newest collection, "Woman Spirit/Woman Soul" and "The Spirit of Womankind," features gifts made from Balinese sweet pine wood, including hand-painted chime earrings that ring against hammered metal. Instantly recognizable, Burch's work is available in major department stores and specialty stores nationwide, as well as in her two personal galleries located in Sausalito and Carmel.
Open daily

NICOLE MILLER
Carmel Plaza, Ocean Ave. level / 408-625-9320

Internationally renowned New York fashion designer Nicole Miller has opened an exciting new store in the Carmel Plaza Shopping Center. The store features her gorgeous designer evening dresses and fun, sophisticated sportswear for women. You will also find Miller's silk print separates, accessories and formalwear for men and women, as well as the best selection of her wildly popular silk theme-print ties.
Open daily

R.K. SHUGART
Dolores btwn. 7th & 8th, Carmel / 408-624-7748

R.K. Shugart is one of Carmel's most exclusive women's boutiques. Fashions by such designers as Thierry Mugler, Iceberg and Versace are expertly coordinated by the staff.

RITTMASTER
Pine Inn Building, Normandy Court, Ocean & Lincoln Carmel / 408-625-6611

The three elegant Rittmaster boutiques offer smart urban fashions by top European and American designers. You'll find a full line of clothing for both men and women.

ROBERT TALBOTT SHOPS
Ocean & Dolores, Ocean & Monte Verde, Carmel
The Lodge at Pebble Beach / 408-624-6604

The Robert Talbott Shops represent more than a quarter-century of tradition and quality in menswear. They also carry elegant, handcrafted silk neckwear and accessories.

VENDETTI
Lincoln St. btwn. Ocean & 7th, Carmel / 408-625-6720

Designed by Monique Vendetti, this exclusive line of coats, jackets, sweaters and pullovers were created as alternatives to fur.

GALLERIES

BLEICH GALLERY
Dolores near Ocean, Carmel / 408-624-9447

The Bleich Gallery features the work of plein air painter George J. Bleich. His paintings, inspired by French Impressionist landscapes, have a special luminosity prized by collectors.

CARMEL ART ASSOCIATION
Dolores btwn. 5th & 6th, Carmel / 408-624-6176

Carmel's oldest gallery owned and operated by artists has a 66-year history. It features the finest paintings, sculpture and graphics by top local artists.

GALERIE BLUE DOG, LTD.
6th btwn. Lincoln & Dolores, Carmel / 408-626-4444

Artist George Rodrigue, famous for his surreal depictions of the Cajuns, began the Blue Dog series several years ago. The artist has won a universal audience with his unique and touching series. What began as paintings of the *loup-garou* or Cajun werewolf has developed into the spirit of the artist's dog, Tiffany, who sat by his side for 12 years while he captured the culture of his native Louisiana. Traveling through time and space, the "Blue Dog" tries to reunite with the artist. The result is often humorous, but its basis is spiritual as the artist explores the concept of an afterlife.
Open daily

HIGHLANDS SCULPTURE GALLERY
Dolores btwn. 5th & 6th, Carmel / 408-624-0535

You are encouraged to "touch" in this friendly and informal gallery, established almost 20 years ago. The contemporary sculptures in stone, wood, bronze and other metals are by California artists, some local. The artists represented include Gordon Newell, Robert Holmes, Norma Lewis, Micah Curtis, Sharon Andreason, Ana Daltchev, John Libberton and Winni Brueggemann and his "Sounding Sculptures."
Open daily

LILLIANA BRAICO GALLERY
6th near Dolores, Carmel / 408-624-2512

To find Lilliana Braico's Gallery, you have to turn up the path by "the tree," a Carmel landmark on Sixth Street. Her sunny, welcoming gallery features her acclaimed florals, portraits, abstracts and vibrant Mediterranean seaside scenes. The artist returned to Carmel after spending seven years on the island of Capri. Working in her own studio, she refined her painting and color techniques by visiting major European expositions. Her joy in exploring color is reflected in her oils, acrylics and limited-edition prints. Braico's work attracts both private collectors and commissions from interior designers.
Open Friday through Tuesday; Wednesday & Thursday by appointment

MAISON VAL DU SOLEIL
8 El Carminito Rd., Carmel Valley / 408-659-5757

Set against the spectacular Los Padres Forest, Maison Val du Soleil is an antique and art collector's dream. Blending fine art and antiques for distinguished living, the gallery attracts connoisseurs. The 18th and 19th century French antiques are chosen in France by the owner, Germaine Lestrade. Maison Val du Soleil also features oil and water-color paintings by French and American artists.
Closed Sunday & Monday

PHOTOGRAPHY WEST GALLERY
Ocean & Dolores, Carmel / 408-625-1587

This attractive gallery features the finest in 20th century photography, including Ansel Adams, Brett Weston, Winn Bullock, Paul Caponigro and other contemporary masters. Photography West also displays the work of leading regional photographers such as Morley Baer and others. The gallery specializes in expert appraisals for private and corporate collections.
Open daily

RESTAURANTS

ANTON & MICHEL
Mission btwn. Ocean & 7th, Carmel / 408-624-2406
Lunch & dinner daily
CONTINENTAL

Sophisticated elegance, old-world charm, a priceless

GALERIE BLUE DOG, LTD.
6th AVENUE BETWEEN LINCOLN & DOLORES
P.O. BOX S-3214
CARMEL, CALIFORNIA 93923
(408) 626-4444

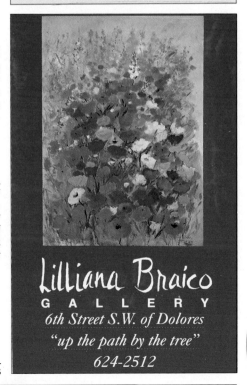

Lilliana Braico
G A L L E R Y
6th Street S.W. of Dolores
"up the path by the tree"
624-2512

CARMEL • MONTEREY

QUAIL LODGE
RESORT & GOLF CLUB
CARMEL, CALIFORNIA

A beautiful resort hotel in a country setting with luxury rooms and suites. An 18 hole private golf course with gardens, lakes, trees, wildlife and mountain vistas. Hot tubs, tennis, jogging paths and miles of nature trails.

PREFERRED
HOTELS & RESORTS
WORLDWIDE

Awarded Mobil Travel Guide's 5-Star Award for the 17th year

Call Val Johnson for color brochure at (408) 624-1581 or for reservations 1-800-538-9516. Quail Lodge, 8205 Valley Greens Dr., Carmel, CA 93923.

collection of original oil paintings and superb cuisine have made Anton & Michel's a favorite with locals and visitors for 12 years. Connoisseurs will appreciate the house specialty: a traditional rack of lamb cooked to perfection and carved at tableside. The attentive, unobtrusive service is offered in a romantic setting enhanced by outdoor fountains and gardens. The extensive award-winning wine list, full bar, and luscious desserts make Anton & Michel the perfect choice for elegant dining in Carmel. Reservations suggested.

Specialties: Grilled Lamb Medallions with Mint Pesto Sauce; Sauteed Veal Piccata; Fresh-farmed California Abalone; Black Angus Beef

THE BAY CLUB
2700 17-Mile Dr., The Inn at Spanish Bay
Pebble Beach / 408-647-7433
Dinner daily
NORTHERN ITALIAN

The setting at the Bay Club is decidedly intimate, and the food undeniably superb. Classical music on Friday and Saturday perfectly complements the restaurant's romantic mood and a choice selection of Italian, French and vintage California wines matches the fine cuisine. The Bay Club participates in a chef exchange program, supervised by award-winning Chef Gualtiero Marchesi of Milan. The program guarantees a menu that is always fresh and innovative, reflecting the best in contemporary Italian cuisine. The prix-fixe menu includes antipasti and several courses. The 17-Mile Drive gate fee is waived with dinner reservations; jackets are requested at this elegant restaurant.

Specialties: Lobster Salad with Black Truffles; Ricotta & Spinach Crepe with Tomato Coulis; Open Ravioli with Scallops, Ginger & White Wine; Pan-roasted Striped Bass; Classic Milanese Veal Chop; Rack of Lamb with Thyme-garlic Sauce

CASANOVA
5th btwn. San Carlos & Mission
Carmel / 408-625-0501
Lunch & dinner daily
CONTINENTAL

Casanova specializes in Country French and Italian cuisine, homemade pasta and a full selection of mouthwatering desserts prepared in-house.

CLUB XIX
The Lodge at Pebble Beach / 408-625-8519
Lunch & dinner daily
COUNTRY FRENCH

In a spectacular setting overlooking Carmel Bay and the 18th hole of famed Pebble Beach golf course, Club XIX is an elegant restaurant for a special dinner. Romantic and intimate, the restaurant is in the world-famous Lodge at Pebble Beach. Jacket and tie are requested for dinner. The 17-Mile Drive gate fee is waived with dinner reservations. Weather permitting, lunch and drinks are

served on an umbrella-decked patio with panoramic views. Casual attire is accepted for Club XIX's more informal bistro lunch.

Specialties: Glazed Oysters with Spinach Leaves & Sevruga Caviar; Consomme of Squab with Squab Breast & Aspic Timbale; Poached Salmon Tournedos with Leek, Spinach Sauce & Garnish of Oysters & Caviar; Rack of Lamb on Striped Polenta with Spinach, Wild Mushrooms & Goat Cheese

THE COVEY AT QUAIL LODGE
8205 Valley Greens Dr., Quail Lodge
Carmel / 408-624-1581
Dinner daily
EUROPEAN

Even though it is part of the prestigious five-star Quail Lodge, The Covey maintains an engaging simplicity in a thoroughly sophisticated atmosphere. The interior features dark wood paneling, duck prints on the wall and a peaceful lake view through the bay windows. The menu includes lots of fresh seafood, light sauces and seasonal vegetables from nearby farms.

Specialties: Muscovy Duck Breast with Red Currants & Brandied Cherries; Salmon with Green Peppercorn Crust & Black Bean Sauce; Turban of Sole with Deviled Crab & Prosciutto; Ragout of Sweetbreads with Mushroom & Flageolets in a Puff Pastry Shell

CREME CARMEL
San Carlos near 7th, Carmel / 408-624-0444
Dinner daily
FRENCH/CALIFORNIA

The menu of French specialties changes seasonally in this intimate candlelit restaurant. A well-conceived wine list complements the excellent menu.

THE FRENCH POODLE
Junipero & 5th, Carmel / 408-624-8643
Dinner Mon & Tues, Thurs-Sat
FRENCH

Candlelight, fresh flowers, a long list of Bordeaux and Burgundy wines, and classic French cuisine highlight this elegant family-owned restaurant.

THE GENERAL STORE & FORGE IN THE FOREST
Junipero & 5th, Carmel / 408-624-2233
Lunch & dinner daily
AMERICAN

Serving one of the best burgers in Carmel, steaks and fresh fish daily, the General Store attracts locals and tourists alike to its outdoor patio with fireplaces and cozy, indoor pub. The soups, salads, breads, and desserts are all fresh and homemade. An easygoing restaurant that delivers comfort and hearty fare, it appeals to every mood and appetite.

Specialties: Charbroiled Filet Mignon With Caramelized Shallot in Red Wine Sauce; Lamb Loin Medallions on a Bed of Fennel, Served au Jus; Mixed Grill (Spareribs, Smoked Chicken & Pork Loin)

CARMEL • MONTEREY

LA BOHEME
Dolores & 7th, Carmel / 408-624-7500
Dinner daily
EUROPEAN COUNTRY CUISINE

A cheerful country courtyard theme, with white fluffy clouds in a pastel sky, accents La Boheme. The restaurant serves a different three-course prix-fixe meal every night, featuring regional recipes from all over Europe.
Specialties: Vol au Vent Marie Rose (Prawns & Breast of Chicken in Puff Pastry); Roast Duckling with a Cumberland Sauce of Sherry, Orange & Red Currant; Beef Wellington; Filet Mignon au Roquefort (Filet Mignon with a Roquefort, Wine & Cream Sauce)

LA BRASSERIE Q POINT OF CARMEL
Ocean Ave. btwn. Dolores & Lincoln
Carmel / 408-624-2569
Dinner daily
FRENCH/CALIFORNIA

With a top-notch chef imported from Maxim's in Tokyo and a truly restful ambiance, La Brasserie Q Point offers a wonderful night out at prices that are a steal.

L'ESCARGOT
Mission & 4th, Carmel / 408-624-4914
Dinner Mon-Sat
FRENCH

L'Escargot, Carmel's oldest French restaurant, has the warmth and romance of old-world European restaurants. Fine meats, poultry, seafood and traditional French fare attentively prepared to order have made this a favorite destination for more than 35 years. Homemade desserts, French and California wines and full cocktail service, offered at tableside, enhance L'Escargot's diverse Country French menu.
Specialties: Escargots de Bourgogne; Fresh Salmon Poached with Beurre Blanc Sauce; Coquilles St. Jacques; New York-cut Steak with Cream, Cognac & Peppercorns; Medallion of Veal with Mustard Sauce; Rack of Lamb; Tarte Tatin

NEPENTHE
Hwy. One, Big Sur / 408-667-2345
Lunch & dinner daily
BISTRO/CONTINENTAL

Nepenthe's redwood pavilion is perched 800 feet above the rocky coastline in a grove of trees. It's a stop not to be missed, where travelers can relax in the invigorating atmosphere, enjoy a drink and dine high above the surf.

PIATTI
Junipero & 6th, Carmel / 408-625-1766
Lunch & dinner daily
ITALIAN

One of seven Piattis in California, this restaurant brings to Carmel the original restaurant's legacy of vibrant regional Italian cuisine. Every dish reflects Chef Zenda Willemstein's interpretation of simple but good dishes.

RAFFAELLO
Mission btwn. Ocean & 7th, Carmel / 408-624-1541
Dinner Wed-Mon
ITALIAN

In a Florentine atmosphere perfectly suited for romantic dining, chef/owner Remo d'Agliano has been serving devoted patrons classic Italian cuisine for more than 27 years. The tiny (12 tables) candlelit restaurant, located in downtown Carmel, features Italian, French, German and California wines.
Specialties: Fettuccine Romana; Veal a la Creme; Cannelloni alla Raffaello; Prawns with Cinnamon; Veal Piemontese; Homemade Spumoni

THE RIDGE
Robles del Rio Lodge, 200 Punta del Monte
Carmel Valley / 408-659-0170
Lunch & dinner Tues-Sun
FRENCH

Overlooking the Carmel Valley, The Ridge offers patrons the combined pleasures of a breathtaking view and traditional French cuisine.

THE RIO GRILL
Hwy. One & Rio Rd., The Crossroads
Carmel / 408-625-5436
Lunch & dinner daily, brunch Sun
AMERICAN

This Santa Fe-style restaurant, with its tall cacti and adobe walls, serves inventive regional American cuisine, with a Southwestern flavor. The menu includes lots of meat, fish and poultry smoked or grilled, great appetizers such as roasted garlic and warm goat cheese, and huge home-style desserts. The full menu is also available at The Rio Grill's casual and friendly lounge, where reservations are not needed.
Specialties: Barbecued Baby-back Ribs; Castroville Artichoke with Roma Tomato Relish & Pesto Mayonnaise; Marinated Rabbit with Yam & Fennel Ragout; Fresh Pasta; Chocolate-draped Ice Cream Sandwich

ROBATA
3658 The Barnyard, Carmel / 408-624-2643
Dinner daily
JAPANESE

Robata recreates a traditional Japanese country inn. Judging by the rustic wood interior, the low ceilings and the quiet grace of Robata, it's a success. The food is as authentic as the decor: fresh sushi, light tempura and delicate morsels of fish, fowl, meat and vegetables cooked on the open-hearth robata grill.
Specialties: Tempura Combinations; Sushi; Sashimi

PACIFIC'S EDGE.

Menus that are spontaneous and creative, drawing from the bounty of the region, changing with the offerings of the seasons.

The dining experience at Highlands Inn. Since 1916 the premier destination for travelers to the spectacular Carmel Highlands Coast.

HIGHLANDS INN

Four miles south
of Carmel on
Highway One

Lunch, Dinner, Sunday Brunch
Reservations Recommended
408-624-3801

MEMBER OF SMALL LUXURY HOTELS & RESORTS

SIERRA MAR
P.O. Box 219, Hwy. One, Big Sur / 408-667-2200
Lunch & dinner daily
CALIFORNIA

The Sierra Mar is in the spectacular new resort, the Post Ranch Inn. Perched on a cliff overlooking the Pacific, each table has an ocean view. Reservations are required.

SILVER JONES
3690 The Barnyard, Carmel / 408-624-5200
Lunch & dinner daily, brunch Sun
AMERICAN/EUROPEAN COUNTRY

An award-winning favorite of locals, Silver Jones beckons with a tantalizing aroma of fire-baked pizza that wafts through its southwestern interior to the cheerful, umbrella-lined patio outside. A wide array of fish, poultry, lamb, beef and local ingredients, including custom-grown produce, is the basis of its distinctive menu, and the restaurant's extensive wine list offers some of the best vintage values in Carmel.
Specialties: Greek Lamb Filet with Eggplant & Spinach Polenta; Penne Pasta Roma with Swiss Chard, Snow Peas & Olive Oil; Salmon Grilled with Sundried Tomato Butter; Roasted Pork Loin with Paprika Pan Gravy & New Potatoes

TERRACE GRILL RESTAURANT
La Playa Hotel, Camino Real at 8th
Carmel / 408-624-4010
Breakfast, lunch & dinner daily, brunch Sun
CALIFORNIA/FRENCH

The Terrace Grill presents California cuisine with French flair against a 1920s Spanish Mediterranean backdrop. Lunch and drinks are served on an outdoor terrace overlooking the luxuriant gardens and the Pacific Ocean. At dinner you'll find fresh seafood specialties and other favorites, as well as fresh pastries baked in-house. The restaurant also has a full bar and cocktail lounge.
Specialties: Artichoke Ravioli with Julienne Vegetables; Salmon & Asparagus in Lobster Sauce; Swordfish with Olive Relish & Blackened, Sundried Tomatoes

TOOTS LAGOON
Dolores btwn. Ocean & 7th, Carmel / 408-625-1915
Lunch & dinner daily
BARBECUE

This casual restaurant serves ribs eight different ways. Toots Lagoon also makes its own pasta and gourmet pizza and serves fresh seafood dishes.

VENTANA RESTAURANT
Hwy. One, Big Sur / 408-624-4812
Lunch & dinner daily
CALIFORNIA

Located 28 miles south of Carmel, Ventana Inn is a Mobil four-star resort, with dramatic vistas of sea, surf and sky. Dine 1,200 feet above the restless Pacific Ocean in Ventana's award-winning restaurant, where a beau-

tifully landscaped terrace offers a 50-mile view of the Big Sur coastline. The exceptional menu features vintage California wines in airy, natural cedar surroundings.
Specialties: Grilled Pacific Salmon Filet; Roasted Rack of Lamb; Grilled Marinated Chicken Breast; Lobster, Scallop & Prawn Stir Fry

ACCOMMODATIONS

HIGHLANDS INN
Four miles south of Carmel on Hwy. One / 408-624-3801

Perched just above the Big Sur coast, rooms at Highlands Inn feature fireplaces and ocean views, and suites have spa baths, fireplaces, full kitchens and spectacular ocean-view decks. Two restaurants also provide fabulous views of the ocean along with award-winning cuisine, and there is dancing in the spacious lounge. Highlands Inn specializes in banquets and is an ideal setting for small conferences — or a romantic weekend.
Singles & doubles $225-$550

THE INN & LINKS AT SPANISH BAY
2700 17-Mile Dr., Pebble Beach / 408-647-7500

Majestic pines, dramatic sea and grass-covered dunes are the setting for Spanish Bay's 80 outstanding residences and world-class golf course located only three miles from the Lodge at Pebble Beach. Built to conform to the site's natural contours, the resort spa and clubhouse, tennis courts, exclusive shops, excellent restaurants — including **The Bay Club** and **The Dunes** — 270 guest rooms and state-of-the-art conference facilities are the perfect complement to this breathtaking coastline.
Singles & doubles $230-$335; suites $500-$1,650

INNS BY THE SEA
P.O. Box 101, Carmel
408-624-0101 or 800-422-4732

Whether you're looking for a quiet, romantic retreat or a great family getaway, Inns by the Sea offers charm, exceptional service, unbeatable value and accommodations to suit every need. In the Carmel inns you'll find everything from spacious family suites with kitchens, to luxury suites with wood-burning fireplaces, down comforters, in-room jacuzzis and fresh flowers. In Monterey you can relax in great rooms that range from doubles to kings, take a swim in the heated pool and wake up to hot coffee and Continental breakfast. You can make reservations at any of the seven inns by calling a single, toll-free number: 800-433-4732. And Guest Services can make your trip a lot more fun by making dinner reservations or any special arrangements you may need. Inns by the Sea offers an excellent value year-round, the convenience and service of a hotel, and all the charm and

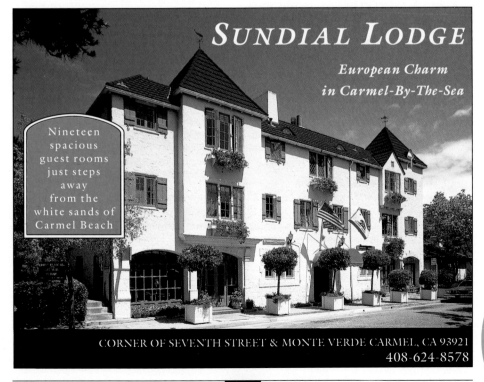

SUNDIAL LODGE
European Charm in Carmel-By-The-Sea

Nineteen spacious guest rooms just steps away from the white sands of Carmel Beach

CORNER OF SEVENTH STREET & MONTE VERDE CARMEL, CA 93921
408-624-8578

personal attention that keep their guests coming back year after year.

Singles & doubles $44-$139; suites $129-$225

LA PLAYA HOTEL
Camino Real at 8th, Carmel / 408-624-6476

Only two blocks from the white sand of Carmel Beach and a short walk from world-class art galleries and boutiques, the historic La Playa Hotel has a storybook charm all its own. The three-story Mediterranean-style hotel has 73 rooms and two suites and five guest cottages nestled among cypress and pine trees. Lush gardens lead to a large, aquamarine swimming pool and the award-winning **Terrace Grill Restaurant**, located just off the hotel lobby.

Singles & doubles $95-$210; suites $300-$425; cottages $210-$495

THE LODGE AT PEBBLE BEACH
17-Mile Dr., Pebble Beach / 408-624-3811

At the sea's edge near the Carmel gate of the Del Monte Forest, The Lodge at Pebble Beach is home to the world-famous Pebble Beach Golf Links. A stay at The Lodge is a lesson in luxury any time of year. From the wide, sunny veranda off the spacious public sitting room overlooking the 18th hole to the tastefully appointed individual rooms and suites, The Lodge offers a completely relaxing retreat from the cares of the business world. Restaurant choices are abundant here also, including the **Cypress Room** and **Club XIX**.

Singles & doubles $280-$425; suites $800-$1,000

POST RANCH INN
P.O. Box 219, Hwy. One
Big Sur / 408-667-2200

A spectacular new resort overlooking the Big Sur Coast, the Post Ranch Inn was developed with a reverence for nature. With just 30 rooms, each nestled into the hills and trees, the resort has a pool, spa, full-time masseurs, acres of trails and oversized private jacuzzis.

QUAIL LODGE RESORT & GOLF CLUB
8205 Valley Greens Dr., off Carmel Valley Rd.
Carmel / 408-624-1581

In a peaceful country setting minutes from Carmel, Quail Lodge Resort is nestled among lavish fairways, lakes and landscaped grounds. The resort conveys a casual elegance with a passion for quality. The only Mobil five-star property between Los Angeles and San Francisco, the lodge offers 100 luxurious guest rooms and suites in a garden setting. The lodge also features a generous selection of private conference rooms. Guests enjoy golf, tennis, swimming and the exquisite **Covey Restaurant** as additional enticements.

Singles & doubles $195-$245; suites from $285

STONEPINE ESTATES
150 E. Carmel Valley Rd., Carmel Valley / 408-659-2245

Built in 1930 as a country home for the Crocker family, this French-style chateau on 330 beautifully landscaped acres is a luxurious, exclusive haven. There are eight suites in Chateau Noel, four in the Paddock House, which can be rented as one unit, and two in the newly added Briar Rose Cottage, all with fireplaces, jacuzzis, antique furniture and Oriental rugs. The private dining room prepares exquisite French cuisine. The oldest working thoroughbred racing farm west of the Mississippi, Stonepine has trail riding and instruction, mountain bicycles, a pool, tennis court, soccer field, croquet and archery range.

Doubles $250-$500; suites $350-$750

SUNDIAL LODGE
Monte Verde btwn. Ocean & 7th, Carmel / 408-624-8578

Located in the heart of Carmel-by-the-Sea, the Sundial Lodge reflects the grace and warmth of a small, European hotel. Nineteen comfortable rooms surround an award-winning, color-splashed courtyard garden, and the hotel is located just a short walk from the white sands of Carmel Beach. Some guest rooms have an ocean view, and all rooms are appointed with private bath, television and refrigerator.

Singles & doubles $105-$170; suite $170

TICKLE PINK INN
155 Highlands Dr., Carmel / 408-624-1244

Nestled high on a cliff, the Tickle Pink Inn at Carmel Highlands offers spectacular ocean views overlooking the Big Sur coastline. Relax by a cozy fire in one of many rooms and suites with fireplaces, view the sunset from your private balcony, and let the sound of the surf lull you to sleep in this quiet, romantic inn. Have the complimentary Continental breakfast delivered to your room with the morning paper, and in the evening enjoy the complimentary wine-and-cheese reception served on the terrace lounge and deck.

Singles & doubles $139-$209; suites $189-$259

VENTANA INN
Hwy. One, Big Sur / 408-667-2331

The Ventana Inn represents a unique Big Sur experience, offering elegant but casual living. Located 28 miles south of Carmel, its dramatic hillside location affords great vistas of sea, surf and sky. Some bedroom suites feature their own hot tubs and there is a swimwear-optional sundeck above one of the pools. The Ventana Inn is a Mobil four-star resort. Its award-winning **Ventana Restaurant** serves lunch and dinner daily in airy, natural cedar surroundings above a beautifully landscaped terrace with a spectacular 50-mile view of the Big Sur coastline.

Singles & doubles $165-$350; suites $310-$475

CALENDAR OF EVENTS

For events in Carmel, call the Tourist & Visitors Bureau at 408-624-1711. For events throughout Monterey County, contact the Monterey Peninsula Chamber of Commerce & Visitors Bureau at 408-649-1770.

JANUARY

AT&T PRO-AM
The tournament pairs celebrities and golf professionals, Pebble Beach golf courses.

FEBRUARY

MASTERS OF FOOD & WINE
Internationally known chefs and winemakers present master cooking classes, gourmet meals and tours, Highlands Inn, Carmel.

MARCH

MONTEREY WINE FESTIVAL
The oldest wine festival in the country features tastings and seminars by top winemakers, Monterey.

APRIL

MONTEREY ADOBE TOUR
Tour of historic adobes and gardens by local historians in period costumes. Free trolley rides, Monterey.

MAY

THE GREAT MONTEREY SQUID FESTIVAL
Squid — in food, arts and crafts, demonstrations and in entertainment shows, Monterey.

JUNE

MONTEREY BAY BLUES FESTIVAL
Outdoor blues festival, Monterey Fairgrounds.

MONTEREY BAY THEATRE FEST
Free theatre festival every weekend through August at Fisherman's Wharf, Monterey.

JULY

FOURTH OF JULY CELEBRATIONS
A morning parade on Alvarado Street is followed by a picnic barbecue on the lawn of Colton Hall in downtown Monterey. The hometown celebration includes food, carnival games and entertainment. Fireworks are displayed over Monterey Bay starting at 9PM. The best viewing site is from Fisherman's Wharf, Monterey.

CARMEL BACH FESTIVAL
A three-week festival celebrating the music of J.S. Bach with concerts, lectures and events, Carmel.

GILROY GARLIC FESTIVAL
Weekend festival in Gilroy, the garlic capital of the world. Garlic is featured in every kind of food and is celebrated with entertainment and an arts and crafts show. The festival is one of the most popular events in Monterey County.

AUGUST

STEINBECK FESTIVAL
Monterey County's noted author is celebrated with films, lectures and tours in his birthplace, Salinas. Some events are also held on Cannery Row in Monterey.

PEBBLE BEACH CONCOURS D'ELEGANCE
Classic automobiles are featured in one of the country's most prestigious concours, Pebble Beach.

SEPTEMBER

CARMEL SHAKESPEARE FESTIVAL
The outdoor Shakespeare festival runs through October, Carmel.

FESTIVAL DEL PUEBLO DE MONTEREY
A grito — a call to arms — opens the festival. The ceremony commemorates the Indian uprising against the Spanish colonizers, which led to independence. The festival features a pow wow, a coronation ball, a fiesta and a parade of indigenous peoples.

MONTEREY JAZZ FESTIVAL
The oldest continuous jazz festival in the United States attracts jazz lovers to Monterey every year.

ARTICHOKE FESTIVAL
Castroville, the artichoke capital of the world, puts on a festival with arts and crafts, food and entertainment.

OCTOBER

BUTTERFLY PARADE
Children parade in butterfly costumes to celebrate the annual arrival of the Monarch butterfly in Pacific Grove.

NOVEMBER

ROBERT LOUIS STEVENSON'S UNBIRTHDAY
The author gave away his birthday to a local girl who was born on Christmas. The "unbirthday" is held at the home where he stayed in 1879, Monterey.

DECEMBER

CHRISTMAS IN THE ADOBES
Monterey's historic adobes are lit with candles and feature music, period Christmas decorations and volunteers in Old Monterey dress.

LA POSADA
A mariachi band leads the traditional candlelight procession through downtown Monterey.

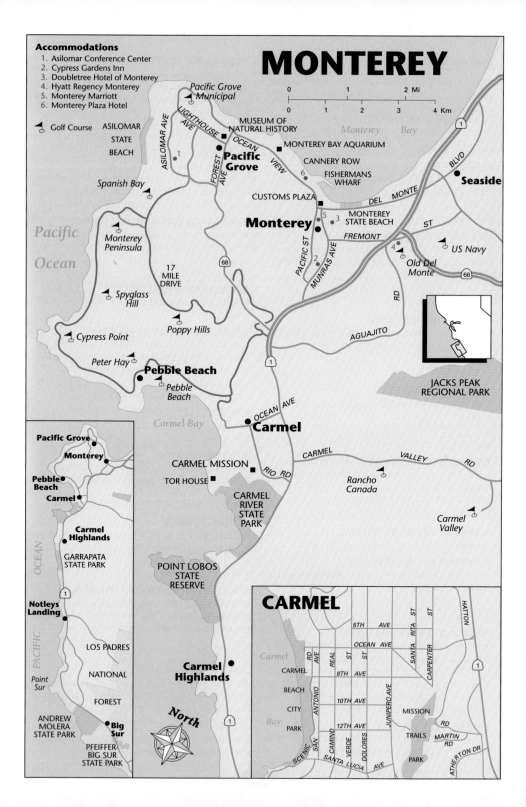

MONTEREY INFORMATION

AAA EMERGENCY ROAD SERVICE
Monterey..............................408-372-8131

AIRLINES
American Eagle/American Airlines
....800-433-7300
United/ United Express 800-241-6522
USAir..800-428-4322

BICYCLE RENTAL
Adventures by the Sea 408-372-1807
Bay Bikes 408-646-9090
Free Wheeling Cycles 408-373-3855

BUS
Greyhound 408-373-4735

CAR RENTAL
Avis..408-373-3327
Budget..408-373-1899
Dollar..408-373-6121
Hertz..408-373-3318
National..408-373-4181

CHARTER BOATS
Adventures by the Sea... 408-372-1807
Chris's Fishing Trips............................408-375-5951
Monterey Bay Kayaks 408-373-KELP

GOLF
Laguna Seca......................................408-373-3701
Old Del Monte....................................408-373-2436
Pebble Beach Golf Links 800-654-9300
Poppy Hills Golf Course... 408-625-2035
Rancho Canada Golf Club 408-624-0111
Spanish Bay Golf Course 800-654-9300
Spyglass Hill Golf Club........................800-654-9300

GUIDED TOURS
California Heritage Guides 408-373-6454
Otter-Mobile Tours 408-625-9782
Seacoast Safaris 408-372-1288
Steinbeck Country Tours 408-625-5107

TAXIS
Yellow Cab 408-646-1234

TENNIS
Monterey Tennis Center... 408-372-0172
Pacific Grove Tennis Club..................408-648-3129

VISITOR INFORMATION
Chamber of Commerce 408-649-1770
Tourist & Visitors Bureau 408-624-1711

MONTEREY DIRECTORY

POINTS OF INTEREST

CANNERY ROW
Monterey Bay Shoreline, Monterey

Formerly an assortment of sardine canneries immortalized by the writings of John Steinbeck, the weathered waterfront structures are now a major tourist attraction of shops, galleries and seafood restaurants. Stretching for a mile along the shores of Monterey Bay, the Row is a fascinating place to visit. There are still empty shells of abandoned canneries, but most have been reconstructed.

COLTON HALL MUSEUM & FRIENDLY PLAZA
Pacific St. btwn. Madison & Jefferson, Monterey
408-646-5640

Under the dominion of Spain and Mexico, Monterey was the capital of California for 78 years. The beautiful grounds of Monterey's Colton Hall and Friendly Plaza in the heart of Old Monterey were the site of the first California Constitutional Convention. The restored two-story Constitution Hall, built of stone mined from nearby hills, was completed in 1849. The second story has exhibits on Monterey's history.

LAGUNA SECA
Hwy. 68 btwn. Monterey & Salinas / 408-648-5111

From the Pope's 1987 visit to headline concerts to one-of-a-kind racing events, Laguna Seca has become a center of activity on the Monterey Peninsula. As one of Monterey County's regional parks, Laguna Seca offers hiking and more than 200 campsites, many overlooking the rolling scenery of the Salinas Valley. For park information and reservations, call 408-755-4895. Laguna Seca's most exciting spectacle is the racecourse, a 2.2 mile-track that brought an international motorcycle Grand Prix to the U.S. — the first in more than 20 years. The course is also famous for historic auto races in August and Indy-500 car races in October. All races are organized by the Sports Car Racing Association of the Monterey Peninsula, and net proceeds go to charity.

MARSH'S ORIENTAL ART & ANTIQUES
599 Fremont St., Monterey / 408-372-3547

One of the most distinctive buildings on the Monterey Peninsula since the 1920s and a landmark for the Oriental-art connoisseur is Marsh's. The first George T. Marsh studied the plans of the Temple of Heaven in Peking's Forbidden City as a prototype for the shop he built to showcase his collection of Oriental art, antiques and treasures. Today, George Marsh, the founder's grandson, still travels to Peking and other Far Eastern cities in search of stock. Treasures can be seen in the main display room, the Moon Room, or in the well-guarded Jewel Room. The Japanese Room, with its screens and exquisite kimonos, opens onto a serene view of the bridge in the Japanese garden.

MONTEREY BAY AQUARIUM
Southern end of Cannery Row, Monterey / 408-648-4888

More than 6,500 marine creatures fill more than 100 major habitat galleries and exhibits — sharks, sea otters, a giant kelp forest, a touching pool and many more — for a startling undersea tour of Monterey Bay. Outdoor observation decks, overlooking the sea, offer visitors sunny spots to admire the bay.

MONTEREY PENINSULA MUSEUM OF ART
559 Pacific St., Monterey / 408-372-5477

This fine local museum features both a folk and fine art collection, closely mirroring the historical development of the region. The works reflect the area's relationship with the sea and its early popularity as a retreat for Bohemian artists, with a survey of important local photography from Edward Weston to Ansel Adams, and changing exhibits of contemporary art. The folk art collection has examples of traditional art from every continent. The museum has expanded its Pacific, California and Asian Rim collections, housed in a newly completed gallery.

MONTEREY STATE HISTORIC PARK
525 Polk St., Monterey / 408-649-7118

In 1602 while searching for a safe harbor for the Spanish fleet's treasure-laden galleons returning from the Philippines, Sebastian Vizcaino discovered the calm waters of Monterey Bay. Many of the gracious surviving adobes of Old Monterey are now part of the California State Park System. The park includes the Cooper-Molera Adobe, the Old Custom House on the Wharf (the oldest government building on the Pacific Coast), Pacific House, Monterey's First Theater, the Thomas Larkin House adobe, the Robert Louis Stevenson House, the Joseph Boston & Co. Store, Casa Soberanes and the Vizcaino-Serra landing site. The California Heritage Guides at the Pacific House, 10 Custom House Plaza (408-373-6454), offer walking tours by appointment.

OLD FISHERMAN'S WHARF
Monterey Bay / 408-373-0600

The first accessible port in Northern California, Monterey's Old Fisherman's Wharf began in 1847 and was the home of one of the world's largest sardine industries. Today, the wharf is a major tourist attraction, with restaurants, gift shops, art galleries and party, fishing and sightseeing boats, many with glass bottoms for shallow bay viewing. Three fish markets offer fresh fish from Monterey Bay, including live salmon and live crab. For information about performances at the Wharf Theatre, call 408-375-1721.

PACIFIC GROVE MUSEUM OF NATURAL HISTORY
165 Forest Ave., Pacific Grove / 408-648-3116

A small, fascinating museum with a large collection of Monarch butterflies, marine and bird life, native plants and Indian artifacts. It's the sort of place you want to visit before you go out exploring the flora and fauna of the Monterey Peninsula. The museum also gives free tours of the Point Pinos Lighthouse — the oldest in continuous operation on the West Coast — every Saturday and Sunday from 1PM to 4PM.

PACIFIC GROVE SHORELINE
Pacific Grove

At the tip of the Peninsula lies the peaceful retreat of Pacific Grove, with its cozy Victorian inns, quaint shops and five miles of coastal parks. For more than a century, Pacific Grove has been known as "Butterfly Town, USA" because of the thousands of Monarch butterflies that winter here. The area began as a Chinese fishing village, then later became a Methodist summer retreat in the 1870s. Neat Victorian homes, dating from that era, sit elegantly along Pacific Grove's coastline. An oceanfront bike and walking path, the only one of its kind in the region, begins at Cannery Row near the Aquarium, passes Lover's Point Park with its crescent swimming beach and picnic area, then leads to the Point Pinos Lighthouse and the crashing surf of Asilomar State Beach.

PAUL MASSON MUSEUM & TASTING ROOM
700 Cannery Row, Monterey / 408-646-5446

At this museum and tasting room in the heart of Cannery Row, the spirit of the Frenchman who developed the oldest continuously operating winery in California lives on. Produced in Monterey County, Paul Masson wines and the new Masson Vineyards premium varietals set the mood for history buffs and wine aficionados who want to explore the art and fable of an extraordinary vintner. Other attractions include a free historical film on Paul Masson and winemaking, complimentary wine tasting and a spectacular panoramic view of Monterey Bay.
Open daily 10AM to 6PM

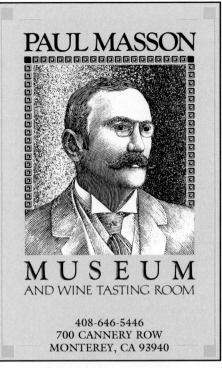
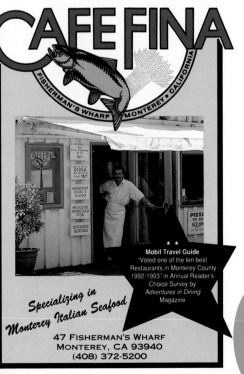

PRESIDIO OF MONTEREY MUSEUM
Cpl. Ewing Rd. btwn. the Bolio & Artillery St. gates
Monterey / 408-647-5536

Located high on a hill with a commanding view of
Monterey Bay, the Presidio Museum outlines the story
of the historic "Old Fort" through dioramas, artifacts
and photographs. The museum is currently open by
appointment only. Visitors are free to take a self-guided
tour of 13 historic sites adjacent to the museum. The
sites include the location of a 2,000-year-old Indian village, the ruins of the first American fort in Monterey,
and Sebastian Vizcaino's 1602 landing site.

SPIRIT OF MONTEREY WAX MUSEUM
700 Cannery Row, Monterey / 408-375-3770

Wax characters dressed in period costumes recreate
moments in California's history such as the discovery
of Monterey Bay and bring to life John Steinbeck's fic-
tional drifters, cannery workers and ladies of the night.

WALKING TOUR OF HISTORIC OLD MONTEREY
Monterey Peninsula Chamber of Commerce
380 Alvarado St., Monterey / 408-649-1770

Maps for self-guided tours of Old Monterey — past some
of the town's fine old adobe homes — are available at
the Chamber of Commerce.

SHOPPING

DEL MONTE SHOPPING CENTER
Munras Ave. & Hwy. One, Monterey / 408-373-2705

A cluster of free-standing buildings with a traditional
Monterey appearance comprises the Del Monte
Shopping Center, filled with more than 90 stores, businesses and services. Shoppers will find **Macy's**,
Mervyn's, a host of fashion and gift shops, restaurants,
bakeries and the largest movie theatre in the area. Beautiful landscaping and a lovely fountain make this an
attractive and relaxing environment for shoppers.

RESTAURANTS

ALLEGRO GOURMET PIZZERIA
1184 Forest near Prescott, Pacific Grove / 408-373-5656
Lunch & dinner daily
ITALIAN

Famous on the Monterey Peninsula for its innovative
whole-wheat-crust pizza and calzone, Allegro also offers
pasta and risotto dishes as well as osso buco and cioppino. Enjoy vegetarian minestrone, Mediterranean-style
salads and Italian sandwiches on focaccia bread in this
casual country trattoria. Complete your meal with a cappuccino or wonderful tiramisu. For those looking for
great-tasting food that's good for you, too, Allegro is the
only local pizzeria with recipes that meet the standards
set by the American Heart Association. On a sunny day,
the outdoor patio is irresistible.
Specialties: Pizza; Pasta; Risotto; Osso Buco; Cioppino

BINDEL'S
500 Hartnell St., Monterey / 408-373-3737
Dinner daily, brunch Sun
CALIFORNIA

Located in an 1840s adobe, this cozy, romantic restaurant recalls Old California. The menu offers regional cuisine, using local seafood, game and produce.

CAFE FINA
47 Fisherman's Wharf, Monterey / 408-372-5200
Lunch & dinner daily
ITALIAN

When you go to Fisherman's Wharf, you expect to make a seafood catch worthy of its tradition and Cafe Fina doesn't disappoint. Owner Dominic Mercurio, from a third-generation of Italian fishermen, presents seasonal fish dishes with an Italian accent. The house specialty, Pasta Fina, combines fresh linguine with baby shrimp. You can also order mesquite-grilled chicken and beef. Cafe Fina makes its own fettuccine, linguine and ravioli. Authentic Italian pizzas are prepared in a wood-burning brick oven imported from Milan, and everything at this casual but elegant restaurant is served by an enthusiastic staff.
Specialties: Eggplant Pizza with Pesto & Roasted Garlic; Oysters Rockefeller; Fresh Grilled Petrale Sole; Combination Seafood Pasta; Veal Stuffed with Mozzarella, Parmesan, Green Onions & Pesto Sauce

CENTRAL 1-5-9
159 Central Ave., Pacific Grove / 408-372-2235
Lunch Tues-Fri, dinner Tues-Sun, brunch Sun
AMERICAN

Inside a 1930s Hollywood bungalow, Central 1-5-9 is a small, intimate restaurant with a crisp white decor and a dedication to the freshest cooking ingredients.

DELFINO'S ON THE BAY
400 Cannery Row, Monterey Plaza Hotel
Monterey / 408-646-1706
Breakfast, lunch & dinner daily, brunch Sun
ITALIAN

Take a romantic dining room with a view, add traditional Genovese seafood and pasta dishes, and the sum equals success. Delfino's serves an outdoor brunch in summer.

DOMENICO'S ON THE WHARF
50 Fisherman's Wharf #1, Monterey / 408-372-3655
Lunch & dinner daily
SEAFOOD & PASTA

What could be more appealing than dining on fresh seafood and top-quality meats cooked on a mesquite grill in a room built on stilts right above the yacht harbor? Enormous windows bring the sparkling beauty of Monterey Bay with its frolicking sea lions right to your tableside. Specialties include abalone, oysters, fresh catch of the day, pasta, Caesar salad prepared in front

CARMEL • MONTEREY

VENTANA
BIG SUR
Country Inn Resort

Hwy. 1

28 miles south
of Carmel

Big Sur

California

408·624·4812

of you, mesquite-grilled Black Angus steaks and home-made ice cream. The service at Domenico's is superb.
Specialties: Domenico's Combination Seafood Platter; Oysters Rockeller; Bouillabaisse; Smoked Salmon Ravioli with Caviar; Pasta Capri

FANDANGO
223 17th St., Pacific Grove / 408-372-3456
Lunch & dinner daily, brunch Sun
MEDITERRANEAN

Fandango will enchant you with its warm ambiance, perfect for both a romantic dinner or a large celebration. Diners can eat outdoors year-round on the restaurant's terrace, surrounded by flowers and warmed by heat lamps. Fandango's spicy and colorful menu is prepared from Mediterranean country-style dishes, such as Spanish paella, Provencal cassoulet, Algerian couscous and other regional specialties. Fandango also serves traditional rack of lamb, seafood and steaks, all prepared on an open mesquite grill, and tops every meal with decadent homemade desserts.
Specialties: Cassoulet Bean Soup; Rack of Lamb in Cabernet Sauce; Cannelloni; Grand Marnier Souffle with Raspberry Sauce; Meringue with Espresso Ice Cream in a Chocolate Sauce

THE FISHWIFE AT ASILOMAR
1996½ Sunset Dr. at Asilomar
Pacific Grove / 408-375-7107
Lunch & dinner Wed-Mon, brunch Sun
CALIFORNIA

If seafood and pasta with a Caribbean accent sound appealing, try the Fishwife at Asilomar, just yards from the Pacific Ocean.

FRESH CREAM
Heritage Harbor, corner of Pacific & Scott, Suite 100C
Monterey / 408-375-9798
Dinner daily
FRENCH

Fresh Cream, a local favorite, serves contemporary French food in an intimate setting. Its new location offers a full bar, four private rooms and magnificent views of Monterey Bay. The menu, based on seasonal ingredients and the chef's inspirations, has a California flair. Rack of lamb Dijonnaise, the house specialty, can be prepared for one.
Specialties: Pate of Foie Gras; Blackened Ahi Tuna with Pineapple Rum Butter; Holland Dover Sole Grilled with Browned Butter & Lemon; Roasted Duckling with Black Currant Sauce; Souffle Grand Marnier

GERNOT'S VICTORIA-HOUSE RESTAURANT
649 Lighthouse Ave., Pacific Grove / 408-646-1477
Dinner Tues-Sun
INTERNATIONAL

Set in an elegant 1896 Victorian, Gernot's features

distinctive European and American cuisine with an Austrian touch. House specialties include local wild boar, venison and seafood.

MELAC'S
663 Lighthouse Ave., Pacific Grove / 408-375-1743
Lunch Tues-Fri, dinner Tues-Sat
FRENCH

This cozy country restaurant's American chef, trained in France, prepares excellent French dishes that are beautiful to look at and generously portioned. The menu changes daily to make the most of fresh seasonal produce, and the wine list is a blend of the best vintage selections of California and France. No smoking is permitted at Melac's.
Specialties: Grilled Quail with Roasted Garlic, Fresh Herbs & Oregon Chanterelles; Seafood Cassoulet; Medallions of Veal with Madeira Wine & Lemon Confit; Roasted Duckling with Port & Fresh Figs

OLD BATH HOUSE
620 Ocean View Blvd., Pacific Grove / 408-375-5195
Dinner daily
CALIFORNIA/CONTINENTAL

Designed to capture the feeling of the 1930s, The Old Bath House offers gourmet dining, an elegant atmosphere and a breathtaking ocean view.

PEPPERS MEXICALI CAFE
170 Forest Ave., Pacific Grove / 408-373-6892
Lunch Mon & Wed-Sat, dinner Wed-Mon
MEXICAN

Fresh seafood and a casual Southwestern decor attract a loyal clientele to Peppers Mexicali Cafe, a small neighborhood restaurant. Its Mexican and Latin American menu features snapper, prawns, chile rellenos, chicken fajitas, homemade tamales and a large selection of California wines and Mexican beers. Peppers Mexicali Cafe has been voted the Monterey Peninsula's "Favorite Best Mexican Restaurant" for four years in a row.
Specialties: Snapper Yucatan; Garlic Prawns; Grilled Seafood Tacos; Daily Seafood Specials

THE SARDINE FACTORY
701 Wave St., Monterey / 408-373-3775
Dinner daily
SEAFOOD

Taste the Sardine Factory's signature abalone bisque or fresh Monterey Bay prawns, part of a continually evolving menu that combines the freshest regional ingredients with European flair and a dash of California style. The Sardine Factory preserves the flavor of "the good old days" when author John Steinbeck roamed Cannery Row. Enjoy intimate dining in the nostalgic Captain's and Cannery Row rooms or step into the lush gardens of the Conservatory for an

CARMEL • MONTEREY

evening of dining pleasure.

Specialties: Abalone Bisque; Fresh Salmon & Swordfish; Monterey Prawn "Baltino"; Rack of Lamb in Orange Port Sauce

SPADARO
The Spindrift Hotel
650 Cannery Row, Monterey / 408-372-8881
Lunch & dinner daily
SEAFOOD & ITALIAN

As waves lap the shore below your window, you can enjoy excellent Italian specialties, a fine array of wines, and a variety of sinful homemade desserts.

TARPY'S ROADHOUSE
Hwy. 68 & Canyon del Rey, Monterey / 408-647-1444
Lunch & dinner daily
AMERICAN

In a charming, vine-covered stone building, Tarpy's Roadhouse features a hearty roadhouse-style menu. Rabbit, duck, venison, fish, fowl and traditional American favorites are served with an innovative twist. The menu is complimented by a full bar and by an excellent selection of California wines. At lunch, the menu includes a variety of salads and creatively prepared sandwiches and entrees. Casual and bright, Tarpy's Roadhouse is perfect for dinner or for sunny dining outdoors, surrounded by gardens.
Specialties: Housemade Rosemary Garlic Flatbread; Grilled Fresh Asparagus with Lemon-roasted Pepper Salsa; Pecan Barbecue Duck; Molasses-bourbon Pork Chop with Braised Red Cabbage; Venison Rib Chop with Green Peppercorn Sauce & Wild Rice Pilaf

TASTE CAFE & BISTRO
1199 Forest Ave., Pacific Grove / 408-655-0324
Lunch & dinner Tues-Sun
MEDITERRANEAN

Locals rave about Taste Cafe's espresso and wine bars and its selection of housemade desserts.

THE TINNERY
631 Ocean View Blvd., Pacific Grove / 408-646-1040
Breakfast, lunch & dinner daily
INTERNATIONAL

A mile from Cannery Row, The Tinnery is a good stop for affordable family dining. The Tinnery specializes in chicken, pasta and seafood dishes.

WHALING STATION INN
763 Wave St., Monterey / 408-373-3778
Dinner daily
MESQUITE-GRILLED FISH & MEAT

The Whaling Station Inn, one block above Cannery Row, is a romantic regional restaurant with Victorian stained-glass windows and attentive service. Owner/chef John Pisto sautees or mesquite-grills meat and game, as well as superb seafood such as abalone and prawns from

the treasure trove of Monterey Bay. His portions are generous, and a complimentary artichoke appetizer is served upon seating. The award-winning wine list includes French, Italian and California selections.
Specialties: Mesquite-broiled Scallops Wrapped in Pancetta; Sauteed Alligator with Sauce Andouille: Porter House Steak; Prime Rib; Rack of Lamb; Veal & Wild Mushroom Ravioli; Peppered Ahi Steak with Garlic Aioli

ACCOMMODATIONS

ASILOMAR CONFERENCE CENTER
800 Asilomar Blvd., Pacific Grove / 408-372-8016

A historical landmark built by Julia Morgan, the Hearst Castle architect, Asilomar is located near Asilomar State Beach in a park full of deer. With 313 bedrooms and 48 conference rooms, Asilomar welcomes both private reservations (based on availability) and groups. All overnight stays include breakfast.

DOUBLETREE HOTEL OF MONTEREY
#2 Portola Plaza, Monterey / 408-649-4511

This modern facility is conveniently located at the foot of Fisherman's Wharf and adjacent to the Monterey Convention Center. The 373 rooms are quiet and comfortable, with a swimming pool, restaurant, cocktail lounge and tennis courts available on the premises.

HYATT REGENCY MONTEREY
One Old Golf Course Rd., Monterey / 408-372-1234

The Hyatt Regency has 575 newly renovated guestrooms, 38 suites, Regency private club accommodations, two restaurants and a huge conference center, plus many pampering amenities: two outdoor heated swimming pools, a racquet club, six championship tennis courts, a pro shop, the 18-hole Del Monte Golf Course nearby, and a concierge ready to assist you with anything — including finding babysitters.
Singles $170; doubles $195; suites $275-$550

MONTEREY MARRIOTT
350 Calle Principal, Monterey / 408-649-4234

Near Fisherman's Wharf, Cannery Row and the Monterey Bay Aquarium, the 338-room Marriott is a reliable choice. For dining and entertainment, the hotel offers **Ferrante's**, a rooftop Italian restaurant and bar with a spectacular bay view, and **The Monterey Bay Club**, a cocktail lounge with live jazz entertainment.

MONTEREY PLAZA HOTEL
400 Cannery Row, Monterey / 408-646-1700

The Monterey Plaza Hotel on Cannery Row is truly a grand hotel. Distinguishing characteristics all point to attention to detail. The hotel's renowned restaurant, **Delfino's on the Bay**, features Italian cuisine with a California influence.

THERE'S
ONLY
ONE GUIDE
YOU
REALLY
NEED...

Your Passport

to Northern

California

AM PM

GUIDE TO NORTHERN CALIFORNIA